The Sandbeetle

By the same author

The Book of Wishes and Complaints – Hutchinson 1991

The Sandbeetle

a novel

ZINA ROHAN

Hodder & Stoughton

LONDON SYDNEY AUCKLAND

Extracts from *The Journey of the Magi* by T. S. Eliot, copyright ©
Valerie Eliot, are reproduced by kind permission of Valerie Eliot.

British Library Cataloguing in Publication Data

Rohan, Zina
  The Sandbeetle
  I. Title
  823.914 [F]

  ISBN 0-340-59340-7

Published by Hodder and Stoughton,
a division of Hodder and Stoughton Ltd,
Mill Road, Dunton Green, Sevenoaks, Kent TN13 2YA.
Editorial Office: 47 Bedford Square, London WC1B 3DP.

Photoset by Rowland Phototypesetting Ltd,
Bury St Edmunds, Suffolk

Printed in Great Britain by
Mackays of Chatham plc, Chatham, Kent

For Georg, finally
and
MWMH

Part I

One

When my father's father was dying it took four men to hold him down, one at each corner. All I said at the time, when they told me what had happened, was 'Why?'

Arriving home after the event I found my parents keening by the bedside. My grandfather's eyes had been closed but his eyebrows were knitted in what looked like a combination of confusion and rage; his hands were pressed down on the covers to either side of him as if he were in the act of levering himself up. His back was arched and could not be straightened. An outsider might have thought he had died in the throes of a convulsion. Indeed, that was my first thought. It was only when I crept out of the room, which was a bad place for a boy, closing the door on my parents' muffled wailing – their faces were hidden in handkerchiefs – that I encountered the four neighbours whose services had been called on to assist my grandfather towards the grave. They were burly men, which is why, no doubt, my father had turned to them first, and they told me with no little admiration how they had struggled to prevent the old man's escape from his deathbed. I listened and then asked my 'Why?'

What did I mean? Since then I have had a few ideas which are, roughly, these: since he was a small man, why did it take four big ones to hold him down? Why were they holding him down at all? Was it because, while they thought he was dying, he disagreed and expired in the attempt to persuade them otherwise? Or was he, on the contrary, anxious to reach the grave more rapidly than was being arranged? Then I have wondered whether it was not the going that troubled him, but the manner of it – that he did not want to die in bed but lying on the floor, or standing up, or leaning out of the window.

I remember him more by repute than from experience because until his dotage I had never seen him at all. We lived in another part of Berlin. He was devout. Every hour of the day seemed to him, if I am to believe my mother, to be a reason for prayer – noisy, obvious, top-of-the-voice prayer, his torso rocking from the waist, its rhythm at variance with the wavering beat of his chanting. Out on the streets he proclaimed his origins and his convictions by wearing what my father called 'fancy dress'. The long black coat, the tall black hat, the beard, the thick glasses – as if he could have dispensed with those by choice – marked my grandfather out and put him firmly in the camp of 'strangers' to which my parents made strenuous efforts to prove they did not belong.

My grandmother I never knew at all. She died six weeks after I was born – relieved, so I was repeatedly informed by my mother, to be exempt from further matrimony. They were both religious people, those grandparents, bound together by mutual hatred. After fifty years of marriage they were thin and bent and arthritic, but they had conserved the energy to throw their domestic possessions at one another – in between prayers – shrieking vile epithets as they did so. My grandfather had selected my grandmother when she was a very young girl in the Polish village from which they came, using as his criteria the width of her hips and the cleanliness of her mother's kitchen. The first of these qualities was under-utilised, as they agreed almost instantly (one of only two things they were ever able to agree on) that such was the intensity of their mutual dislike they would attempt the business of procreation only until a son had been achieved, and then stop. To their good fortune my father was set in train at the first try. The kitchen quality was of greater value because it proved to be longer-lasting.

Probably my father wished he could have remained a dutiful son. I do not think he decided actively to rebel; he always seemed much too accepting by temperament for that. My theory is that on some occasion when his parents were engrossed in hurling the milk pans my father, grown supple from frequent ducking, slithered from the household and skedaddled across the city to another quarter where he had himself apprenticed to a cabinet maker. Briefly my grandparents' voices were joined in vociferous lamentation

4

when they discovered his escape, but this unison was evidently so alien that they returned to safer ground and instead of bewailing their misfortune blamed each other for being its single cause.

Embassies were sent to my father – pride prevented both his parents from pleading in person – to prevail on him to return. He didn't argue with them but merely asked, with uncharacteristic acuity, 'In my position, what would you do?' And the plenipotentiaries went home empty-handed, as it were, for there was no answer to a question like that.

While he was learning his trade my father discarded his faith. He did not lose it but jettisoned it because his experience suggested that you could not have piety without domestic warfare. This apart, he also concluded, looking about him, that being outlandish was unnecessary. The future lay with Germany, secular solid Germany, with whose citizens one might sensibly merge.

He married late, fearing the experience and thereby prolonging my grandmother's life well beyond her intentions. She had vowed that until she had a grandson who might be induced to make up for the apostasy of his father she would not budge from this earth. Her vow and my father's dilatoriness were burdensome to both my grandparents, who had seen the departure of one of them as the only means of obtaining relief. I do not know by what process they decided that she was to be the one to go. I know only that this was the second point of agreement between them, which has always appealed to me on aesthetic grounds: a marriage buttressed by a pair of complementary moments of concord, the first over a birth, the second over a death.

My father's marriage did not improve matters. Elsie Goldstein was a year older than he was (one bad mark) and came from a family whose Jewishness was almost incidental (no doubt part of her attraction for him but earning her many more bad marks). Worst of all, Elsie's robust mother, joyfully aided by her father, had contrived to produce so many children, more than eleven, that Mrs Goldstein had to go through their names in chronological order to arrive at the one she needed. This was an insult. Abraham had been instructed to go forth and multiply, and my grandparents saw the heirs of Abraham as themselves and not the Germanising petite bourgeoisie who were not ashamed to carry their house keys in their hands on the Sabbath.

Having finished his apprenticeship, learning much about quality furniture but nothing about how to make it because he was essentially cack-handed, my father took out a loan and began his own, very modest furniture business. It kept us in adequate comfort. My parents aspired to no more.

We had a spacious kitchen which my mother kept spotless but not kosher, although she would not cook pork. 'And why should I,' she asked, 'when there is so much else to eat?' There was plenty of mahogany to polish, and a glass-fronted tallboy in which she displayed the objects that proclaimed our participation in bourgeois Germany: an immense cut-glass bowl cradling an unwieldy ladle; a pair of statuettes, naked but for the sculpted swathes over their genitals, Greek athletes caught in a spasm of Olympic glory. A shot putter with the shot cupped under one ear, back muscles sweating; a discus thrower, head down as he swung his eternal saucer back along his straightened arm: nasty little vacant-eyed, bloodless tributes to the sort of physical prowess that made my parents uncomfortable. Why did they have them? Maybe they were a fashion like the angel chimes on the clock that stood on the piano none of us could play. You lit the candle underneath and a quartet of golden cherubim, puffing on celestial trumpets, set off on their circular travels, pinging as they went. We were unaware that these ornaments and the heavy furniture represented only the first part of our acceptance as associate members of a club that was already changing its rules of affiliation.

I have always understood that all these objects belonged in spirit to my mother with my father's collusion. Perhaps growing up as one among so many had made her jealous of her possessions, fearful of their sudden disappearance into someone else's room. Whatever the reasons, she kept everything, by which I mean everything, under lock and key. The keys were carried at her waist, on a belt, and looked, I'm afraid to say, ludicrous. In my memory my father was always bald, small and stout. My mother was smaller and stouter still. She had yellow hair in curls and a small, cheeping, cherry mouth which let food in and words out in unregulated quantities. Her little legs were slender at the ankles, bearing the weight of an enormous shelf of a bosom and a high, round stomach. She had no discernible waist, as if her creator, in the act of slapping on the clay, had been called away and subsequently skimped on the job to meet his deadline. Her littleness and her tubbiness were accentuated by that bunch of jailor's keys protruding spikily from her midriff.

She locked all that could be locked in our apartment. The desks, the glass-fronted tallboy with the cut-glass bowl and the Greek sportsmen. There was also a wardrobe, floor to ceiling, filling the hall. Late one night, when I should have been asleep, I spied her selecting its key, unerringly, in the dim light of the heavily shaded bulb. My father had just returned from a business trip, bringing her, as he always did, a gift. She let him walk past her into the dining-room where his meal expected him, and pulled the door to behind him. Then she inserted her key and opened the wardrobe. Handbags came tumbling out, toppling her, crashing around her, so that I forgot I was supposed to be in my bed and went to help.

'What's that noise? What are you doing, Elsie?' my father called.

'Nothing. I've knocked something over. Nothing,' she called back, and for once did not ask me what I was doing out there in the night.

Snakeskin, crocodile skin, beaverskin, even – God help us – pig-skin handbags lay around us, brand new, many still in the bags in which they had been purchased, bearing the names of the towns my father had visited in his efforts to expand his business. Every animal that could be made into a handbag had fallen out of my mother's wardrobe and each, although I did not yet know it, represented one of my father's infidelities. In silence we gathered them up and my mother stacked them, a red-head, a blonde, a little brunette, neatly one on top of the other, including the one my father had just brought (who was she?), back where they belonged in the wardrobe, and locked them in. So she locked the cupboards and the rooms in which those cupboards brooded. She even locked the lavatory door – on the outside – and when either my father or I needed to pee we had to ask her for the key. I remember my father hopping from foot to foot as he roared his frustration.

She locked me in my trousers, tailored to her specifications, sleek at the hips and fastened by a row of a dozen tiny buttons clamped into even smaller buttonholes, sewn up the back. I could do nothing without my mother's help. Was that her intention? It was never a question I could ask. Or should I admit it was simply a question I never did ask. I cannot say how much those buttons and their location made me suffer at school. I drank as little as I could and urinated as infrequently as my bladder allowed. A kidney infection resulted.

'Retention,' said Dr Meissner. 'Is there a reason why?'

My mother was mystified. Not so my father. 'A reason?' he shouted without rancour, being quick to shout because he still thought that was how married people necessarily communicated. 'Of course there's a reason.'

My mother was used to the noise. 'Not so loud, Heinz,' she said. 'Don't shout.'

'I am not shouting,' he bellowed. 'I am only asking a question because my only son has a kidney infection because his mother has sewn him into his trousers because I don't know why. All I know is that he needs a nursemaid to widdle. He can't get his widdler out by himself.'

'Heinz, don't be crude.'

'I am not being crude. Dr Meissner understands these terms. How else could he be a doctor? Isn't that right, Doctor? I am describing a situation and it is intolerable. The boy is going to be a man birthday after next and his mother keeps him in nappies. I won't have it, do you hear, Elsie? Enough. He's been yours for the last twelve years. The next twelve will be mine. Starting from tomorrow. Understood? Kidney infection! How could you?'

Naturally, my mother wept. The awful accusation that she, of all people, could have caused a kidney infection, or the thought that my father might believe it, would have been reason enough. She was so fearful of accident and injury that I had never been permitted to handle sharp knives, efficient scissors, hammer or nails. Now she was being charged with what amounted to negligence. So she cried. Perhaps, though, she was devastated to learn that her son was hers no more, that his care was to be passed into hands she did not entirely trust to do the job properly – but the newly diagnosed infection removed her right to say so. Perhaps, also, she regretted the loss of the rear-fastening trousers.

8

'Tomorrow' – my father's voice was still louder than necessary – 'we will go to *my* tailor, with or without infections, and we will buy this boy men's clothes in which he will not need to retain anything. Understood? And these' – lifting the miscreant trousers disdainfully by one leg – 'go into the bin tonight. Now.'

My mother still had her triumph. 'Good,' she said, passing Dr Meissner a cup of coffee and a piece of strudel on our best petal porcelain, 'and what will he wear to the tailor's? Pyjamas?'

Then began my life with my father, although it was not to be the twelve years he had promised. True to his word, even if he waited for my fever to abate, he took me to his tailor, to whom he had already sent measurements and instructions as detailed as any my mother might have compiled. When we arrived a dark suit on a satin hanger was waiting for us, still unfinished, still only tacked and chalked, 'for a suit that does not fit is a suit you do not wear – the first rule for a man, Leo.' I was ushered into a changing-cubicle, the tailor and my father exchanging winks. There, alone but surrounded on three sides by mirrors, I had my life altered for ever.

I had got so far as to remove my old trousers – my father having tussled, swearing, with the buttons – then I was transfixed. I saw in that three-sided mirror what I had never seen before: my profile; my nose. I knew my face – at least, I had thought so. I was white-skinned, with pale-blue eyes, widow's peak and curling blond hair that my mother said looked well on the collar of the sailor suit. I had a neat round chin and, until that day, I had had a nose that merely separated my eyes and permitted me, sometimes, to breathe through it without conscious effort. Now I discovered that seen from the side it was very nearly immense and markedly hooked. I was looking at a person I did not know.

I leaned forward towards the mirror in front of me and pushed my chin out, taking sly glances in the side mirrors as I did so. I pulled my hair further down over my forehead, puffed up my thin cheeks. The nose remained, unimpressed, immovable, grafted on while I had been asleep as punishment for a crime I was unaware of having committed. There was to be no remission. I was sickened by the injustice of it, for the size of my nose in my pinched face (it

9

looks better these days, I believe) was in inverse proportion to its effectiveness as an organ. I had no sense of smell. A faulty sinus had been operated on when I was small, the operation had failed, and I was left with the sinuses still blocked and no means of making a distinction between the aroma of a rose and a turd. With the ability to smell had gone my ability to taste, and mealtimes were a distress. That triumvirate of mirrors, cackling in judgement, said as clearly as anything that someone had played a dirty trick on me.

'What are you doing in there?' my father roared. 'Doesn't it fit? Can't you do the trousers up? Must I come in and help you even with these?'

I hadn't got so far as to take the trousers from their hanger. I was rooted with my reflection, pinching, prodding, tweezing at the interloper on my portrait and filled suddenly with foreboding. Consider the date. It was 1933 and the cartoonists were already busy. It was clear to me, in that cubicle, that I had been their unwitting model, a boy with two completely different faces – the one you see from the front and the one you see from the side. My classmates had been more than tactful not to point it out, and I had imagined my trousers to be the pinnacle of suffering! I was touched, remembering the day when the whole school had been assembled in a fidgeting, gassy but silent block to hear the guest speaker's lecture on the properties of the true Aryan. He had spoken of blondness, widely spaced eyes in a long head, the clear honest look. He had scanned the rows of upturned faces gaping at him, examined the rows slowly from right to left, left to right; we had followed his scrutiny from bust to bust, curly, brown, black, mousey. 'Yes,' he had said doubtfully, 'yes, you are all very nice-looking children.' Then his voice surged with triumph. 'There! There I see a boy. Stand up lad, will you? Now *that's* what I mean, that's exactly what I mean, just what I've been talking about.' His finger, of course, was pointing directly at me. I stood up and stared at the lecturer, my face burning. Around me my friends, who were already giggling, knew what he didn't know, that I was the only Jew in the school. But they also knew something *I* didn't know: that the lecturer, had he been standing to one side of me, would not have awarded me that coveted racial prize. And nobody had said a word.

My father ran out of patience. He stormed into the cubicle where I was still standing, with my nose, among the tell-tale mirrors. My old trousers lay on the floor; the new suit on its satin hanger was draped over the back of the chair.

'What's the matter with you? Are you ill? You don't like these trousers? You want to keep the old ones, like a baby? Crying like a baby!'

I was, and I thought I would tell him why. But as I tried to find the opening words I realised the endeavour was futile. What should I say, after all? Why didn't you tell me about my nose? He would think I was either mad or hopelessly vain. A little vanity was all right. Everybody had to be a little vain in order not to look a mess; looking a mess was disrespectful to others, like dirty fingernails. My father hated people who had dirty fingernails. He took it as a personal insult. Whenever he was introduced to someone he would bow over the hand he was shaking, seemingly deeply courteous, but in reality inspecting the owner's character through his fingertips. However, the sort of vanity that had you crying in front of a mirror because of your nose . . . I dared not tell him that my nose was the original of the cartoons he pretended not to see. I was not to draw his attention to them lest he be forced to acknowledge that they referred to him, to my mother, to me – and not only to the strangers in the dark coats and black hats from whom he supposed he had made his escape: his own father, stubbornly insisting on parading the attributes that had 'Jew' written all over them at a time when a little moderation was all that was needed.

We bought that suit. My father was so embarrassed by my snivelling that he pushed me out of the shop.

'Doesn't it fit?' The tailor, whose reputation depended on following measurements exactly, was disconcerted by the scene we were making.

'It will,' my father snarled, no doubt leaving the poor man more puzzled still. 'Here,' he pushed a wad of money into the tailor's hand. 'I'll collect on Thursday week.'

'Perfect.' The tailor was mollified. 'A new suit for a young man just in time for Pesach.'

Outside the shop my father threw up his hands. He had forgotten all about the Passover, which in our household had long been abolished. He turned to me, averting his eyes from my childishly tear-swollen face. 'You know what I'm going to do with you? I'm going to take you hiking in the Black Forest. It's good for the constitution, if kept within limits, and you need to get away from your mother, from the city and from those mirrors you're so fond of preening yourself in front of. We'll leave tomorrow and we'll be back in a fortnight.'

'But what about my new suit?'

'It won't run away. Old Schneider can't sell to anyone else, can he? Whom would it fit? But you have a point.' And he veered off the pavement into a store where people bought clothes off the peg. He kitted me out in the long baggy shorts and rugged socks favoured by urban people preparing to pit themselves against rural air.

We would fill our lungs with the fresh, uncontaminated breezes of our Fatherland, he promised gloomily, a man who felt most at ease with the pavement for his pathway and the clanking of trams as his birdsong.

Almost immediately he grew grumpy and restless. After a week I came upon him in our hotel room packing our things.

'On the other hand,' he said, pursuing some inward conversation, 'we should be getting home to see how our Mutti is doing, *ne*?'

We had been out to walk under the trees only once, where we stepped aside for a band of real hikers whose legs were downy with golden hair.

On the way home from the station we stopped off at a shop selling luxury items where my father bought a black patent handbag from a sales-lady with a blonde bun who recognised him. When we got home my mother took the bag and wedged it without question into her wardrobe.

I did not know my grandfather, only that now, whispered my mother behind her hand, the old man was unhinged, deprived of the life-enhancing skirmishes that had sustained him, berating the angel who had run out on him, leaving him to live out his last years on his own.

The burden of caring for him had fallen on his neighbours, good people, for he had never had to do anything for himself. They understood – up to a point. Other men's wives were prepared to bring him food he could accept from trusted kitchens; they were prepared to sweep and clean and take in his washing. They were not prepared to be shouted at in recompense. The old man had a son, a daughter-in-law, a grandson even. Logic dictated, more than logic, that he ought to go to them. What were families for but to take care of their own? How could an old man not wish to enjoy his last days in the household of his only boy? All right, there had been differences of opinion, but only God could be the judge and everybody knew, everybody had been able to hear only too well, why the boy had been driven out into that other world where he probably had not wished to be. By all accounts the daughter-in-law was a good enough woman in her way, from a family to whom God, for reasons of His own, had given many children. The old man had only himself to blame. It was up to him to compromise and make amends.

Poor grandfather. Compromise and making amends were not in his nature. He had prayed, which was right, argued with his fellows, which was also right, walked in God's ways, observed the Commandments and much else with conscious attention. It should have been sufficient but had turned out not to be. No wonder he was annoyed.

My mother fussed over the laying of the table, bought in all the required foods, set out the candles. She stood over me in my bedroom while I brushed my hair, pinned on my crown the skullcap she had hurried out to buy, inspected my fingernails and cooed with satisfaction when I paraded for her in my new suit, to which she had reconciled herself. She made reproachful faces at my father, who would not help but sat chewing his lips.

My grandfather was both smaller and more frail than I had expected, and needed a stick to walk. His face looked grimy under its beard, his hands were not clean, his overcoat was greasy. 'My God, he smells,' muttered my mother under her breath. I was not surprised that my father had run away from this unkempt, wild creature who was standing in our hallway, breathing noisily, the phlegm rattling in his nostrils. He shook off my mother's attempts to help him and gave me a single morose glance. We positioned ourselves round the table, my grandfather seated in my father's chair at its head, and said nothing. In the silence I busied myself examining, with my fingers, the three fat fly buttons of my new trousers. I fastened and unfastened them first with one hand, then with the other. They responded magically to my command, slipping from their buttonholes, creeping back again with a minimum of manipulation. I could not keep my fingers from them.

'Is that what the boy does all day in your household? Play with himself?'

'Leo, put your hands up on the table,' commanded my mother.

'He likes his trousers,' explained my father.

I stared rudely at my grandfather as he wagged his profile between my parents, seated to either side of him. It horrified me to think that I might have got my nose from him. But his was narrow, straight, with nostrils slim as a girl's. My hands were now on the table. I bent my head and slid my nose between my raised palms.

'What's he doing now? Is he praying like a Christian?'

'Leo, put your hands down on the table.'

'Of course he isn't.'

'Of course he isn't,' mimicked my grandfather. 'Well, let's see what you've been teaching him.'

There was another silence while I looked from one parent to the other. What did the old man want? Mathematical formulae, the history of Germany since Bismarck, the poems I knew by heart? Did he want me to relate the exploits of my favourite literary figures, Karl May's Old Shatterhand and Old Surehand?

He did not wait for an answer but raised the glass of wine by his elbow, looked into it, looked up to the ceiling and began to moo a nasal spell: '*Borooch ahto ahdonoi ehlohaynu mehlech hoholom bohray pree hagofen.*' On and on he went, glass aloft, and I watched fascinated, waiting for the golden liquid to spill on to my mother's damask, mesmerised by his swaying and his skill with the glass. The wine remained in place. Suddenly he stopped and tipped some of it into his mouth. Then he dabbled his fingers in a small bowl of water my mother had placed by his plate. He reached forward to a platter of undressed salad, plucked out a leaf and swished it in another bowl of water, back and forth, the way my mother rinsed

14

towels, shook off the excess drops and stuffed the greenery into his mouth too. He nodded fiercely to us.

'What's he doing?' I whispered.

'Shhh.' My mother's forefinger was on her lips. 'Do what he does.'

I soaked a piece of lettuce, waved it vigorously as he had done and ate it, shocked to find it salty. Some of the salt water dripped on to my suit leaving a stain. My mother's eyebrows contracted.

My grandfather reached into the centre of the table to the plate of the matzos my mother ate for breakfast for her diet. There were just three there. He chose the middle one ostentatiously, broke it in two, dropped one half and slipped the other under his napkin. The mooing began again, so that I waited for the hidden piece of matzo to emerge from his napkin as a rabbit or a pigeon.

He refilled his glass and nodded to my mother, who filled our glasses as well. My grandfather sat in silence, shuffling his feet under the table. Minutes passed. Suddenly he banged one hand on the table. 'Well? And what sort of people have you become?'

It was my mother, not my father, who understood what was wanted. She leaned across and whispered in my ear.

Somewhat confused, I turned to my grandfather and asked, 'How is this night different from all other nights?'

'Finally we have it,' he was crackling with sarcasm. 'But which of the four sons have we here?'

Four sons? I looked at my father. His face was white; he was chewing his lips and twisting his napkin.

'There's only me,' I explained, thinking that my grandfather, who had never been to visit, might be mistaking us for some other family.

'Leo, ssh!'

'There are always four sons, and it is your parents' misfortune that you are the last.'

'I'm not,' I insisted. 'I'm the only one.'

My grandfather grimaced. 'There are four sons', as if I had not put him right. 'One is intelligent, one is ill-mannered, one is indifferent and one is not even able to ask a question. You are three of them in one, the second, the third and the fourth.'

'But I did ask a question. I asked about tonight.'

My mother had her head in her hands. To my amazement, my father was smiling.

'And I will tell you why,' hissed my grandfather. 'You are ill-mannered because you think this has nothing to do with you.' I agreed. I couldn't fathom why I should be expected to listen to the outlandish noises he had been making, and then be chided for it. 'And you asked the question because your mother told you to. Don't think that because I am old I am also deaf. I hear what is said and I have heard tonight a great deal that has not been said. I have heard the silence of years and now, clearly, the Lord has laid upon me the duty of breaking it.' He took a breath. 'All of this' – he pointed to the plates on the table – 'is because of what the Lord did for me when I came out of Egypt.'

I gasped. No one had told me my grandfather had been to Egypt. We had seen pictures of the pyramids in school, and men in white dresses on camels. Was this the food people ate in Egypt, which my grandfather wanted to eat again, to remind him of his journey?

'What was it like there?' I asked, interested and eager.

My grandfather was appeased. He settled in his chair, leaning against the cushion at his back. 'Since you don't know, I'll have to tell you. And since you don't know, since no one has bothered to tell you before, I'll have to tell you from the beginning, which is irregular. When is his bedtime?'

'Tonight is different,' said my mother unwisely.

'Precisely,' he agreed curtly, and to me he said, 'but I expect you to listen and to remember. There was a time', and his face grew softer, his voice rounding like a dumpling, 'when we were enslaved. Four hundred and fifty years of unremitting menial work for the Pharaoh and his Egyptians. We made them bricks from straw, we built for them, we drew their water and fed their cattle so that they didn't have to do any work for themselves. They lived in their palaces, leaving only huts of mud for us, and whoever didn't do what they wanted was beaten and starved and humiliated. It had gone on too long and it couldn't last. It had to be stopped. How? you ask. Well, I'll tell you.

'Although the Pharaoh was so powerful he was also afraid. Of whom? Of us, of course, because the Lord was sending us more children than he was giving to the Egyptians, and Pharaoh said to himself one day, "If I'm not careful there will soon be more of these Israelites in my land than Egyptians." So you know what he did? He gave an order that every baby boy born to our people should be murdered. Well, you can imagine what people thought, how they were running about to find ways to protect their children. But it wasn't easy. The Egyptians had their spies everywhere, they knew when a boy was born and where to find him. So there was nowhere to hide. The mothers tried everything, believe me. They tried to put their babies behind the sacks of grain, even sometimes in the sacks of grain when the soldiers came looking, but the babies would cry or sneeze because of the dust in the grain, and the soldiers would pounce on the bags with their knives, rip them open, rip open the bodies of the newborn babies and throw the bodies into the street for the dogs. But the dogs knew what was what and wouldn't touch the little corpses because, I tell you, the Lord was already in them.'

My grandfather had moved his chair round the table close to mine; he was holding my hands in his and staring at me in excitement. In equal excitement I stared back. I could feel the heat in the air; his voice seemed hoarse with dust and sand. Then it boomed from the burning bush, like the Lord's, and I wanted to unlace my shoes just as Moses had unlaced his sandals in order not to profane holy ground. Flies, frogs, lice, locusts, hail, rivers and vats of blood clogging Egyptian mouths. That stubborn Pharaoh still wouldn't give in and let the Israelites go, he wanted to keep his slaves so badly. It was only when he got a taste of his own medicine and the firstborn child of every Egyptian household was found dead in the morning, but the Israelites' children were spared because the Angel of Death had passed over their houses, that Pharaoh finally shouted, 'All right then, go! Get out. Take all your animals and your children and your women and go!' And they went. Away they went, no time to pack, no time to let the bread rise before baking.

'So they had to eat it flat, like this.' My grandfather broke off a piece and gave it to me. Festooned with the riches of the Egyptians as the Lord had commanded they should be, they drove their cattle before them. 'Think of it, thousands of people carrying their children, the cattle all running the wrong way, and they get to the sea, with the Egyptians pounding behind them on their horses, because even then Pharaoh hadn't really given in.'

I saw the horror on the faces of the Egyptians as the waters unfolded, I heard the gasping and the choking while on the further shore the cattle of the Israelites were already looking for places to graze.

My grandfather pushed his hot face even closer and whispered harshly, 'Don't forget. Don't ever forget.'

'Will you tell me another story tomorrow? The way you told me that one? It was wonderful.'

'Story?' He slapped the flat of his hand on the table, his glass rocked and some wine leaped over the rim on to the tablecloth. My mother surreptitiously poured salt on the stain and blushed. 'Story? This wasn't a story. This was the truth. Stories are a waste of time.'

I can't say that my grandfather took immediately to his bed but certainly he retreated to his room, insisting that his meals be brought to him there, served on his wife's crockery, cooked in her utensils from the kosher ingredients purchased only from the purveyors he named. So my mother carried his meals through to him on the desired plates with segregated cutlery, and went to the designated shops – once, in order to keep in her kitchen the bags and packets that would prove she was obeying orders. Into them she decanted the ordinary groceries she bought locally against the possibility that one day my grandfather might venture into her kitchen to check up on her. He never did, for kitchens were not his territory and it did not occur to him that his wishes could be so sneakily ignored.

He would creep to the bathroom when he gauged we were other-wise employed, carrying the chamberpot he kept in his room. He mopped at himself (my mother said, having peeked through the keyhole), standing naked in a basin on the floor. Every week he left a small heap of dirty laundry outside his door. My mother would exchange it for clean linen which disappeared once she had vacated the corridor. She set out his midday meal on the deep-sided inlaid tray he had brought with him, which my father detested, identifying it as one of the objects his parents had so enjoyed lobbing over the dinner table. When he had eaten – and he scraped his plate clean – my grandfather would leave the tray on the floor outside his room as if he were in a hotel.

On Friday evenings he left his cell and hobbled down the corridor to invigilate over our Sabbath meal. He broke the bread in his unscrubbed hands and passed it round. We put the unhygienic fragments in our mouths and chewed slowly. Sometimes the only sounds were my grandfather's mutterings and the moist movements of his tongue on his food. The mounds on my plate had no flavour, having no smell. I forced them into me, as I had been brought up to do in order not to offend my mother, gagging on the mouthfuls as my grandfather mashed his supper into a wet mess before swallowing it down.

Mine was an indoor life lived behind heavily curtained windows, padding in soft-soled slippers to spare the parquet, dipping into the leather-bound books my father kept shelved in order of height but did not read. I stayed at home for lack of alternative venues, and lay on my bed, arms behind my head, creeping with Old Shatterhand through the forests, leaving no trace, cracking no twigs underfoot.

The children who had chosen not to betray my nose because, as children, they had not yet discovered that they should, were being warned off. My closest friend, Friedrich, told me that I wasn't to come to his house after school for the coffee and cakes and the afternoon gluing stamps into his album that had been our regular Wednesday appointment. I told my father.

'Your mother makes cakes as good as any you'll get in the Müllers' house. And if you want stamps, Leo, I can bring you plenty home from the office.'

After school on Thursdays I had expected to start learning to ride, round and round in an indoor *manège* with the equestrian club organised by our favourite, the gym teacher, youthful, muscled, tanned Herr Schelling. The first springtime afternoon they turned me back at the door, advising me not to bother to present myself there again. I ran home and told my mother.

'Horses,' she said dismissively, handing me my grandfather's evening tray. 'Who wants horses?' But she added, 'Tell Pappi.'

My father followed me down the corridor. My grandfather held out his hands for the tray. I set it across his knees and he began drinking his soup, bending his head low over the bowl, sucking and dribbling.

I turned to go but my father was behind me, knuckling me in the back. 'Tell your grandfather.'

'Tell me what?'

'They've said I'm not to learn riding after school. I'm not to do sport with them.'

My grandfather put down his spoon. 'And what is your opinion, Benjamin?' – the first time I learned that my father had started life with a different name.

My father patted my shoulder. 'Well, never mind, we were never too keen on sport, were we?'

The old man raised his head from his plate and gazed at his son with myopic contempt. 'It is not a question of what we are keen on. It is a question of who decides what we will or will not be keen on. As from this moment, we are keen on sport, but also as from this moment our desire to become athletes is irrelevant. You're a fool, Benjamin, trying to run away as if you could leave behind the thing you run from and become something else. There are no choices about who you are, nor should there be, and you should give thanks for it. And while you're about it, ask the Lord to restore your memory. Without it you shall surely perish.'

By this time he was jabbing towards my father with his fork, frowning so hard that his eyebrows grew into a single grizzled hedge bisecting his forehead, and he was shouting. But old and frail as he was, the voice emerged as a petulant squeak and I wanted to laugh.

Behind me my father exhaled a hiss of irritation. 'This is ridiculous,' he said. 'Come on, Leo. Suppertime.'

He closed the door on the old man's contorted expression. Through the crack I saw his raised fork with a piece of beef speared on its prongs, and it brought to my mind a grotesque little devil with a comical trident in his hand.

As we sat down to our meal my father dusted his hands together like a streetfighter who has floored his opponent with a left and a right, and I sensed he was proud of himself. I was certainly proud of him. We wouldn't be so timid in my grandfather's presence in future. He was just a noisy old man who slobbered his soup and pulled awful faces.

The following morning Herr Schelling beckoned me into the shadows of the main stairwell. 'I'm sorry about the riding,' he whispered. 'It was nothing to do with me and, frankly, I think it's a disgrace. I promise you, Leo, I won't stand for their rubbish. Count on me. Watch me.'

I watched him. They had taken to singing the Horst Wessel song at the start of each school day, right arms raised at the diagonal, the stuff of black and white archive documentaries. There were times when I wanted to join in. They sang so well and that damned tune was so catchy. But I kept my eye on Herr Schelling, his mouth clamped shut, his hands rammed into his pockets. Morning after morning after morning. Until the day he closed his eyes and sang, his arm as high and stiff as anyone's.

Under the stairwell again. 'I'm sorry, Leo. I wouldn't have done it for anything but my wife's expecting. I hope you understand and won't think ill of me.'

When I got home I told my mother. '*Ja*, Leo. I know,' she said. 'Go and do your homework.' Then she went into her bedroom, closed the door very quietly behind her and locked it.

My grandfather went to bed and did not get up again. He did not eat the meals we brought him, he did not drink. But at night we could hear him railing in his thin voice, 'You and your promises. You stupid, thoughtless fool.' Then he died on his bed and they had to call in the neighbours to hold him down.

Two

My mother consulted no one, which was probably wise. My father would have impeded her, slowed her down. As for me, not only had I not been asked what I thought, I hadn't even been told what she was up to until it was too late to make any changes. In this, however, I do not believe she had either me or my father in mind. If there was anyone who might jeopardise her project, it was herself. After all, here was a woman who had locked me in my trousers to ward off I don't know what imagined danger. All of a sudden, giving herself no time for reflection and second thoughts, she arranged to send me away, to live in London with people she did not know, on my own, at the age of twelve, possibly for ever. And why? Because Herr Schelling's expectation of fatherhood had weakened his resolve.

There was a man called Gross who owed my father a minor but uncomfortable sum that he had borrowed on impulse at a sticky time. In his turn Gross was owed by a man in Holland who could not pay his debt because a man in Manchester was holding back on his, and the man in Manchester pleaded that he couldn't move until an Englishman in London, by the name of Chapman, had handed over what he had felt the need to borrow. But Chapman, like so many, had hit hard times and showed no sign of being able to pay, so my father – who did not need the instant repayment of his loan, who had in fact forgotten all about it because Gross was an old friend, and when you lend money to a friend you must tell yourself it was a gift, Leo, and put it behind you – was not going to get his money back, said my mother. Unless. What was her method? I never found out but I would suspect her of everything – veiled threats, direct threats perhaps; pathetic stories of persecution, of a boy taunted and bullied; flattery: the Chapmans had been recommended to her as an exceptional pair, such an exemplary household that a mother forced to part with her only son might comfort herself to know that he was in hands as good as her own. For their part the impecunious Chapmans might be prepared, in return for the clearing of their debt and a regular sum, to take me on.

They were.

My mother packed my trunk with more suits from my father's tailor, and a quantity of new white handkerchiefs. My father inserted a box of shoe-cleaning materials, as if reminding me that keeping my extremities gleaming – feet and fingernails – would be both my chief protection and my primary duty to my hosts.

A house, not an apartment. A black wrought-iron gate flanked by a pair of black birds; a red-tiled front doorstep, and a black front door with a heavy lion's-head knocker. A strange window that jutted from the front of the house, its three panes facing to the sides as well as forwards. On the threshold a man and a woman whose anxious faces expected little pleasure.

The man was extraordinarily tall, and knock-kneed. His feet were large and his shoulders sloped. His hair was smoothed across the top of his head. The woman was holding the elbow of her right arm in the palm of her left hand, soothing her left upper arm with the stroking fingertips of her right hand. Her brown hair was waved, her face wreathed in an old disappointment. She wore a tailored grey skirt and heavy black shoes, like a nurse's, on dainty feet. At her knee squatted an ugly white dog. Husband and wife spoke to me in words I struggled to understand. Having come to know them, I feel sure this is what they will have said.

'How do you do. I am Henry and this is my wife Elisabeth.'

'How do you do, Leo. We are very pleased to have you.'

'Is that your taxi? Have you paid him? Let me pay him. Oh dear, Elisabeth, have you any money? . . . I don't seem to have . . . oh, how awful . . . oh, thank you, dear.'

'Now come on in, Leo. Put your case down there. My goodness. That's a big trunk, isn't it? What a lot of things you must have.' She spoke to me as if I were very young as well as foreign and ignorant. 'Let me show you your room. I hope you like it. Or would

23

you rather have a wash and something to eat and drink first? You must be tired after your journey. How did it go? Was the sea rough? But perhaps you're a good sailor. I'm afraid I'm not and poor Henry only has to look at water and he's . . .'

She led me upstairs to a room organised as a small child's den, clean, wistful, decorated with blue bunnies. She moved over to the window and closed it. 'I was only giving the place a bit of an airing. It smells a little musty, doesn't it?' She reopened the window. 'It's nice to have someone in here.' Her indrawn breath quavered.

They hauled my trunk up the stairs, Elisabeth panting but urging Henry to be careful of his back. On the landing Henry remained hinged at the waist over the trunk waiting for his wife to massage him upright again. The key to the trunk was hidden in my suitcase, wrapped in a handkerchief in the toe of a sock wedged into a slipper.

'Well, well,' said Henry, holding the key up to the light, afraid it might be a dud.

Elisabeth was unpacking my things. I stood.

'Dear, dear,' said Henry, when Elisabeth handed him my three new suits. 'Those won't do at all, will they?'

My suits were not right. This couple agreed immediately that my new suits were somehow not right.

'We'll leave him now, shall we? Let him settle in by himself for a bit. When he's ready for tea, he can come down, can't he? He'll find the way, won't he, do you think?'

'Smell his way down. Sardine sandwiches today, for Thursday, haven't we?'

They closed the door behind them very slowly, very quietly, as if I were finally asleep after a racking nightmare. I stood in the centre of the rug where I had come to a halt, a rug laid on floorboards painted brown. My hair moved in the breeze. Automatically I closed the window, looking in vain for the double casement. Elisabeth had pushed the emptied trunk to the foot of my small child's bed. I put my hands on the mattress and pressed, sat down, lay down with my arms behind my head. Fine lines mapped the ceiling, all the countries of the world tumbled together so that none was recognisable. How did they know my suits were wrong, so well made by Mr Schneider even at the special rate?

24

I could not imagine what I was going to do in this house. I did not know for certain why I was here. Herr Schelling's salute had roused my mother, set her organising to send me away. My father would have preferred me to stay, but it was too late, she had seen to that. Then I realised that a journey made one way could be reversed. The Chapmans were not happy people, and I wasn't likely to make them happier. I would find my way downstairs to their sardine sandwiches, but afterwards I would write to my father, at his office where my mother would not find the envelope first, and we would arrange my return.

'Ah, Leo. There you are. Found your way down. Well done. You'd better come and meet my irascible mother.'

Gloomily, Henry steered me into the dining-room where a table was laid for four. There was a low cake on a plate in the middle. Another plate with pieces of white bread already thinly smeared all over with butter. There was a pot of jam with a spoon in the pot. A plate of small cakes with some white stuff on the top. There were the sardine sandwiches. Elisabeth was bringing in a teapot which was wearing a woollen hat. Behind her, tall and upright, was a thin woman with iron-grey hair set in immovable ripples. Her mouth was thin and vermilion, her nails long as claws, brighter than her mouth. The ugly white dog pressed against her legs.

Henry spread an arm towards her. 'This is my mother, Mrs Chapman. Mother, this is Leo Beck.'

'The debt child,' she said. 'What an enormous nose you have. All the better to smell us with?'

'Mother!'

'It's all right, Henry. Oh really, can't you see he can't understand a word? Besides, I have said nothing that isn't true. Now.' She approached, step by step, making for me. 'Leo.' I nodded. 'Good. Jason.' She pointed down at the dog. 'Say hallo to Jason. Jason, say hallo to Leo.'

The dog couldn't help being ugly. I knelt and put out a hand but the lumpen animal whined and cringed behind Henry's mother.

'Never mind, he'll get used to you. He's a terrible coward, as befits this house. Shall we sit?'

Elisabeth poured tea for everyone. Henry's mother stopped her. 'The boy won't drink that. Germans don't know what tea is, do you?' I nodded. 'You see?'

'No, mother, he's nodding because he does know.'

'He doesn't.'

'He must do.'

'Why must he? Don't make assumptions, Henry. Germans drink coffee all the time, don't you? You see? Now, Leo. Will . . . you . . . drink . . . tea?'

'Please. Milk.'

'Oh, excellent.' Henry's mother clapped her hands. 'A diplomat.'

After the meal Henry's mother opened a drawer and pulled out a box. 'Do you play? Do you know how?'

Draughts. Who could not play draughts? She set the board out on the table, snorting with impatience at Elisabeth, who was slow to brush the crumbs from the tablecloth.

I beat her, chilled, thinking it was rude, but she interlaced her bony fingers, stretched her claws and set the pieces out again. 'At last! We shall play every day.' I beat her again.

Elisabeth hovered. 'I think Leo ought to get ready for bed, Mrs Chapman. He's had a long journey.'

'Oh, nonsense. You know nothing about continentals. They never go to bed.' But she yawned. 'I shall go and read.' She raised herself and departed, the white dog Jason leaning on her ankle.

In the morning I was woken by a flushing lavatory and weeping. I opened my door. Henry stood stooping in sad pyjamas, striped blue, patting Elisabeth's bent head as she snuffled over a handkerchief. 'There, there, dear. Never mind. We must just keep trying, that's all.'

There was something important they couldn't do, so upsetting to Elisabeth that it was making her cry. I wondered if it was my fault and whether, as their guest, I should offer to help. I stepped forward, but the door opposite opened and Henry's mother emerged, already encased in a dark-green dress buttoned tight at the neck, her grey ripples undisturbed by sleep. 'Oh dear me,' she cawed, 'have we failed again?'

'Mother. Do you have to?'

'I was only making an observation. Good . . . morning . . . Leo. Did . . . you . . . sleep . . . well?'

'Thank you.'

'Henry. You'll have to get the boy to school. We don't want him under our feet all day.'

'Yes, mother. When school starts. In a week or two. It's all arranged.'

At breakfast she said, 'Now. Leo. I want you to call me the Queen Mother. It will make Henry feel better. A king without an heir, oh dear, oh dear.'

'Please?'

'The Queen Mother.'

'Mother, don't be ridiculous. You'll confuse the poor fellow.'

'Perhaps you're right. He'd better call me Ma'am. Can you say Ma'am? Say it. Say Ma'am.'

'Marrrm?'

'Oh, Henry. Did you hear that? I am Marrrm.' And so on.

I wrote to my father. The Chapmans, I pleaded, were peculiar. I suggested the house was dirty, which he could not verify, but which seemed to me to be true, for nothing gleamed with my mother's polish. I said they did not want me to stay. I said they had the windows open in my bedroom, where there was no heating. I said they let the dog sleep in the bedrooms. I said that I could manage my voyage home myself, and if my mother were against it he and I could live somewhere together. Meanwhile, however, he might persuade her that she had made a mistake.

Elisabeth took me to a department store where I was fitted with a black blazer and grey shorts, thin grey socks, black shoes, a striped tie and grey shirts to wear to the school that had all been arranged.

My father's letter had been written from home. He had discussed its contents with my mother. It was natural, they concluded, that I should be homesick and find a stranger's household unusual. The best thing to do was to fit in with the strangers as quickly as possible. 'Pretend,' insisted my father, 'when you have to.' He recommended opening the window after I was dressed and ready to leave my room, but advised me to be sensible and keep it closed at night. If I did not allow the dog into my room its germs in

27

another's were not my concern, but I should remember to wash my hands after contact with the animal. Of course the Chapmans wanted me to stay. They were English, though, and would need getting used to, but it was I who must get used to them, not the other way about, for I was the outsider. There was no question of any return. 'Try to make the best of it. When we see each other again, you'll be glad you did. You'll understand it was better this way.' He did not say when we would see each other again. He had been talked round.

I was angry. Pretend? Very well. I would pretend. I would pretend so well they would not recognise me. I would not get used to the Chapmans, I would become a Chapman, and when the time came my parents would see what they had done and be sorry.

On Saturday mornings Marrrm 'did out her room' and downstairs Elisabeth fluttered with anxiety. Marrrm, who told me you never ask a lady her age, may have been very old. She was angular, gaunt, taller than Elisabeth. Where Elisabeth's monthly disappointment was steadily sapping her energy, it had the opposite effect on Marrrm. When she heard her daughter-in-law blubbing behind the bathroom door she was ignited with impatience. She would wait for Elisabeth to emerge with swollen eyes and a brave smile, and she would pat her vigorously on the arm and console her. 'Never mind, never mind. It's not your fault. We all know that.' So that Elisabeth would renew her sobbing in Henry's defence, while Marrrm bounded off for the carpet sweeper.

On Saturday afternoons Henry listened to the sports results on the wireless while Elisabeth was out singing 'Sheep May Safely Graze' with the St Saviour's Housewives' Club choir. Two copies of the local newspaper were delivered in the morning so that, at teatime, they could read bits to each other. Marrrm snorted. 'This is the nearest they get to marital bliss, Leo. Observe it.'

On Sunday mornings Henry and Elisabeth went to church and did not ask me to accompany them although I would gladly have done so. Henry was hesitant, thinking of my soul. 'Would you care to go to the . . . um . . . synagogue? There is one near here, I'm told.' 'No thanks,' I said. After lunch Henry walked round the block with his head hanging down as if he were scanning the pavement for

28

dropped coins. Once a fortnight he took Jason to the vet, who put drops in the dog's ears.

Little was asked of me for reasons of compassion, perhaps, or because they could not forget that I cost them something less than the monthly sum they received for their pains.

Marrrm snorted. 'Bad for the boy. Give him something to do, Henry, for goodness' sake. Or he'll grow up thinking he's a guest.'

They gave me Jason, who required walking twice daily. He was a bull terrier, built to be a terrorist, with bloodshot eyes in his misshapen head. But he was neurotic, afraid of everything, outdoors especially, and he would scream in panic as I hauled him to the corner and back, his massive shoulders quivering, his hind legs skittering over the pavement. Marrrm watched gleefully, knowing that the neighbourhood would interpret the animal's shrieks as evidence of ill-treatment at my hands.

Upstairs in my nursery I leaned over my homework while blue bunnies hopped about the wallpaper. I liked maths best because I excelled at it – why pretend otherwise? – and numbers are numbers wherever you are. Numbers were safe. But I also steeped myself in the language of the country I had adopted, sucked the sense out of new sounds and made them mine. I was clever. 'Above average' was the term they used.

I had ceased thinking about my parents except when my mother's letters arrived, like hospital visitors, not unwelcome, but disturbing our closed community.

'. . . and Pappi has brought home a little budgerigar, all yellow with a patch of blue on his head. He cracks his beak when I call him and I promise you he understands every word I say, Mrs Weiss agrees, and we have decided to call him Fritzi because he seems to be saying that all the time . . . Pappi is away a lot . . . Mr Goldschmidt, you remember, the man with the two big sons you said you didn't like, is leaving Berlin. He says he is leaving Germany altogether and letting one of his apprentices take care of the shop. But Pappi and I have told him that when he comes back he won't recognise the shop because people only take care of what is theirs. Pappi says that once you have made yourself a solid base you have to be a fool to turn your back on it . . . Tell Mrs Chapman I will send her some recipes if she would like them. I don't know how to bake "rock" cakes but I wouldn't like to eat them every week . . . Such good people. I must remember to tell Mr Gross how happy you are there . . .'

Probably the letters smelt of home, of my father's cigars or my mother's toilet water. But for six days of the week I was remaking myself into a Chapman. On the seventh, the postman rebuked my hubris.

Dr Shapiro, teaching geography, was not listened to. He gobbled his words and at the back of the class a row of boys gobbled back at him. He had a milky gaze through thick lenses, the curved brown teeth of a rabbit, sparse hair and a waddling walk. They said his breath was thick. People drew lewd cartoons, accentuating his thick glasses and heavy lips, and tittered. I didn't join in, lacking the stomach for it, nor did I demur. Whenever I heard his wide-hipped trundling steps approaching along a corridor I slunk away for fear my classmates might invite me to take part in baiting him. But I had all but joined them and sanctioned their thoughtlessness, even if it was not calculated cruelty, when I knew what I should be doing.

To me my classmates were not hostile. Nor were they especially welcoming, lacking curiosity. I remember some names, some faces. A Philip, whose mouth was perpetually ringed with toffee. Michael Harrington – about whom I can recall nothing else. And of course Jeremy Benson, who smiled at me, offering himself generously, when others would not, as a potential friend. But he was square and dull with a wide, amiable face. His hair was the colour of sand as the sea retreats and his shoulders were already broad. For no good reason that I could fathom I could not bring myself to like him and his well-planted feet. Instead, I plunged into the collective of my peers, where, as one among many, one swims unnoticed.

The one thing I most looked forward to was the school morning assembly: the routine, knowing that we would file into that hall always in the same order, alphabetically; the script – a hymn, a reading from the New Testament, another hymn and the jostling to sit cross-legged on the scratched parquet for the announcements; the nudging, the whispering, the hissed 'Tsst!' from the teacher at the end of the line; above all the massed singing. We did not sing well. I, particularly, did not sing well, having little voice and scant musical memory.

> All things bright and beautiful,
> All creatures great and small.
> All things wise and wonderful,
> The Lord God made them all.

That was for the younger ones. Then we sang for them.

> Oh hear us when we cry to Thee
> For those in peril on the sea.

Poor voices were lost among the fine ones in our ragged rhythms, each verse lagging behind the piano, the accompanist struggling to find us and hold us to his beat. But we sang together. And although I knew mine was a singular joy, that everyone else, staff and pupils, considered the whole business tedious, I was invariably uplifted by the end, suffused with affection for all those other bodies around me. No doubt it was a purely physical well-being induced by breathing more deeply and in a more measured way than usual. It did not seem so at the time.

Slowly I made the acquaintance of Jesus Christ, until then little more than a name. Everyone else had already been introduced. In the weekly lesson devoted to religious instruction our teacher, Mr McKechnie, eschewed the story in favour of pointing out the occasions in history on which its injunctions had been ignored. What's the use of it, he seemed to imply, but would not say so, leaving me entertained but dissatisfied.

These are the moments when the well-assimilated refugee realises that his cover is no more than camouflage over an alien core. I was fourteen. Deciphering Jesus was, to me, the same as learning the nursery rhymes I was too old to wish to sing but without which I had no English childhood. I tried both in private. The nursery rhymes proved the more difficult, for while the words were to be found the tunes were closed. I couldn't read music. Nor could I ask anyone to sing them for me and retain my dignity. That small failure gave the Christ story a head start. And what a story! God's son, conceived by the union of a pure virgin lady and the spirit of God, visited by wise men, feared by a wicked king who, like Pharaoh, slaughtered male babies in a paranoid burst of mistaken self-preservation. This baby survived because it was intended that he should. He grew up and spent his days wandering about in the heat with a band of rough-hewn followers, healing people, working magic, talking endlessly. Arguing. He was very bright. He had shown enormous early promise, trouncing the bemused Pharisees at their own game, aged only twelve. Shafts of light from the heavens illuminated him at significant moments and he pleased his father, who was with him one and the same person, but who nevertheless allowed him (and, therefore, presumably himself) to die horribly on a cross on the top of a hill. The cross bore a sign saying that this man was the King of the Jews. On either side of him a burglar was lashed, rather than nailed, to a similar cross. One repented and was saved. The other did not.

Mr McKechnie was also teacher of history, which he expounded with a sort of anger, listing the Kings of England and the dates of their glories in his nasal tenor voice, writing for us to copy from the blackboard the clauses of the Factory Acts of 1833 and 1844, a challenge to risk the smallest error. He stood in front of the class, small and morose, and dared us to find what he was saying interesting. It was rumoured he was a communist.

He was also a stickler for the rules, whatever they happened to be. Sitting on his chair at assembly, he swivelled his head, eager to spot the fidgeter, the giggler, the tell-tale heads too close together, implying speech. 'Tssst!' And he would thrust out his right arm, index finger like an unsheathed dagger, so that across the hall the culprit felt the stab. He was seen to sing the hymns with emphasis.

Sometimes, when I was foolish enough to turn my head towards him and would find him looking at me with his eyebrows raised, I felt my pleasure draining away. Yet never quite. For I imagined myself on a hill, talking; all around me sat the multitude, straining to hear, straining unnecessarily, for my whispered words reached each one individually. I put a hand on a dying man, who revived. People fell silent as I passed and tremulously fingered the hem of my robe, drawing strength from it. Tiny children in distress smiled when I turned to look at them. Wherever I went people were made

32

better, their complexions changed, the emaciated grew plump; crutches were discarded, the blind opened their eyes, the deaf sang, Elisabeth conceived. But I wanted more than that. No one was ugly, no one was gnarled or roughened. No one was lonely.

It is in the nature of daydreaming that the dreamer improves on his world alone, locked in himself at that moment more than at any other. During classes I sat at my single desk, a boy in front and another behind, each at his single desk, and was on my own.

It was on my own that I discovered the zoo in its grassy park and began going there every Sunday afternoon. I found it both desolate (the awful pacing behind the wire) and consoling (every week the animals were where I expected to find them, still alive and in motion). First of all I was delighted by the looped rhythm of the monkeys swinging arm over arm, never faltering, never glancing up to select where to fling their leathery hands. I clasped my hands behind my neck in admiration at the loose shoulders of the big cats and longed to see them flexed on some wide grassy plain. The great seductive eyes of the giraffes, the sheer size of the elephants' flat feet, the mosaic of the snakes astonished me at each visit; they made me smile, I suppose with pleasure.

Eventually I found my way to the reptile house where a chameleon behind its glass fused with a sliver of rock in the rectangular desert world someone had created for it. It out-waited me. I could not stay to watch but I became besotted with this creature that appeared to have decided not to move. Every visit the chameleon was motionless, but somewhere else. And always I could not control the urge to sidle away and keep company with something more entertaining, knowing that when I turned my back the chameleon would flit to a new location to freeze there, disingenuously, disdaining even to swivel its bulging eyes to take pleasure in my frustration.

Hour after hour it sat on its rock, indistinguishable from it, gauging the distance between the end of its nose and an imagined perched insect, computing that distance by the length of its sticky tongue and the speed with which it could launch the tongue on to the insect. I thought it was thinking about me just as I was thinking about it; I thought it waited for me, that it was, in its way, playing

33

games with me. It did not yet occur to me that not only was it not thinking about me, it was not thinking at all.

Every Sunday I moved from cage to aquarium throughout the zoo and grew increasingly confused. So many creatures, so many species, the warty and the speckled, the lithe, the slimy, the spined, and the pulsating bladders of existence. Why so many? Why some so lovely and others so ugly?

I couldn't sing but I could whistle adequately and did so, as one does, through my teeth, impelled, without knowing why, to a tune.

> All things wise and wonderful
> The Lord God made them all.

'Stuff and nonsense, actually, Beck.'

I had come to rest, as always, by my chameleon. In the glass of its container I saw behind my own weak reflection the face of Mr McKechnie. He carried a small girl on his shoulders, his daughter.

'Take it from me, lad. There's nothing wise about the Lord God's creatures, nor about the Lord God himself. Nothing wonderful either, nor nothing made, or if it was it was a botched job. A mess, the whole thing. And if that's so – and it is so – then I'd call it a bit of a wasted effort, wouldn't you say? A waste of time.'

'Can you talk about God wasting time?' I retorted, and bit my tongue.

Mr McKechnie was tickled, however. 'Well, I imagine it's possible to be profligate even with eternity. Come on, Lucy. Time for your ice cream. That's the sort of time that matters, isn't it? Don't hang around here too long, Beck. A watched chameleon never budges, hah?'

They moved away, the child clinging to her father's sandy hair, legs locked over his shoulders, sandalled feet hooked under his armpits.

Then why do you sing along with the rest of us at assembly? I thought.

Three

They asked me to select a profession. 'I'll be a doctor,' I said. Hasty words because some were required, and it was done.

'Yes, yes. Good profession. Tough one, that, but you'll manage, I dare say. Doctors in the family, have you, Beck?'

Not one. But naturally the choice would be welcomed. I had spoken and could not – or would not – take the words back and a chill of regret coursed through me. I heard, suddenly, my mother's voice exaggerating proudly to Frau Weiss next door. I saw her ordering clothes from the tailor. I wanted to tell her to stop, that she didn't understand, that I was not going to be the sort of doctor she expected, and wanted me to be. Frau Weiss had no doctors in her family either and so she, too, would be impressed. How could she fail to be, with Dr Meissner living only two streets away and so courteous out and about when you met him?

My mother had no idea what being a doctor in England would entail. She was clasping her hands under her chin at the image of a younger Meissner, not so tall perhaps, thinner for sure, still only a boy but receiving his patients in a wide, high-ceilinged, sun-filled consulting-room whose polished floor was a museum of oriental rugs, or so said people in the know. The furniture was antique. 'No reproduction rubbish, Leo,' my father confided. 'Dr Meissner is a cultured man, he knows what's what.' Where furniture was concerned, so did my father, but in himself he counted it merely trade.

Dr Meissner wore his lightweight, tailor-made grey suits with casual formality. He led the conversation everywhere. He played the viola in a string quartet that rehearsed twice weekly in his apartment. He published articles in a historical journal on the subject of ancient runic writing. He skied. He could dance better than any man she had met, Frau Weiss whispered, and rolled her eyes. And she should know, my mother agreed, she can dance, that woman. When Dr Meissner recommended a visit to the theatre or mentioned, by the way, the work of an up-and-coming musician of whom no one had heard, everyone put themselves out and underwent the cultural experience with serious expressions on their faces. And when it failed them, as it was bound to do, they blamed themselves. They were not as educated, not as clever as Dr Meissner. He had never been known to have a medical failure.

I could have told my mother, that's no way for an English doctor to behave. 'No?' She would be amazed. 'Then how?' 'How?' I would say impatiently. 'Like Dr Hoop, of course.'

Only a few times had Dr Hoop been called in to treat us. Once I had a chesty cold. Twice Marrrm complained of rheumaticky pains in her legs. 'Look, I can't walk,' she moaned, bowing her legs out at the knees and bending to see the effect. Once Dr Hoop came to see Elisabeth when she had stomach-ache in the middle of the night. He came to see us willingly and straight away. It was not so everywhere, but Henry, who had known him long, if not intimately, had learned the rules. The doctor arrives, steps through the front door, bag in one hand, hat in the other, lays the hat on the hall table but keeps his worsted coat on. Henry points up the stairs to indicate the whereabouts of the invalid and asks casually if Dr Hoop might care for a drop of Scotch. Dr Hoop is apparently taken aback and says 'Um . . . ah . . .' and hesitates over a tricky decision but quickly makes up his mind. 'Well, I can't say I wouldn't . . .' But he keeps his drop of Scotch for afterwards so that, as far as his visit to *us* is concerned, all the proprieties have been observed. He cannot be faulted; no drinking done until the patient has been carefully and soberly considered. It was always well played by them both, except, remarked Henry, for the hint of whisky on the doctor's breath as he came through the door.

He was a big man with a long square head. He had begun his medical career in the navy, and on the walls of his surgery were paintings of a troop ship in heavy seas, thick with waves of cracking oil paint. Dr Hoop would sit on the bed and pat his patient on the thigh he had pushed aside to make a space for his own buttock. 'And what seems to be the matter?' he would say. He prescribed bland food and bed rest, nodding from the neck to emphasise the correctness of his remedy, and set off downstairs for his Scotch and a chat with Henry. I cannot comment on his expertise, for by the time he was called in whichever one of us it was that needed his services was already, as he put it, 'on the mend'. His name conjured up neither scandal nor spectacular success. My parents would have to understand that, since I was now an Englishman, I would be a doctor like Dr Hoop.

My blurted vocation provoked an invitation to tea from Mr McKechnie. 'Tea. Sunday. Five o'clock at the above address.' I accepted. Refusal did not seem an option.

They lived in a basement, in a street without trees but with dust on the pavement and small girls, thin in longish frocks. Steps through an iron gate in iron railings led down into a narrow area. The front door was narrow and black.

I saw a large room, the further end curtained off, not squalid, but painfully provisional. Without the genteel shabbiness of Henry and Elisabeth's, where the surfaces were dusted rather than polished and the furniture well used, it had about it the feel of a repository of other people's goodwill. It seemed that every item – the armchairs, the fireside rug, the table – had previously been scattered in the households of other, unknown people who had unexpectedly come up in the world and could therefore afford to distribute their unwanted possessions among those who were still waiting.

Lucy, with tightly plaited mousey hair, sat opposite and did not speak but stared at me while she pulled her sandwiches into tiny pieces between her fingers before eating them. Mrs McKechnie wore a flowered apron and gave me hard-boiled eggs and salad cream. The table was covered with a yellow oilcloth cracked at the corners.

'You'll be wondering', said Mr McKechnie, who had not greeted me, pacing the length of his table, 'to what you owe this tea. And come on, lad, help yourself. Jean's made the effort for you so you must do her work justice.'

'Squash, dear, or tea?'

'Squash, please, Mrs McKechnie.'

'You only have to say.'

'I was in two minds, I'll not pretend otherwise. I don't, as a rule, entertain my pupils at home, and that's not because it is against school policy to do so. On the contrary, that in itself would be an incentive to issue invitations on a regular basis.'

'Bob. Now, dear.'

'Tush, Jean. No, in your case, Beck, there was a reason, a reason almost amounting to duty.'

He reached the end of the table, turned on his heel and paced back again, eyes down, heel to toe, as if he were taking the dimensions of the room.

'It has come to my notice that you have expressed a wish to study medicine. Now, of course, I know that every teacher is jealous of his subject – we tend to take it as a compliment if a boy chooses to pursue further the thing we have been teaching him. I am different. And why? Because no lad with a head on his shoulders such as you have would consider continuing the study of history if his sole experience of it were the drivel I teach. Well, yes. You don't need to look so surprised. I have a job to do to earn my weekly wage to keep my family, that and no more.' He guillotined the air with his hand. 'My contract requires me to ensure that a reasonable percentage of the boys attending the school pass their matriculation in my subject with good enough marks to encourage the parents of another generation of boys to send their children to the school. I am not asked to fire you with enthusiasm, I am not asked to turn you into budding historians. On the contrary. Budding historians must ask themselves all the time not only what happened but why, through whose agency, and in whose interests? And that, Beck, as you will have noticed, has nothing whatsoever to do with learning by heart the dates of a succession of kings who took it in turns to misrule these islands as of right. I can tell you now that you will pass your examination. I can also tell you that I couldn't care less how well or how feebly, because all you will be demonstrating is your useful memory. Go on. Take another sandwich. They were not made for me, I can promise you that.'

'Bob! You'll make him think I don't feed you.'

'Och, Jean. He'll think no such thing. But anyone can tell an ordinary sandwich from a plate of special ones.' They did not seem out of the ordinary, but they had been arranged in concentric circles. Perhaps by Lucy. 'That memory of yours will come in handy for medicine, I don't deny it. So far as I can tell, that is three-quarters of what medicine is about – remembering large amounts of information. And at the end what will we have from you? The world will be richer by one doctor, even though I am not aware that there is a particular shortage of medical practitioners at the present time. What we are short of, Beck, is people who will stop for a moment and ask the questions other people so earnestly wish not to have to answer. These are times, these are going to be times, you mark my words, when we shall be needing as many of those people as we can find, and the sooner we begin preparing them the better it will be for us all.'

'Bob! You're confusing the poor boy, I know you are.'

'I am not, Jean.'

'You are. Just look at his face.'

'What's the matter with his face? Beck, are you confused?'

'Um . . .'

'All right, then. Let me go back a step. What did you do yesterday in Mr Willis's biology class?'

'We dissected a frog.'

'You dissected a frog. Why did you dissect that frog? To find out what its inner structure is like, I dare say. Did you learn a lot from that? I trust you did, or Mr Willis is not doing his job as he should. So now you know all about the innards of one deceased frog.' He paused, sucked in his breath and trudged back to the opposite corner. 'And what would you think if it entered the head of the frog to dissect you? But of course you don't have to worry about that, do you, because you know the frog has not enough head, and not enough power even to entertain the idea, luckily for you.' He turned again, retraced his first journey and came to rest behind Lucy, who was dismembering her sandwich with serene concentration. Mr McKechnie leaned forwards and put his hands on his daughter's shoulders, tickling at her neck with his fingertips. 'But we are different, Beck, aren't we? We are capable of those ideas. We can dissect a frog even without his kind permission, so we are allowed. Because no one can prevent us. Or perhaps I should say because no one can prevent some of us. Now you are

39

fortunate. You are among the number of that "some", your attendance at our school proves it. You are well fed, well housed, I don't doubt. You are lucky, Beck, lucky.' He leaned forwards, tapping me on the chest with a knuckle. 'Have you thought about that? What it is to be lucky as you are?'

'Now, dear. Enough of that. You're not to tease the poor young man. Sit down now, and eat your tea.'

Mr McKechnie snorted but sat. Mrs McKechnie set his plate of egg and buttered bread before him. He took a bite of bread. 'I'm not teasing, Jean, and he knows it.'

'Well, you shouldn't be putting ideas in his head.'

'What d'you mean, woman? I'm his teacher. It's what I'm paid to do, put ideas in his head. Or, rather, you're quite right. It's what I'm paid to prevent – the arrival of ideas in his head. But where would they come from if someone didn't put them there?'

'Not *those* ideas.'

Mr McKechnie sighed, shrugged, gesticulated into the air. 'I'm being silenced, Beck. My wife thinks there are things you talk about to growing boys and things you don't. Among the things she approves of are their families, their aptitude for sport, their cat or their dog and what they want to be when they grow up. It is unfortunate that in your case this last issue may not be raised here because I would have to bring into the discussion all those things my good wife thinks are unsuitable, including my belief that mankind is about to go mad – as a whole. And that if you, Beck, put your serviceable brain into the business of keeping people alive longer than is absolutely necessary you will be doing yourself no favours.'

Mrs McKechnie leaned over and pulled a mess of grey wool from a basket on the floor. 'Maybe the boy is thinking of others in wanting to be a doctor. Maybe he's not thinking of doing favours only to himself.'

Mr McKechnie slipped his hands into the wool and stretched it so that his wife could begin winding it into a ball. 'Don't you believe it. In this society, the only reason for doing anything is as a favour to oneself. It's what keeps us going . . . in this society. What do you say, Beck?'

40

What could I say? I mumbled something about wanting to heal.

Mr McKechnie cackled, spraying the oilcloth with his last mouthful of finely minced egg yolk. 'Hah! The laying on of hands, is it? You want to wander among the common folk and make them all better. Is that it? Is it? Well, is it?'

I said it was something of the sort and averted my eyes from the little blob of egg yolk on the oilcloth.

'You see!' Mrs McKechnie was rejoicing as if she had found her first ally. 'Not everyone is as sour and cynical as you.' She drew the words out, enjoying them.

'You think not? Then let me ask him. Why do you want to make all those poor sick blighters better? Why, Beck? Answer me that.'

Why? I did not want to be a doctor but I still dreamed of that magical healing. Why? I shook my head.

'Because you want to be loved, that's why. That's why any doctor does it. Because he wants to be loved. If you don't need the whole world to love you then you don't need to go about trying to cure it of diseases which are anyway mostly self-inflicted. It's a lot of cant, Beck. I tell you. Vocations. Rubbish. There's no such thing. And in case you're about to ask, why do I teach, believe me, laddie, it's not that I'm called to it.'

'Eat your tea,' said Mrs McKechnie.

Later, on the doorstep, she shook my hand. Her husband had remained sitting at the table. 'Don't you take too much notice of Bob and the things he says,' she whispered. 'You know what he wants of you most? He wants you to stand up to him. He's chosen you, somehow, and he wants you to be worthy of that. He's really very pleased you want to be a doctor. It's just his way. He's not always like that, you know.'

'Oh, yes I am,' he called out. 'At least I hope so.'

'Listen to him,' she said, sounding fond.

I turned to go, then turned back. 'Thank you for the tea.' She smiled and nodded, don't mention it. I looked over her shoulder. 'Goodbye, Lucy.' Lucy, who was sitting curled into her father's lap, stared up at me but did not reply.

Mrs McKechnie said, 'You must come again.'

'Yes, do that, Beck. Sunday after next. Five o'clock. After the chameleon.'

Mrs McKechnie raised her eyebrows at me, seeking an explanation, but I shook my head as if I were as mystified as her.

Behind her, Lucy was fitting pieces into a jigsaw puzzle, her father cajoling her to look not at the picture but at the shapes that formed it. After the door had closed and I had climbed the area steps to the pavement I waited a moment, then bent to look down into their dark parlour. The McKechnies stood face to face, their arms wrapped around each other. Lucy had wormed her way between the two motionless bodies. I envied her.

I walked back to Henry and Elisabeth's wondering why Mr McKechnie had invited me; thinking I did not much like him; wondering what little Lucy thought about; wondering whether he was right. But I was chosen, burdened by this privilege, and buoyed by it. Being the object of someone's choosing drew me to the chooser, as happens so often.

My teas with the McKechnies became a regular once-a-month affair because Mr McKechnie so decided on it. But at school he continued to behave as if we had never so much as exchanged words outside its gates. He glared at me in assembly as before, hissed his disapproval at me as much as at anyone else, paid me no more attention in class than my efforts deserved. I was offended, almost annoyed. He ought to signal something to me, something that others could intercept and decipher, so they might discern here a relationship subtly different from theirs. But he knew better. Teachers and pupils were not supposed to fraternise; even boys from one year were discouraged from mixing with those of another. Had it emerged that one of the invisible frontiers was being breached, once a month on a Sunday afternoon, during which time things were said that were well beyond the requirements of the curriculum, Mr McKechnie's position would have become delicate indeed. He could not afford that.

I knew when I had been fully accepted. A summer Sunday, when the flat was all the darker for the light outside, and as I came through the door opened for me by Lucy, she said, 'Hallo there, Beck', in her father's voice.

The Olympic Games had been staged in Berlin. We had seen at the cinema how impressively. Germany seemed to make the

London streets around us tawdry. The young Germans, girls thickly braided and bright-eyed, the muscled young men with polished teeth, made us feel, as we raced up and down our bleak playing ground, that we were a disordered bunch of boys whose limbs were no longer quite in control, whose voices had deepened but were still without weight. 'You're German,' they said to me, curious now for the first time. 'So what's it like?'

Germany was admirable, driven with an energy that was awe-inspiring. My classmates equated me with that Germany, and I revelled in it. What that meant, however, was that like everybody else I must see only what was wholesome. In this my mother was helping me. Her letters, dozens of letters by now, indistinguishable one from another, chattered inconsequentially and, to my shame, I did not even read them through. I did not keep them. I did not want them. I thought I did not need them. Even now I am not sure whether she wrote only about Mrs Weiss, about the budgie, about business, about Dr Meissner because she was protecting me or – conceivably – because she was trying, by writing, to create other circumstances. She had sent me to safety. Therefore she had expected a danger from which I must be made safe. But she was not attempting to avoid that danger herself. Could it be that the more events around her vindicated her first decision, the more she was determined to ignore them, will them away? Whatever the truth was – and I never found out – both of us contrived to affect an astonishing ignorance.

The changes in the nationality laws, whereby Jewish immigrants who had arrived later than 1918 were de-naturalised, left my parents unmoved. 'We have always been here. Nearly always.' Jews were banned from the civil service, from teaching in the universities and the schools, excluded from legal practice. But my father was in trade. The tax laws were altered. My father must have shrugged, '*Na ja*, so we have to pay a little more.' The pressure on Jews to leave – 'Only a fool goes when he doesn't have to', the Nuremberg Laws – 'We're already married, Elsie. It's not our problem.' None of it was enough to make my parents consider quitting their apartment, their business, their neighbourhood. The neighbourhood thought much as they did – until November 1938, the huge swastikas on the shop doors, the splintered glass of Kristallnacht. There could be no more pretending. I, however, saw to it that I knew nothing, which was not, after all, so very difficult. Henry's local newspaper had other stories to tell.

I might have been able to retain my innocence had it not been for Mr McKechnie, whose patience suddenly snapped.

'And where the dickens are your parents, Beck?'

We had never before mentioned my family, never referred to the strange arrangement by which I was housed in London, never, for that matter, once alluded to my German birth.

'My parents?'

'Yes, yes. Come on, boy. Don't you care? Don't you worry? Time's running out and you're not doing a thing.' In what way was time running out? I must have looked perplexed. 'If they stay there much longer they're going to be in trouble, your people. Old Adolf will see to that. Get them out of there, Beck, or you'll have it on your conscience.'

'Why?'

Mr McKechnie was sitting on a kitchen chair, knee to knee with his wife, winding the grey wool as if he never did anything else. He stopped winding and her hands froze at the diagonal, her movements lashed to his. He looked at me in silence with his cool tawny eyes for so long that I blushed.

'Tell me something,' he said at last. 'Do you really not know anything about this world, do you really never ask yourself questions? Have you not listened to a word I've been saying to you, have you not stopped to ask yourself why you're here, in this town, in this country? Why your father sent you –'

'It was my mother.'

An irritable toss of his head. 'Your mother, then. A woman with foresight. Why do you think I invited you to tea in the first place, when was it, last February? Did you think yourself such an irresistible individual? No, laddie. It's where you come from that was interesting to me, where and from what sort of family, even if you think you can go about incognito. But don't fool yourself. It's where you come from that makes you who you are. If you don't know your past you don't know anything and you might as well give your future to someone else – which you seem to have been quite happy to do. But you're nearly grown now, and it's your turn to get up off your backside and do what needs to be done. Act on it or never come here again.'

Mrs McKechnie put her hand on his arm. 'Bob. Stop it. Stop it, please. What is the boy supposed to do, at his age? He's only seventeen.'

'You know what you should be doing, my lad? You should be using this a bit more.' He tapped the side of his nose. 'You're not short of it. Not lacking nose, Beck, are you?'

'Bob!'

'So listen here. Not very far from here, in fact two streets away, is a small synagogue. You pass it every time you come here but I expect you haven't bothered to notice it. Go there. Go and ask the people there what you should be doing. They are your people. They'll tell you if anyone can. There are organisations bringing people in but they won't be able to much longer because nobody wants any more Jews. Don't you read the papers? If you let it lie too long your parents may not be allowed in, and it will be your fault.'

'Bob! He's still only a child. You're frightening him.'

'Frightening him! I hope to God I am, frightening him enough. Now go on. Get out of here.'

I went. I scuttled out as if Mr McKechnie was behind me with a knife. I ran from the flat with tears of anger in my throat, affronted by his tone, by his contempt. At the corner of the road I looked back expecting to see him shaking a fist at me but the pavement was empty.

To my relief the synagogue was locked. It was Sunday. 'So?' he would say. 'Then go on a Saturday. Simple.' Indeed.

Instead I kept faith with my caged intimates at the zoo, pacing back and forth with them, to their rhythm. The chameleon perched dully on its sliver of stone, rehearsing its tongue, otherwise motion-less; and for the first time I accepted that whatever it was doing while I was watching it was also doing in my absence. Once I leaned forward and tapped on the glass, heaving myself up on the bar especially placed to restrain visitors from such an action. The chameleon's head flicked upwards in alarm and instantly I had lost it. Now I waited with greater patience than I had ever waited in its presence, holding my breath as if my breathing might be sensed on the other side of the glass, willing myself to blend into the grey-green light of the reptile house, thinking to fool the chameleon with its own trick into believing I had gone elsewhere in search of better fodder.

Outside it must already have turned to dusk. They rang the bell to warn lingering visitors that the gates would soon close. Alert to authority rather than to the message of the bell, I left. On the way out I paused by the cage I had always hurried past. In the dimming light I thought I saw a sceptical glint in the humiliated eyes of the old lone gorilla, cradling his paunch on his concrete bed. In some jungle somewhere they had laid a snare and netted him. None of them powerful enough to take him on his own terms, in their numbers, in their certainty and with a great deal of shouting and excitement they had plucked him out for me to see. I stood in the dusk and apologised for the life sentence that had so abruptly curtailed his biography.

A month later, without my intervention, my parents sent a message to Henry and Elisabeth through Mr Gross announcing their imminent arrival. 'Tell the boy his parents have decided to move to England after all.'

Maybe Gross believed that if my guardians were to hear the news from me they would be offended, possibly even upset. Perhaps he had decided, on the contrary, that they should be the ones to break the good news to me. It was anyway a shock, a transparent shock, and boundless for being so unexpected. My first thought was that this was an intrusion. I was in England. My parents were supposed to be in Germany. That had been the arrangement to which I had agreed to accustom myself. To disturb it now seemed inconsiderate, churlish. The second thought exiled the first as Mr McKechnie's challenge filled my ears again and ordered me to ask myself who the dickens I thought I was even to think that way.

We sat round the breakfast table in our usual places, Henry, Elisabeth, Marrrm and I, and passed the letter between us. Marrrm said what I did not want to hear: 'Well, so you'll be moving along.' Under the table Jason was snoring.

Mr Gross wrote again. My parents would be taking over a small house in Cricklewood, helped by the Jewish Welfare Foundation.

Would we be so good and go there to see that everything was in order, wash the windows, sweep the path – he understood there was a path – and receive the crates should any arrive? But it was my parents who arrived, came to our house and sat in the lounge. My father wept.

They thanked Henry and Elisabeth with every observation they made, although they – like Henry – seemed unable to look me in the eye. They commented on how tall I was, thank you, so well grown, we're so grateful, how healthy, you have been so kind, we can't tell you . . . They said all this in German, of course, which Henry and Elisabeth didn't understand. It wasn't necessary to understand. They told me to my face all over again everything they had written, and my mother tongue sounded obsolete, belonging to another time. It sat uncomfortably in my mouth as I made my stiff replies.

I had never seen my parents out of place before. My mother perched very still in this stranger's home, looking about her only in order to be doing something but without the critical curiosity I could have expected. She picked up her handbag from the floor, nursed it in her lap and set it down again. She sat bolt upright, knees and ankles together, rather near the edge of the easy chair – partly from nerves, I guessed, but also because she didn't want Henry and Elisabeth to notice how her short legs would dangle if she sat herself back. She wore a small brown hat set straight on the top of her head; it screened half her face with a tiny brown veil, strewn with what appeared to be the brittle fragments of autumn leaves.

My father was bald. His head was square with a remnant hem of hair tacked on to it just above his neck. How silly, I thought, aware of thinking this in English before I recognised the injustice of the thought. But he had become smaller; he deferred to Henry, whom he had paid. He was shy, admiring of my English, and he made me pity him. I did not want to pity my father and I was angry with him for it. The tips of his shoes still gleamed with polish but his folded hands were draped across his knees like a pair of empty gloves. He sat peering up at Henry from between hunched shoulders with little round eyes. He had had to run away, with my mother scrambling after him. That was not the man he had schooled himself to be. He ought to have looked out for his woman, taken on whatever it was, whomsoever it was, single-handed if need be. Instead he had watched her pack their belongings into the crates, some of which were never to cross the German border, and said listlessly, but with growing irritation, 'Yes, yes', when she asked him, as she incessantly asked, 'And should I pack this too?' He had watched her write the letters. He had probably not listened while she assured him he would start all over again in England: people needed good furniture there too, and Leo would help. He might, perhaps, have said, 'Yes, but the furniture I made at home was good then and people liked it well enough.'

When the crates arrived they filled the front room of the small house in Cricklewood, blocking out the light from the window and announcing to the neighbours that new people were moving in. We shifted the contents back and forth until my mother was satisfied. She made an office for my father in the upstairs front bedroom where he sat looking down into the empty street. 'He'll start again, Leo, you'll see. But it will have to be in a small way to begin with.' She had locks fitted to all the doors, making herself at home.

With her things around her, she was restored. Her carpets were brushed, her pieces of mahogany gleamed, and behind their glass the little Greek athletes surveyed their alabaster musculature. Within a month she seemed to have traced every German-born woman in London and was out having coffee with them as if her flight had been no more than a change of venue. I thought: women's lives are so transportable. If they don't do much in one place, it doesn't matter to them if they don't do much in another. It was different for my father.

My mother's new friends could be heard coming and going, wearing their hats and good coats. Did they have husbands? I didn't know. Only that her husband still sat in the upstairs office, at the pristine desk topped with pockmarked red leather on which no papers lay, cupping his temples in his palms and listening to the piping female voices in the living-room below.

Then one morning my mother toddled up in triumph and told him, 'Herr Goldschmidt is here for you. Hurry up, he's in his car.'

My father raised his head and gazed dopily at her but lifted himself from his chair and tottered silently but obediently down after her to the waiting Herr Goldschmidt, whom he did not know, let himself be bundled into the car like a confused geriatric, and disappeared.

My mother was purring. 'You can make any man do anything if you do it through his wife,' she said.

When my father returned with Herr Goldschmidt I saw him arguing in the passenger seat, wagging his finger, tapping it on the steering wheel while Herr Goldschmidt tried to park. Herr Goldschmidt had the air of a man who has accomplished what was expected of him and hopes, now, to be thanked. They came together into the house carrying boxes of stationery which they bumped up the stairs.

'I am going to be very busy tomorrow,' my father declared in a loud voice, setting out his boxes of paper in important piles. 'I must not be disturbed. And next week I shall be away. I have an appointment in Birmingham.'

'You see?' my mother explained.

'Now then,' said my father, back from Birmingham, and spreading a large sheet of paper on his desk, 'I am taking on a partner. There will be small premises for storage here.' He stabbed at a point on the map with his middle finger. 'Everything is cheaper in Birmingham. But I will organise from here. This is where the people will be buying. *Ja*. And Elsie, I forgot. I brought you something.' As he handed it over, my father's eyes briefly met mine, then looked away. Although the handbag, wrapped in tissue, was only of plain brown leather my mother took it with pleasure and locked it in the empty tallboy on the landing. All her other handbags had been packed in one of the crates whose passage across the frontier had been stopped. She too was beginning again.

Four

I gift-wrapped my mother and father to present them to Mr McKechnie at the last parents' meeting before I left school, the first I was to attend, and led them into the assembly hall, one on either side of me, my head the apex of the triangle, feeling as if I were the parent. They were better dressed than other parents, which was inappropriate. My father's shoes shone as if they were wet; his suit was immaculately pressed and, for this English occasion, formal with its pocket watch and waistcoat. My mother had brought out the highest heels she had managed to pack and clicked her way across the scraped parquet, adding traces of her own, her slender ankles incredibly bearing the weight of her enormous bosom. Both my father and my mother wore, pinned to their right shoulder, the label handed to them as they came in: Beck (Mr), Beck (Mrs). All the parents were similarly tagged, for it was understood the staff could not be expected to know who belonged to whom.

Jeremy Benson stood at the hall door, acting as usher to show people to their seats. No sitting cross-legged on the floor today. He beamed at me, 'These your folks?', and nodded me away to his right where the boys were to be seated. Parents went to the left.

I returned to Jeremy. 'Can't I sit with them? They won't understand what's going on.' They might, I feared, do something to embarrass me, in their ignorance.

'Sorry. Rules. It would look odd.'

Nothing could be worse, I agreed. They looked to me odd enough already with their round, curious gaze. Meekly they followed the direction of Jeremy's chin to the places indicated. 'What a pleasant boy,' my mother said. 'Is he your best friend?' But I turned and went to a centre seat on the other side of the aisle where it would be hard for my parents to catch my eye but from which I could monitor their gestures none the less. Their heads were together, whispering where others talked. My father was pointing as if he were tapping, with his middle finger, towards Mr Flint's trestle-table on the platform. I saw it with his eyes. A mediocre piece of furniture, unworthy of a man of the headmaster's position and a poor advertisement for the grand school he had been informed I attended. How would I explain to him that here, the more august the establishment, the draughtier its buildings, the more meagre its accoutrements?

Mr Flint, the headmaster, swept in in his gown with a heavy file in his arms, and for a moment I feared my parents might applaud the arrival on stage of the conductor. 'Ladies and gentlemen. School. As you all know, this is the last such occasion we shall celebrate together before our Upper Sixth leave us for the world of work or academe. In short, to become, finally, men. We, I and the staff, trust that you, their parents' – his head switched to the rows on the left, mothers and fathers seated like paired birds – 'will regard the years your sons have spent with us without regrets and that you, the boys' – back to us in our black and grey, ranged according to age – 'will look back on those years with affection and . . .'

My father's hands lay in his lap, the pads of the middle fingers rubbing the pads of the thumbs, but he was sitting straight-shouldered, attending to the alien words.

Mr Flint nodded to the boy waiting with hands poised over the keys of the piano, and we got to our feet. I glanced across but my parents, well used to doing what those around them did, were already standing, their hymn books open. Someone, Jeremy no doubt, had placed a marker in the correct pages of the books provided for the parents.

The Lord's my Shepherd, I'll not want . . .

On my side, the boys' side of the dividing aisle, I stood and sang as tunelessly as ever, but with an aching nostalgia for the present moment. For the three verses of the hymn which, like those around me, I knew by heart, I forgot my mother and father again and sent

51

my slender baritone forwards towards Mr Flint on his platform, beyond him and out through the wall.

When we closed our books I felt my parents' astonished eyes on me. To avoid them I turned my head to the right and met the sardonic gaze of Mr McKechnie, blushed, and turned from that too.

'Let us pray.' Mr Flint closed his eyes. There was a moment of muttered unison, then his two hands patted the air with gentle downward pressure like someone modestly calming an ovation. We sat.

'Just a brief announcement for those of you who will be coming back in September. As you know, the autumn term starts again on Monday the fourth. There will be a sale of second-hand uniforms on Friday the first here in the hall. Please label any items . . . For those of you not returning, please be sure that you have given in all, and I mean *all*, your library books.' Around me my classmates were mimicking Mr Flint in silent and exaggerated unison. 'The staff have quite enough to do . . .' I alone had not heard this speech before, but I envied those who would hear it again. '. . . And now, may I wish you all a very enjoyable summer, weather permitting. There will be sherry in the library for the parents of the Upper Sixth and perhaps even a small glass for their sons.'

My mother clasped her sherry glass about its narrow waist, her little finger extended, the glass positioned in front of her lips as if she were preparing to take a sip. My father stood close by her side, his shoulder pressed against hers. He held his glass between fingers too wide for the little stem so that it seemed to me the sherry might spill out at any moment. I had refused the glass offered me. Sherry goes straight to my knees, as I had once discovered at Henry and Elisabeth's, parents-in-lieu who had never presumed to be parents.

Teachers circulated expertly, drinks in hand, pausing to suck in tiny amounts of the sweet stuff through lips pursed round holes as small as straws. I thought of courting birds dipping their bills, or anteaters probing with their sticky tongues.

Planted amongst them stood the groups of parents whose sons, made gawkier by the circumstances, clustered together, jostling one another, exchanging school talk to distinguish themselves from the paired adults with whom they felt, here, embarrassed. The parents registered the presence of those they had last met at a previous function with wide smiles, looking for their sons, comparing their sons, while the sons prowled the library's circumference and compared the parents. In all this Mr and Mrs Beck stood out sorely, never before scrutinised, come from Germany, funny and foreign in alien hats.

They stood quite still, waiting to be approached by the men who had been teaching their son. Jeremy Benson held out a platter of cheese straws. My mother took one and put it in her mouth. My father watched its passage, also took one but kept it between finger and thumb like a furtively held cigarette. Jeremy beamed as before and almost bowed. My mother was about to speak when Mr Flint slipped towards us, his hand already extended to take my mother's. Some of her sherry spilt as she transferred the tiny glass to free her right hand, leaving a sticky stain on the court glove she was still wearing. '*Ach!*' she said. My father exhaled through his teeth.

Mr Flint pressed her gloved fingers, ostentatiously noticing nothing. He put a hand on Jeremy's stolid shoulder. 'And this is our Head Boy, Jeremy Benson. You'll have met him at our little assembly?' I realised the statement was put as a question because he was unsure whether my parents could understand. Proving they could not, their heads turned simultaneously to me.

Impelled to some mischief I translated. 'Jeremy Benson is the boy's name. He's very important. He's a *Junker.*'

My parents took an alarmed step back as if he had clicked his heels, wielding a duelling pistol. They had thought him pleasant.

Mr Flint smiled, seeing them impressed. 'Enviable thing, that. Two languages. That's something I've never managed to get under my belt.' He turned away, scanning the library for a suitable and unencumbered pedagogue. 'Ah!' Arm raised, snapping his fingers like a man in the rain hailing a taxi.

My heart sank. Obedient to the headmaster's summons, Mr Shapiro was waddling his soft buttocks across the room, clacking his brown teeth. I saw my parents' expressions relax in recognition. From all corners the Upper Sixth were watching. And so, framed in the library door, his empty sherry glass dangling upside-down from his knuckles, was Mr McKechnie.

Mr Shapiro halted in front of my mother and father and bared his smile.

My mother was tugging at my elbow. 'Leo. Little one. Help us. The Herr Doktor Shapiro doesn't speak German.' She was astonished.

We formed a square, our backs to the rest of the company.

My mother was voluble in paragraphs: the house in Cricklewood; the missing crates; the huge swastika daubed across my father's shop doors; the fate of the budgie she had had to leave behind; Mrs Weiss and Mr Weiss; the good Chapmans, so kind but so incomprehensible; her son who was doing so well but of course Mr Shapiro knew that; my father's new business venture with the partner in Birmingham but the trouble was you never knew whom to trust and it was impossible to work out how much things really cost . . .

My father put a hand on her arm. 'Elsie! The boy can't keep up with you. One sentence at a time.'

But Mr Shapiro encouraged her with his brown-toothed smile. Her veil bounced and she set off anew: what a wonderful stroke of luck that I had found a place at this school which was obviously a cultured place, she thought it must be; and just imagine, studying to be a doctor, and at Oxford too . . . Whom should she thank especially for that?

'Not me, tell your mother,' said Mr Shapiro, looking at me so directly that I blushed. 'Our man's right behind you, Leo, in a manner of speaking. Best of luck.' And he shuffled away, his message untranslated, my parents watching his departure with the distress of people who think they may have caused offence.

My throat tightened as I heard Mr McKechnie's high voice at my shoulder. 'I'd say that was more like it, Beck. I'd say you've taken your time but well done anyway. Some day you must tell me what you did. In the meantime, introduce us, please.'

My mother clasped her hands in front of her bosom, the two huge breasts nestling in the angles of her elbows. The biology teacher? No? But *ach*, Leo, *Kleiner*! Surely the man they had to thank for turning me towards medicine. Tell him . . .

Mr McKechnie put his hand on my arm, and nodded. 'Say I

did my damnedest to stop you, and I'm not proud of the result. Go on. Tell her.'

I turned back to my parents, standing there waiting, my mother's hands still clasped in supplication, my father's grasping the brim of his hat. 'Mr McKechnie is very pleased you're so happy.' Their eyes shone. 'He says he thought he'd never talk me into it, he almost gave up but he's glad he didn't.'

My father reached out and pumped Mr McKechnie's hand up and down. Mr McKechnie pumped vigorously in return. Then he pulled back his left cuff and made a show of looking at his watch, miming the act exaggeratedly as if people who didn't speak English might also be limited in their grasp of small English gestures. 'Good heavens,' he said in flawless German. 'My wife will have cooked the dinner and here I am keeping her waiting. Please excuse me. We must meet and talk again.' Then in English to me: 'Tea next Sunday, Beck?'

It was a hot, heavy midsummer afternoon, the streets dusty where the McKechnies lived. The little synagogue on the corner was closed, as silent as if it had long given up on its clientele. In the small courtyard in front of it a group of children were playing hopscotch, their game chalked inexpertly on the paving stones. They stopped and watched me pass, a girl in a long pink skirt frozen on one leg, the other bent under her like a crane at the water's edge.

There was no discernible movement in the McKechnies' flat, so one could suppose there was no one home. At the top of the area stairs I stopped, thinking I could still turn back and escape past the hopping children.

The door was flung open. Lucy stood there shouting, 'It's Beck, Daddy. It's Beck. Beck's here.' She beckoned me with her entire arm as if I were a long way off and likely to lose my way. 'Come on, come on quickly. We've got something for you.'

'Yes, come on down, Leo. What a long time it's been.' Mrs McKechnie loomed behind her daughter from the murk of their indoors. 'Lucy's impatient. I wanted to send her out to play but she wouldn't go. She thought you might creep by without her noticing. Silly, isn't she?'

The table was laid on the yellow oilcloth, my place distinguished from the others by the folded paper napkin Lucy always arranged for me. The McKechnies each had their own bit of cloth rolled in a wooden ring. Surrounded by sandwiches and buttered bread was a large white cake with 'Congratulations!' iced in bright blue. A red fabric rose with two small dark-green leaves was poked into one side. Mr McKechnie sat in his armchair, in judgement on my entrance.

Lucy grabbed my sleeve and pulled me to the table. 'We made you a cake. I did the icing, didn't I, Mummy?'

'Well, most of it.'

'Do you like it? It's a lovely cake. I'm going to have one just like that when it's my birthday.'

'Yes, and you've got a bit of waiting to do before that. Now let poor Leo sit down and have his tea.'

I stood behind my chair and held its back with both hands. The cake was enormous. They would expect me to eat a large piece. I liked cake but my throat was blocked with apprehension. 'It's wonderful,' I said. 'But what's . . . ?'

'What's it in aid of?' Mr McKechnie had left his armchair and was unfurling his napkin. 'What would you like it to be in aid of? As I see it you have three possibilities. One, it's the end of your schooldays. Two, you have got yourself a place at the gentlemen's university. Three, you have brought your parents over to safety. Which will you choose? And do sit down, for God's sake.' He nipped off a corner of buttered bread and waved at me with the decapitated remains.

Mrs McKechnie held out both the plates of sandwiches and the bread for me to help myself. Lucy took a sandwich as the plate passed her and pulled it into tiny pieces, instantly laying them out into the pattern of a face. I watched her place a pair of eyebrows on the rim and nibble round the edges of two more pieces for the eyes. Mr McKechnie, chewing silently, waited. I took a piece of bread.

Mrs McKechnie set the plates down again. 'What's wrong with choosing all three? That's why the cake's so big. It had to be to hold three such good reasons.'

Mr McKechnie had finished his bread and was reaching across

the cake for a sandwich. 'No. That's too easy. Let him choose just one.' Like a crone in a fairy tale, offering a single wish.

'Cup of tea, Leo? Or squash?'

'Squash, please.'

'Same as always, like me,' said Lucy.

'Bob?'

'Tea, tea. You know that, Jean.'

'Lucy, you forgot to put the sugar on the table.' Lucy scraped back her chair and brought the white china bowl.

'Have we got everything we need now? Well, thank heavens for that, at least. Beck?'

Only one reason would be acceptable. He was trapping me. He was humiliating me, and enjoying it. But school was over, I was going to Oxford in the autumn, I need never face him again. I would drink the squash, eat my cake and decamp.

'I choose the second.'

'Then here's to Oxford,' said Mr McKechnie, raised his teacup and took a large, scalding swallow.

'But what about your parents, Leo? Surely.'

Mr McKechnie was sucking in air. 'No, Jean. He's chosen very wisely, I'd say. Well done, boy. I'd have thought less of you otherwise. Eat your cake now. Lucy will cut you a huge piece if you don't stop her, eh now, Lucy?'

Mrs McKechnie stood behind Lucy, her hands on the child's hands, guiding the knife as if they were newly-weds. A large wedge was put before me and I ate it all. With pleasure.

Five

War was declared, a siren sounded and everybody stood transfixed in the street. Then came the all-clear and they moved again. Nothing more.

I needed money and, seeking it, went to answer a small advertisement, displayed in a shop window, requiring a grocer's delivery boy. Passing Willesden Green police station, my mind occupied with the possibilities of travel the delivery boy's bicycle might provide, I heard, in the wings of my attention, the querulous lamentation of an old man accusing someone. '. . . Stupid, I call you, stupid. Couldn't you have been more careful after all this time, letting something like this happen? You're going to have some explaining to do. Idiot! Idiot! Getting yourself robbed at the first moment!'

Only after I had turned to the source of the complaint, seen a bent figure the size of my father but older and in gaberdine and spattered shoes, did I realise that he had spoken in German and I had replied: 'This is a police station. You could go in and report it.'

He seemed not to hear me but stood quite alone in the middle of the pavement thumping at his forehead with the palm of one hand while the other rotated wildly, egging himself on. I repeated my advice and this time my voice yanked him from his monologue. For a moment he was clearly unsure where he was and he retreated a pace, his back to the railings of the police station. I pointed at the building behind him and said again, 'It's a police station. Go and tell them you've been robbed.'

'How?'

Language, of course, would be the problem. I was rash. 'I'll help you.'

We mounted the steps side by side and therefore, to the eyes of the sergeant on duty, we entered as a pair.

'Yes, sir?' The old man was too unkempt to be granted a fully respectful tone, and I was too young. But the sergeant was not uncivil either.

I said, 'This gentleman has to report a robbery.'

The sergeant pulled a piece of paper towards him and asked my companion, 'Have you witnessed a robbery or are you the victim?'

The old man turned to me, the question in his eyes. Facing him, I translated and from the corner of my eye saw the sergeant step back from the counter. 'Just one moment,' he said and rushed through a door in the far wall, leaving the two of us unattended and unsupervised.

'What's the matter with him?' My question, foolish and rhetorical, was in English.

The door opened and the man who preceded the sergeant through it wore a suit rather than uniform, suggesting seniority. He was solid and wide-faced. He did not smile, but he did not scowl either. Here, perhaps, was a man who could be trusted. He approached us quietly but with almost menacing authority, opened the flap of the counter, turned, closed it and walked round us so that we were now between him and the sergeant, who had resumed his original position.

The man in the suit did not introduce himself but looked down into the face of the old man and glanced briefly at me. He held out his hand. 'Passports.' It was not a word that needed translating.

The old man made a show of rummaging in empty pockets before he remembered me. 'Please explain. I've been robbed.'

'Yours, then.'

'I'm English. I live here,' I protested. 'I don't carry a passport around.'

'That's what they'll all be saying. Anyway. Bring the old man through. Questions to ask him. You interpret.'

The flap was lifted again and with forward flapping motions of his outspread hands he shooed us to the other side, across the sergeant's office and through the closed door opposite. The sergeant followed and stood inside the room with his back against the door. There were four wooden chairs pulled back from a pale, scratched wooden table. There was no other furniture. The floor was mottled maroon linoleum, cracked around the legs of the table.

'He wants to report a robbery.'

'So you said. First things first. Sit down. You here, tell him there.'

We sat. The old man wrapped his gaberdine coat round him although it was warm. The tips of his feet tapped up and down, pecking at the linoleum.

The man held a pen poised over a large sheet of paper with official markings along the top and down the margin. 'Name?'

'Silberstein, Friedrich.'

'How's he spelling that? . . . All right. Where's he from?'

'Austria. Vienna.'

'How long's he been here?'

'Thirty-seven days.'

'Thirty-seven days? That's very precise. How does he know?'

'He's been counting them.'

'Why?'

The old man rubbed his eyes with the backs of closed fists and sighed. 'What am I supposed to say?' he asked me. 'I've been alive thirty-seven days longer than I expected.' To my ears it was melodramatic. It embarrassed me and I toned it down.

'He says he likes it here so much he's been counting the days.'

'Yes? Well, we all like it here.'

The sergeant stepped forward. 'Ask him if he's got a map of England.'

'Not yet, Sergeant. Not necessary, I don't think.'

'It's the rules, sir.'

'I know the rules. All in good time' – irritated by the interference of the policeman. 'On the other hand, go ahead, if you must.'

'Have you a map of England?'

The old man indicated his pockets again.

'Ask him: has he got a zeppelin?'

'What?'

'Just ask him.'

Friedrich Silberstein stared. 'I've been robbed, I came in here to say.'

'Satisfied, Sergeant? No zeppelin about his person.'

'Said he was robbed, sir. Might have had one before.'

'And where would he have been keeping it, Sergeant? In his trousers?'

'Perhaps he's got it at home.'

'Well, perhaps. Find out soon enough.' Then to me, 'We'll be needing an address, proof of residence – how did he get here? Who helped him?'

The old man wrote an address on a piece of paper and named a Jewish welfare society.

The man in the suit coughed. 'Them again. All over the place, like damned beetles. Who's he got over there?'

'What do you mean?'

'Who's he got? Parents? No, too old. Wife? Siblings? Children? Who's he got?'

'No one, he says. He says he's on his own.'

'Lucky for him. Have to get that Jewish lot to vouch for him but after that, tell him, he's class C. There's many that won't be.'

'Class C what?'

'Enemy alien class C. Do what he likes . . . within reason. Get him off home, now. Tell him to clear off.'

The old man left gratefully, his robbery unreported. I made to follow him.

'Whoa, there. Not so fast, young man. What's he to you, the old one?'

'Nothing. I've never met him before.'

'Lucky, wasn't he? Bumping into you just like that?'

'Yes.'

'What were you doing outside the station?'

'I was looking for a job.'

'A job? Here?'

'No, this one.' I showed him the advertisement I had copied down.

'Grocer's boy, eh? We can do you better than that. More of the same. There are plenty more like him, you'll see. Got people interviewing every day now. Need an interpreter. Your English is very good. Useful.' I wished he had chosen to compliment my German and taken the English for granted, but I had found employment. 'We'll have your address too, by the way.'

'I'm with my parents.'

'Yes? And? Live locally?'

'Melrose Avenue.'

'Oh yes. Number?'

'A hundred and eleven.'

'A hundred and eleven Melrose Avenue. Very nice, too. Eight o'clock tomorrow morning, young man. Be punctual.' He was writing again as I made my way out.

I was paid fifteen shillings a week as interpreter to the North London Tribunal headed by the man they called simply 'the Magistrate'. He gave me the money out of a tin which stood on a shelf with a kettle and a tea caddy. With my first earnings I bought myself a heavy black bicycle on which I would henceforth pedal importantly to my place of work. Cycling home, as upright and self-conscious as a child in his first uniform, I passed Tolini's, the Italian restaurant, which I had never entered, lacking the money and fearing to order food that I would most probably not eat. Now it was different. I would go in and ask for a cup of coffee, sit with it as I had seen others sitting in the window. If they wanted me to eat, well, I would pay up and leave, as only customers with cash can.

I propped my bicycle against the window and chose a seat precisely on the other side of the glass, the only customer. It was early afternoon and the midday diners had gone. The restaurant was a long thin room with a narrow aisle between the tables. At the back, away from the window where the light was dim near the door to the kitchen, two men leaned in their shirtsleeves among the ashtrays and cups of a small square table. They gave me a glance and began slapping each other's upper arms, each trying to urge the other to get up and serve me. Their reluctance to break their conversation brought the sweat out on me. Money was all very well, but I had disturbed their afternoon break, made myself conspicuous, and all for a single cup of coffee.

'Yes, sir?' It was the older of the two, his belly balanced on his belt, his arms as round as a leg of lamb. 'You goin' to 'ave somethin'?'

I swallowed. 'Actually, I only wanted coffee, if that's all right.'

'Everythin' is all right. You only 'ave to ask. I call the chef and 'e does what I tell 'im. That's because 'e's my son. But 'e would 'ave to do what I tell 'im anyway 'cos I'm the boss. So you not eatin'?' I shook my head. 'You eaten before?' I shook my head again. 'You ill? You not 'ungry?' He took a step back and surveyed me until I blushed and shifted on my chair. 'You don' like to eat? You don' like food?'

'Not much. Not when it's cooked.'

'But why? Wass wrong with you?' He was indignant on behalf of all cooks.

Mr Tolini was a stranger. He knew no one whom I knew. 'I don't eat because I can hardly taste, and I can't taste because I can't smell anything.'

'Nothin'?'

'Nothing.'

'Nothin' at all?'

'Nothing at all.'

'I don' believe you. Is not possible. Eh, now we gotta do somethin' about this. Wait a minute. Giusè!' – shouting towards the closed kitchen door – '*Due caffè!* Yeah, we gotta do somethin'. Lemme think, will you? Now, look. First we gotta be sure, I mean you can never be too sure, you understand me? You wait 'ere. Don' go nowhere.'

He swung round and almost ran to the kitchen, his stout legs struggling to keep the pace he had set them. A moment later he was hurrying back with a vast tray piled with pots. Behind him hurried Giusè with a cup in each hand. Tolini balanced the tray on one palm and with cavalier conviction swung the pots, one after the other, on to the table. He sat.

'Now, we gonna begin.' He swept the lid off the nearest pot. Steam rose. 'Put you face in this and tell me what it is.'

'Hot,' I said, droplets collecting on my nose, 'but that's all I can tell you.'

'Incredible.' He shook his head. 'Try this one, maybe. Is really strong.' Off came another lid.

'I'm sorry.' And I was. He was so disappointed.

'You know what I put in this? Peppers they sent from 'ome, and so much garlic' – he spread his arms – 'and basil and *origano* and everythin' that is a good taste and a good smell is in 'ere. An' you tell me you smell nothin'.'

'Not a thing.'

'Incredible. Eh, boy, this is a tragedy.' He laid both hands on my arm. 'I never met someone with a problem like this one. What we gonna do for you, eh? Tell me that.'

My deficiency had never made me feel so interesting and I laughed, embarrassed also by his misery. 'I'll just drink my coffee.'

'I gonna get you a brandy to go with it.'

'Oh no, don't do that. I've got my bicycle outside.'

'Is you bike? She nice, a good one. But you can drink one brandy with a bicycle. An' if you don' feel so good, 'cos you not eaten, you can push the bike.'

'But I don't want to push it. I only just bought it, with my first money. I want to ride it home.'

Mr Tolini gripped both my arms so that I knew there would be twin bruises next morning. 'You first money! You buy the bike and you come 'ere to celebrate with you first money, but you ain't got no smell so you can't eat nothin'. Is 'orrible. We gotta do somethin'.' He sat with his head in his hands. Then he looked up. 'Hey, wait a minute. Sometimes you eat somethin' otherwise you dead. Now, okay, you tell me, when you wanna eat somethin', when you so 'ungry you gotta eat somethin', what you like?'

'Soft-boiled eggs,' I said, 'and bread and butter and salt.'

' 'Ow many soft-boiled eggs?'

'Three.'

'Okay! You gonna get three soft-boiled eggs and bread and butter and salt. On the 'ouse. No, don' thank me. I gotta reputation to keep up.'

Tolini brought them to me, each egg in its cup, but cannily bringing an empty glass as well. Behind him came Giusè and the other man. All three sat at my table to watch me eat. I tipped the eggs into the glass, buttered my bread, sprinkled salt on it and dipped it into the soft-boiled eggs.

'Is what kiddies like,' said Tolini mournfully, 'but it make you 'appy?'

'It's wonderful. I wish I could try all your other dishes, but I'd only be pretending.'

'Thass no good. I don' like pretending. You come 'ere when you want an' I make sure you get the eggs an' the bread an' whatever. Eh, Giusè?'

And Giusè, taller than his father and scarcely older than me, gave me a thumbs-up and said in richly London tones, 'Right, mate. Any time.'

Some of them were elderly, the men and the women, the lawyers, oculists and shopkeepers; the qualifications they pressed on us were of little interest in the small back room where I was their mouthpiece. The Magistrate decided that all answers were to be relayed through me, and even those who could have spoken in English for themselves, who explained energetically that they wished to, were silenced by a shake of his head. When they asked his name he merely stared at them. Giving a name might be mistaken as a sign of intimacy – which could, at some later date, be abused. So they turned to me, but I must have looked like a supercilious child to whom they had to defer.

With my help the Magistrate wrote a large A, B or C by the names of the people who obediently delivered themselves to him to be so classified.

The As – there were only two of them – were deemed dangerous. They were immediately accompanied to their place of residence, invited to pack a suitcase and escorted away somewhere. Both said they were German nationals in London on business and trapped by the declaration of war. One claimed to have been on the point of concluding a deal to buy large quantities of embossed labels made by a factory in Fulham which also sold to the Japanese and the French. The other said he was buying textiles. We doubted all that. They were so evidently different from the others, and they argued, proof of malign intent. These were the sort of people with whom we would be doing battle.

The Bs were a problem. One couldn't be certain about people like them. Awkward types, they'd got into scrapes at work; one of them had tried to lead a strike. Some were socialists. They were allowed home, nevertheless, on condition that they first wheeled their bicycles to a police pound and undertook not to visit coastal regions. You needed to be able to keep tabs on the ones who might turn out to be untrustworthy.

The Cs were different. So long as they could prove that someone would pay for their keep and so long as we could be sure they hadn't left behind parents, or children or siblings for whose sake they might, in the event of an invasion, be persuaded to perform unfriendly acts, they could do as they pleased. They were refugees, after all, grateful and uncomplaining. The Magistrate and I were courteous and cool. People like us did not knock on one's door after dark. Even as we allocated the future of the shabby foreigners with the guttural accents, they were charmed.

Then I would pedal to Tolini's for my soft-boiled eggs, which Giusè had dubbed 'Beck's Special'. Tolini's brother wheeled my bicycle into the restaurant and I sat with them at the back, by the kitchen door. We played cards and smoked their cigarettes. Sometimes Giusè sat on the crossbar of my bicycle and we wobbled like kids to the cinema, where Europe was on the march. Men who knew what they wanted bellowed from their podiums, and the crowds, who wanted the men, bellowed back. We saw them, dressed in black but wreathed in joy, streaming to answer the Duce's beckoning arm. Giusè leaned forwards, smiled, spat and smiled again. 'Ain't been back in years,' he said. 'Wouldn't mind nipping over for a bit, if I could. My gran's getting on and Papa thinks she could kick the bucket any day. Don't fancy that lot, though, even if Papa says the country needed a shake-up. So does this one, I shouldn't wonder.'

My job with the tribunal lasted one month. In that time I ate sixty excellent eggs. When the time came for me to leave London for the university Tolini gave me a plastic flower. 'You keep that in you room. 'E last for ever, an' you don' care if 'e don' got no perfume.' Then I was on my way, a different man, a departing student with a suitcase outside Paddington Station.

Ahead of me were my parents, already positioned at the platform gate, and in dispute. They were a small couple physically, these conspicuous, arguing people, the man in an overlong coat and a Homburg, the woman solid of body, spindly of leg, her hair in close yellow curls under her veiled hat. Between them stood a bulging bag with smaller bags tied to its handles like a donkey with panniers. These objects seemed to be the cause of the quarrel which was being carried on in a language against whose people we had recently proclaimed ourselves to be at war. The woman was using more words than the man and at a more agitated pitch. Her voice penetrated into the deepest corners of the station. Men with pipes and newspapers were roused and turned to look.

I considered creeping behind them and on to my train which would lurch away from their public disagreement. But the curiosity around them was tangible and sidling closer so that they broke off and, in glancing round, saw me.

My mother hoisted her little arms in joy. 'Leo! *Kleiner!*' – abolishing my anonymity. Over her shoulder I saw my father also make as if to approach, then hesitate as he remembered the mound of bags, which held him, and he guarded them uncomfortably.

'Come with me and you can tell him yourself,' my mother was urging me, confident of victory, her voice radiant with unconcern. 'I think he really doesn't understand, sometimes.' She was hanging on my arm, pulling at it with a weight that balanced the suitcase on the other. 'Heinz, look who I've found! Now we can sort this thing out. Leo, you tell him.'

'What? What am I supposed to tell him? Pappi, what's going on? And we don't have to shout, do we? Now, here, on the station?'

She put her hand over her mouth and whispered between her fingers, 'So, now tell him.'

My father took this instruction as his. 'Elsie is coming with you to Oxford, to help you settle in.'

'No, she isn't!'

'Leo, you said not to shout on a station.'

'I'm sorry. But I'm going on my own.'

'You see, Elsie?'

'No, I don't see. It's ridiculous. How can the boy go to Oxford by himself? He's never been there before, he doesn't know his way about there, he doesn't know anyone. Someone has to make his bed up, sort his clothes out. You're both stupid. You never think, either of you. *Ach*, I don't know.'

'Elsie. Elsie, he's been in England since he was twelve, where you sent him on his own. Now you think he can't go from one English town to another without you. It doesn't make sense.'

'That was different.'

'How was it?'

'Because he was going to the Chapmans.'

'But we didn't know the Chapmans would turn out to be such good people.'

'Of course we did. Herr Gross recommended them.'

'Herr Gross didn't know a thing about them except that they needed the money and would be willing.'

'And that's all?'

'Of course that's all. You should know, Elsie. You arranged it.'

'You should never have let me.'

With that my mother's retrospective imagination caught up with her, her legs buckled and she would have found herself sitting on the ground had not my father swiftly kicked my suitcase under her. She breathed heavily, eyes closed in an ashen face. This was no play-acting. Her distress at having put me in such jeopardy six years before eclipsed the feat of my survival. I was not going to persuade her into making the mistake a second time.

'Oh, all right, then. Come with me if you must. But you can't stay. Women aren't allowed in college.'

'You think I don't know that? I already bought a return ticket. Look.'

A young man in loose trousers rolled up to the calves walked diagonally across a square of lawn surrounded on all sides by stone arches. His arms stretched behind him as if manacled to the broad, stiff-bristled broom which he was dragging over the grass. It left contrasting stripes of dark and light green in the perfectly mown surface.

My mother stopped to watch, enchanted. 'And they do all this just for you,' she said.

'Don't be silly. Not just for me.' Having thought the same. Mr McKechnie's nasal voice twanged in my mind.

My rooms were off a winding stone stairway in the further corner. The key they had given me weighed importantly in my hand. My door was dark wood, heavy, and swung on its hinges without a sound. Inside, the bedroom was small with a casement window;

68

there was a thin piece of patterned carpet on the black-stained floorboards, a narrow bed already made up, a table under the window, a chest of drawers, a narrow wardrobe and an empty fireplace. Next door was a study with a table, a bookshelf and three armchairs. There was a scuttle of coal-dust by the grate. In its emptiness, its stuffy silence, my accommodation was less than we had both expected after the performance on the lawn outside.

'*Na ja,*' said my mother and opened my case, smoothing the creases of the trousers as she hung them away, adjusting the shoulders of the shirts on the pink satin hangers she had brought in her bag. The university, she had predicted, wouldn't think of such things.

When I saw her back to her train, on to the train, she waved leaning from the window, heedless of the smuts. She had satisfied herself that I had safely arrived. I had assured myself she had safely departed.

My mother's unpacking had put a stamp of domestic familiarity on the alien furniture of my rooms. She ought to have let me come on my own, but she had not, I thought, been seen.

Someone knocked on my door. It was Jeremy Benson, offering cocoa. I turned the offer down politely and regretted it. I like cocoa.

Six

I think I tried to persuade myself otherwise, but I was not enjoying my medical studies. What I learned about the workings of a healthy body made me queasy. I was repelled rather than challenged by the uncountable varieties of its possible malfunction. But to be honest the problem lay elsewhere. I had not realised that in order to become Dr Hoop I first had to be student Hoop. Within the space of little more than the first half-term it became clear to me and to my fellow Hoops that we were not going to get on.

There was a familiarity among them, a recognition which they brought with them to their first encounter with one another from all the different cities of which they were natives. Like Masons they eyed each other with appreciation across the street. Medics knew other medics at sight, they could smell each other out at a distance. Only I, with my botched nose, failed to detect the whiff on the breeze. They spoke in full bellowing voices, rich sonorous voices that could have done service on swaying trans-atlantic vessels – and indeed were to do so. They played rugger with sweating enthusiasm, slapping meaty arms around meaty rumps, head under crotch. They lurched together on the night-time pavements in comradely clusters, beer-loosened arms across one another's shoulders, and whooped at the tight-lipped windows of the townspeople who wanted to sleep. They thought little of Leo Beck.

So what did he do? He affected disdain, grew a beard which emerged several shades darker than the blond silk of his head, and he spent many minutes in front of a mirror curling this beard around a pencil until it began to look as if it had been chiselled from a Greek statue. He bought a cloak lined in red from a theatrical costumier, who smirked and persuaded him to buy a silver-topped cane to set off the cloak. He then took to striding alone, muttering aloud with indrawn cheeks and reciting poetry in the presence of passers-by. It was intended to look as if the solitude had been selected.

Much of the poetry was my own. Some of it was not bad, I believe even now. I wrote it by candlelight on offcuts of wallpaper which I had to hold flat with my left elbow and forearm while I wrote. Each piece sprang back into a scroll as soon as it was released and I tied the separate pieces with ribbon like legal documents. My room grew a honeycomb of loose tubes in whose crevices the dust collected.

Jeremy Benson, who had always been an excellent rugby player and was, therefore, also a medical student, was still inexorably amiable. His smiles indicated good humour; the immobility of his eyebrows masked neither arrogance nor self-doubt. His shoulders were wide, his spirit a stranger to malice. I couldn't stand him. He was unaware of my dislike.

Together we might have made what he called 'a good team' if I had been content to ride the thermals of his unhurried, easy manners. Women were attracted to him initially and – realising, presumably, that he must soon be called up – chose to ignore the dull mind enclosed in his handsome head. The same women overlooked me altogether and therefore did not question whether I, too, would be asked to fight, or for whom. I saw myself as a diminished Cyrano, parrying with words but unequal to the swashbuckling, wooing the women Jeremy's face brought within reach of my wit. To my chagrin it was even a role he proposed to me, saying, if I remember this correctly, 'What say we wet our whistles at the Trout tonight? I'm sure I'll find you a lady or two, and you can read your poems out.' This was not showing off. This was Jeremy in honest invitation, the good neighbour whose rooms were on the same stairs, old classmate turned fellow student doing his bit where no one else would.

'Kind of you,' I muttered, in imitation of his pattern of speech. 'Bit busy tonight. Can't make it.'

'Good to hear it.' Jeremy, who no more noticed slights than

made them, sounded disappointed. 'Have fun.' I would watch him put on his blue blazer with two silver buttons at the cuffs in imitation of naval uniform. His shoulders grew. 'Be seeing you, then. If you can't be good . . .'

'I'll be careful.'

''Course you will. Not to worry, anyway. My kid sister'll be up next year, I shouldn't wonder. Caroline. Blonde as you.'

It didn't do to be in of an evening and anyway our exchanges precluded it. Once I gauged he had left the college grounds I would slip out to evensong and, wrapped about in my gown, sit brooding like a raven in a rear pew. Prohibited by convention from singing with the exquisite choir, I mouthed the familiar hymns and with closed eyes imagined myself returned to school assembly. You could not be more careful than that.

Later, after dark, I would feel my way along the river bank, listening to the light movements of the deer in the park and thinking that I held between my hands the black-stockinged calves of the women who milled around Jeremy and his many friends.

It was on just such an evening that they found me out. I was sitting in the dark between the arthritic roots of a wide willow, watching the V of light the landing ducks left on the black water. I was furled in my theatrical cloak because the spring sunshine hadn't yet percolated to the evening air, and held, through the material of the cloak, my copy of Donne's sonnets, from which I was quietly declaiming – by heart as it was too dark to read, for the benefit of the river, its ducks and what I generally supposed to be Nature. From a distance I may have looked like a gnarled outcrop on the giant trunk except that, for some reason, I was swaying slightly, backwards and forwards to the rhythm of my own voice.

I was not so entranced by this performance that I failed to hear the approaching babble of tipsy talk and laughter, but I pretended none the less. They can't have heard me over the noise they were making but they must have made out the black rocking silhouette at the water's edge. There was a sudden silence, and in that silence my voice emanated from the silhouette:

72

'When I am dead, and Doctors know not why,
   And my friends curiositie
Will have me cut up to survay each part,
When they shall find your Picture in my heart,
   You thinke a sodaine dampe of love . . .'

There was a roar of joyful medical fury and shouts of 'Get him!
Damp him!', which they did at such speed that I hadn't even the
time to throw my book to safety. I was, as it were, pre-packed for
my attackers, my arms trapped inside the cloak. I remember many
hands wielding enough muscle between them to swing me back
and forth three times ('One! Two! Three! Go-ooo!') and throw me
right out into the middle of the river, where I began promptly to
drown.

The folds of cloak yanked me under, my arms straitjacketed by
the weight. I was being rolled over and over like a log in rapids,
I couldn't breathe, I couldn't shout.

Then I was lying on the bank face down in the black grass and
they were tugging the cloak off me. Someone was pounding me
between the shoulders, there was a continuous booming in my ears
and my ribs were being pulled apart. Things were done to me of
which I have no memory. When I came to again there was a weight
on my back, my ribcage was being jolted up and in and everything I
had ever held in my body was pouring from my mouth into the grass.

I wanted to stop this helpless dripping and drooling, and raised
my head feebly to say so, but a hand came down over my cheek
and pressed me back into the river bank. Voices seeped into my
ears as the booming faded and with eyes grown used to the dark I
picked out the forms of some ten people, men and women, standing
nervously not far off.

Someone said, identifying my saviour, 'Well done, Jeremy. We
ought to get you home and dry too.'

'I'm fine. Need to make sure he's still with us, though.'

From behind me, from my back, a girl. 'You're nothing but a
pack of kids, throwing somebody in without an idea of what to do
after. Some doctors you'll make.' Her two hands squeezed another
pint of water from my raw throat.

'We weren't to know he couldn't swim.'

'Nobody can swim if they're all wrapped up in material.' Another squeeze.

'Jeremy fished him out pretty smartly.'

'Oh, good for Jeremy. It might have been cleverer not to throw him in in the first place.' More water.

'We didn't mean any harm. We weren't trying to do him in . . .'

'Well, you very nearly did . . .' And more.

'Yes, but, Eleanor. You don't know this chap. He was asking for it. He's been asking for it for months.'

'How?' The question was a grunt as she threw her body behind the force of her hands and another wave was pumped out of me. I wanted these recriminations to end so that I might be left in peace with whatever portions of the river I still contained. I tried to move to indicate to the life-saver that I was adequately alive but her knees were gripping my sides with awesome strength, and her hands were holding me down.

'Well, I mean, look. Look at him. Sitting in the dark in a cloak and reading poetry to the ducks. Does it all the time. Runs about looking for moonlight and twirling that damned cane and stroking his beard. A beard, I ask you.'

In the dark I blushed at the accuracy of the description and lay very still. The weight of the girl sitting astride me was shaking slightly and the pressure on my ribcage eased. She was laughing, changing sides, wooed from her impatience back into Jeremy's circle. Angry self-pity lent me a moment of strength. I flipped one of my legs up at the knee and kicked her sharply in the back with my heel.

'Ow!' There was a warm trickle on my spine. 'Hell!' She dismounted and pulled me over on to my back but in the night could no more see me than I could see her.

I tried to speak and offered 'How do you do?' but she can only have heard a damp croaking in which the words struggled and sank.

'Come on, you lot. You threw him in, now get him home.' Two people, one of them undoubtedly Jeremy, scooped me upright and looped my arms over their shoulders. I put my feet on the ground to prove I didn't need their help and my knees collapsed under me. But for their hands clasping each of mine at the wrist I would have folded on to the grass.

They bumped and stumbled me back to my rooms, past the porter's lodge.

'What happened to him?'

'Fell in the river.'

'Shouldn't drink so much, tell him. You young men. And when there's a war on. You wait till you all get called up. Any minute now. Then you won't be fooling about any more. They'll learn you something new, you'll see. Tell him that when he comes round.'

'We will,' they said, laughing.

I left my head where it was, chin on chest, at first faking unconsciousness, then slipping into it. They deposited me on my sofa, I heard Jeremy being urged to depart to change into dry clothes, my soaked ones were somehow removed and they rolled me into bed. The room seemed crowded with the large, upright forms of the medics and their molls. They stood rather still, looking at me as if my body, prone in bed rather than on the river bank, transformed horseplay into manslaughter. I kept my eyes closed to mask my embarrassment but also to increase theirs. They were muted suddenly, and whispered like people in church. They wanted to leave but did not know how to begin.

'I can manage. You lot, clear out now.' The girl's voice rescued them from their indecision and they jostled at the door in their eagerness to remove themselves, leaving behind them a desert silence.

I slept, woke and slept again, perhaps for only seconds at a time. A scraping by the wall brought me fully awake. The girl was crouching by the fireplace building a bed of coal in the grate, laying rolls of paper across it, lighting it with one match after another. Then she was standing, holding my gown in front of the fireplace confidently close to the first guttering flames. The coal sizzled like a trapped wasp and was alight. She turned her head over her shoulder to look at me, still holding my gown out to keep the fire drawing.

She was tall, it seemed from where I lay, and very slim in a dark pleated skirt and pale cardigan. I can't recall the colour exactly because all I noticed was her hair, twisted about her head in a deep-red mass, almost maroon in the dim light of the single bulb.

'Can you speak?' I nodded. 'D'you think you want some tea?' I shook my head. 'Coffee?' No. 'Cocoa, then?' No. 'I'm sure you ought to have something. Well, look. I'll have some, and you can try.'

She boiled a kettle and pulled things from my small cupboard, unerringly choosing the right doors and drawers for the teapot, the tin caddy, the cups. I thought of my mother, who would have been boiling up water not for tea but for a hot compress for my chest, who would have pulled a thermometer from her sleeve, who would have been wringing her hands, discussing her anxiety with herself and in the process augmenting it. I thought this cool, efficient girl was taking my condition too lightly, without even sympathy. Yet I was also relieved. I had never been alone in the company of a girl, for all Jeremy's assurances, and I did not know what to say. Now, here I was, weakened, discomfited and – the phrase occurred to me – at her mercy. Why did I think that, I wondered. What was I expecting? Sisters of mercy. I saw nuns gliding about the room, wheels not feet under their habits, passing objects from one to another, bending over mounds in beds, hands on foreheads. This girl had not approached me. She was making tea, heating the pot, spooning in the leaves. The mound of red hair on her head seemed to be held in place by a single long pin; it hadn't been disarranged even by her exertions over what had nearly been a corpse. She alone had known what she was doing, and her anger on the river bank had been provoked not by the stupidity of the act itself but by the subsequent incompetence of its perpetrators. So she had not really been disapproving of Jeremy. Perhaps she had admired his swift plunge into the water, the one sensible, manly action. Now she was merely completing the task of prolonging my life on this chilled evening. It was not mercy. And the body in the bed might have been anyone's.

'I've put in rather a lot of sugar.' She sipped at her tea and made a face. 'Too much, I'm afraid.'

Her face was, forgive the cliché, heart-shaped, wide at the cheekbones, two wings of the soft maroon hair curving back from her forehead. She was white-skinned, lightly freckled, with dark thin eyebrows and dark lashes. Her wrists were almost bony. As she leaned forwards proffering the cup, her blouse moved over the ridge of her collar-bones, which just then seemed more prominent than her breasts. She was quite unlike the women I had been brought up to find attractive.

'Come on. Try a bit. You really need it, you know.'

If I didn't she would have failed. She was holding out the cup from which she had sipped, having turned it so I could grasp the handle. I tried to sit up and hold it but my hand shook and tea spilled on my sheets. The girl took the cup back.

'Now you wait,' she said, as if I had been too greedy. She put the cup down and draped my gown over my chest, tucking it round my neck like a barber preparing his client for a shave. The corners of her curved lips twitched. 'You could do with a haircut, as a matter of fact. And I do believe there's nothing you could do to stop me.' She scissored two long fingers menacingly in the air in front of my nose. 'Now then.'

Then her arm was round my shoulders supporting my head while she held the teacup to my lips. I bent my head and sucked. The sweetness of the tea caught the back of my ravaged throat and I coughed, then choked, and the tea emerged not from my mouth but from my nose.

'Oh dear. Sorry.' She patted at my face with a corner of my gown. 'Let's give it another go. Come along.' I shook my head and turned it away, the most vigorous gesture I could manage. 'Oh, please.' She was nearly pleading. She put her fingers up to my face and gently pushed it back again.

I could feel the lines of each finger separately along my cheek, and under the blankets my body stirred. Had she noticed? I looked into her face and met her eyes staring directly into mine. In the wan light they looked violet. Maroon hair and violet eyes. A poet's after-death delirium.

For a moment we held our gaze, then she dropped her eyes, released me back on to my pillow and withdrew her arm. 'I'm sorry. I apologise, for the whole thing. For the lot of us. I'll leave you be.'

I wanted to say: Don't go. But she wasn't going. She took the cup away and settled herself without another word in my armchair, leaned back and closed her eyes, inviting me, instructing me to follow her example.

'For the lot of us', she had said, still allied to the medics. If ever I had set myself a task, breaking that alliance was it.

Seven

I woke in a hissing hot room, an eiderdown of air over my mouth. But for the vermilion crevices around the cinders in the grate there was only darkness, and my tight, raw throat. My arms lay pinioned under something massive that would not countenance any movement. I had been strapped down. I flexed my wrists but felt no bindings. Surreptitiously I worked my hands towards one another across my chest until my fingers touched. No one prevented me. Holding my breath so that my captors shouldn't hear, I slid one hand with its forearm sideways away from my body until all of a sudden it was released into the heavy air. I twisted my wrist to probe what was holding me and felt some coarse cloth. I tweaked it but it didn't respond.

Again I held my breath to make out the movement of an alien presence and realised, after a moment, that I was quite alone, in my own bed and surrounded by the looming figures of my pieces of furniture, darker even than the darkness. My free hand groped for the switch on my bedside light, tangled in the flex and sent the ugly object topple-crunch to the floor, where it lay, shadeless and on its side.

Yellow light pooled out over the floor. My room was empty and I was bibbed by my gown, tucked under my chin and into the blankets, and spreading down over my knees. I couldn't remember why I had put it there.

I sneezed, coughed and thought I was depositing all my gullet on to the gown. Then I remembered the girl with the cup of sweet tea, the maroon hair and violet eyes. The long cool fingers. I craned my aching head towards the armchair where she had settled down but it was vacant. I had learned nothing about her.

Taking the weight on my elbows then my hands I cranked myself upright and the gown fell away. Foot by foot I made a naked exit from my bed and, holding the bedside light in my hand like a torch, I itemised my room. There was nothing to suggest anyone had been there and so I must have blacked out when Jeremy and the others brought me home and covered me in my gown. The girl was no more than the product of a quirky imagination under stress. It was unforgivably unfair.

'Hallo?' I said all the same, as if she might be hiding in deference to my nudity. 'Hallo?' louder, and coughed again. My legs began to shake and I could feel the skin on my forehead tighten with fever. My armpits were sodden. I sank into the armchair, gripping the arms in fury and panic. Something crackled under my naked bottom and I paddled my fingers under it like someone in the theatre trying to scratch without being noticed. I had flattened a scroll of paper, one of my poems, but too small to be one of my poems.

Planting the bedside light between my watery knees I unrolled the paper. 'I read some of your poems. I put them back where I found them. What do they mean? E.L.'

E.L.

EL.

What do they mean?

Irritation gave me strength and on my feet again I prowled along my honeycombed wall minutely examining the position of each scroll; but since I had stacked them with deliberate carelessness there was no way of telling which red ribbon had been untied, which scroll opened, read and refastened.

Was there anything in any of them of which I should be ashamed? It had never occurred to me that a stranger might ogle my words. I found I couldn't remember what I had ever written; under my fever, cool appraising eyes smirked at my thin white body.

But she had not understood. What did she mean 'what do they mean'? They were not supposed to mean. They were. That was surely enough. They were there, sonorous, incantatory, celebrating the power of syllables piled on syllables. Meaning in the sense EL appeared to need was pedestrian, earthbound, the chains around the ankles of a falcon. Gasping in my armchair I began to plan her education.

A gentle tap on the door as it swung open. I commanded my voice into a bass register. 'Meaning', I croaked, 'is beside the point. First there is music. Only then, if absolutely necessary, need one look for meaning.'

The door hesitated on its hinges, then crept a touch further. Jeremy's face mooned whitely round at the level of the handle. He must have been on his knees. One by one, each a head higher than the last, the medics joined him in a vertical line, mouths open so that I thought they were about to address me in close harmony. They gazed mutely at my nakedness and I played a nonchalant hand out for my gown but it was beyond my grasp. Rugger players knew each other's bodies. They did not know mine. I returned my hand to my groin with dignity.

'I say, are you all right?' Jeremy's voice was shaking. Laughter? Guilt? 'I'm sorry. I can't tell you how sorry.'

'Never better,' I squeaked as a cough welled up and shattered my words in a surf of retching.

'We ought to get a doctor.'

'What will we say?'

'You . . . are . . . doctors . . . aren't you?' My hands went up and down like paddles trying to ride the wave.

'Fools! If you call a doctor, you'll all be sent down.' EL's rebuke flung me from my chair on to the floor curled like a foetus, willing my gown to descend over me like night. 'It's all right, I'm not looking. I brought you some soup because I expect you need it. You lot, do go away now. You're not helping, standing there gawping. What's the matter with you?'

'That soup. Smells good,' came a male voice. 'You haven't got a bit more of it somewhere, have you?'

'It *is* good. What d'you think it is, Leo? Have a sniff.' She knew my name and swung the tureen towards me.

'I . . .'

'The way he's been coughing and sneezing, I shouldn't think he could tell.' For the first time I felt genuine affection for Jeremy, who had rescued me in all his ignorance.

*　　*　　*

81

EL carried in more coal and kept the grate rosy, rearranged my pillow, aired the room and provided what must have been succulent soups. I dared not tell her I should have preferred her to keep her cooking to herself, that I was an uncommitted, intermittent eater who could not be wooed with food. She was not, however, wooing me. She had undertaken to restore my health without the intervention of professionals and in direct competition with Jeremy.

They passed occasionally, EL leaving with her tureen in her hands, lightened by my willpower, Jeremy arriving with cocoa into which he was going to pour the brandy he got from his father. They stopped on the threshold and from my sickbed I catalogued the mutual challenge in their eyes. Then it seemed to me my body was simply the terrain for a rebarbative courtship; they parried and lunged and scored points over me. For all I could tell, I was of no personal interest to either of them except in so far as either one could claim to be the sole agent of my recovery.

Jeremy talked about Eleanor Laing with bitterness. I could see he was a man in love. He spoke of nothing else, pulling the armchair up to my bedside, moodily watching the stream of brandy filling the mug of cocoa. EL was reading chemistry. Everyone was after EL. He studied my face as he spoke, gloating, I thought. I wiped all expression from my features to deny him his satisfaction.

Beginning to feel better I tried to make up my mind how well it would be wise to appear. If EL were to find me robust and on my feet she would presumably dust her hands together and remove to some riverside pub with Jeremy to dispute the merits of general female competence over laced cocoa and masculine conversation. It was time to remind EL that I was more than a medical experiment.

'All right, then,' she said, releasing me from her ladle, 'read me your poems aloud. Convince me.'

She passed me a scroll at random. I scanned it and my palms grew moist. Multi-syllabic adjectives were stacked on a bed of abstraction. I couldn't recall having written them, I couldn't remember what had prompted me to write them. I didn't know what they meant, so how could I read aloud and give shape to the music of the words?

I shook my head. 'Not this one. It's rubbish.'

EL suppressed a smile. 'The poet says so himself, does he? What about *this* one?'

'It's even worse.'

'Oh dear. And this?'

'You wouldn't believe it.'

'Oh yes, I would.'

'That's not very kind.'

'I didn't think kindness was compulsory in literary criticism. Come on, there must be one.'

She filled her arms with scrolls, turned on her heels and opened her arms over my bed. Dust hung in the space between us. Together we pulled off the red ribbons, I unrolled my creations, winced and deposited them one by one on the floor.

All of a sudden I had it. Eight lines tangled into a single convoluted sentence in which the individual wandered in a cosmic solitude, elbowing a path through the Milky Way as he toiled up an invisible ladder to the Heights. It was perfect. It was in German.

I felt my voice gliding into a lower register as I began to read. Without thinking I clambered out of bed without pausing in my reading and directed my words to the window over EL's head. There was rhyme, there was rhythm and, as far as I could make out, no meaning whatsoever, but it wouldn't matter.

'Crikey!' she said.

It was early summer. The lecture hall was emptier, students transformed on request into soldiers; those still left behind looked out of the windows and waited to be asked to join in. Elderly Austrians cluttered the cheaper restaurants and jangled the air with their guttural accents. My gown sweeping from my shoulders, I stood with the townspeople and watched them from across the road.

'I'm going to visit my parents for the weekend. D'you want to come?' EL stood at dusk by my writing-table looking down at me, her hair loosed in a floating mauve mass to her shoulders.

'Me? Why?'

'Why not? Don't you want to? It's a lovely place, in the country . . . very poetic.' She laughed.

I had never visited the English countryside. 'Have you got binoculars?'

'My father has. He goes out birdwatching.'

'Oh. Thank you.' I heard the nervous formality of my response. 'I'd love to.'

'Good. I've already told them to expect you. We'll take the train on Saturday morning. I'll come by and pick you up.'

'EL?'

'Don't call me that. What is it?'

'Sorry. Who are your parents?'

She laughed again, almost grimly. 'My parents are exactly like everyone else's. You'll see. By the way, my father's only got one leg but he doesn't mind people noticing. He lost it bravely in the war . . . the last one . . . fighting Germans.'

I shrugged. 'I'm not German.'

'Not?'

'Not according to me. Not according to them, either.'

'Have it your own way. If you don't say much he won't notice your accent. He's a bit deaf as well.'

'What accent?'

'Ze vay you shpeek English,' she mocked.

'I don't sound like that.'

'No, you don't . . . more's the pity.'

I didn't ask her what she meant. 'What about your mother? How many legs has she got?'

'The normal quota, and all her faculties, and a hairnet. We . . . she breeds New Forest ponies. I hope you like horses.'

'I've never met one. I was going to learn riding once.'

'Why didn't you?'

'Oh, it sort of fell through.'

'Never mind. I'll teach you, if you like.'

I wasn't sure I wanted to become EL's pupil in anything, least of all where courage might be required.

That night I gathered up all my scrolls and crushed them into the back of my cupboard.

The house in which she had grown up spread quietly in a shallow, unremarkable valley. Purple flowers draped the creeping plant that

84

sucked the moisture from old red-gold bricks breathing back the sun. A tight brick porch was paved in dusty red tiles brocaded with moss. 'We never use the front door,' said EL, but generations of wellington boots, ranked by size and grey with old mud, stood witness to the steady growth of her feet and to her mother's reluctance to pack the boots off to a jumble sale. High in the gables the small-paned windows flashed the reflection of stationary clouds.

All around the house the garden was well kept but without love, as if only social requirement saw to the cutting of the grass, the planting out of lobelias and begonias. Spent wallflowers drooped among them. A broad-backed elderly black labrador lay in the sun like a sack of charcoal. He came waddling with rheumatic excitement to greet EL, offering her his old breath and clouded eyes. She paddled her fingers on his head. 'Hallo, you old Bounder, you pong even worse than before. Where is everyone, then?'

The dog escorted us round the corner to a side door and the kitchen.

Something was bubbling in a casserole. Peeled potatoes floated in a large, blue-flecked, white enamel basin of water on the draining-board. The table, long, functional, its wobble corrected with a wedge of folded newspaper under one leg, was a mess of paperwork – timetables of some sort and copies of a local journal.

I looked at EL. She was leaning, bent from the waist, forearms on the table, reading the local paper. 'Hah! Got him at last.'

'Got who?'

'Bob Bold. Calls himself a breeder. More of a horse thief, though. They actually caught him altering a brand.'

'A brand of what?'

'No. A brand. A brand on a pony.' I stared at her. 'So you know who it belongs to. Oh, never mind.' With an edge of impatience in her voice.

We stood silently in the empty kitchen. I think I was not alone in wondering what I was doing there. The room seemed content to do its chores unattended. It gave off a familiarity with its own routine; like a horse that knows its way home, it managed without human direction.

Uneven footsteps outside. Hearing the approach of her father EL slipped her arm through mine and laid her head on my shoulder. She had not touched me since that first cup of oversweet tea. 'Why are you so scrawny?' she whispered, then called out, 'Daddy, Daddy. We're here.'

EL's father, Major Derek Laing, demobbed because of the leg, was as bald as my father. My father's bald head was as square as a loaf of sliced bread; the major's was quite round and his fringe of neck-hair was a strip of dark, tight curls. A pair of bifocals on a string round his neck gleamed at me from his chest. He put them on to examine me but arched his eyebrows over the tops of the frames to see better. In his retirement he had been teaching young boys in a nearby prep school and none of them, said EL, could believe he had ever been a major. His voice wasn't loud enough.

'Ah,' he said, and shook my hand. 'You're very welcome. The girl doesn't write as often as we'd like. Good of you to bring her.'

'I brought *him*, Daddy.'

'What's that? Yes, of course. Marjorie's outside somewhere. She'll be in in a minute, I expect. Eleanor, take your young man out and find her. She'll be with Belinda. Had twins, you know.'

EL's hand still gripped my upper arm so I pressed it tentatively to my side, feeling my palms grow moist, the blood flooding my face. 'Who else lives here?' I asked as she nudged me into the sunshine.

'What d'you mean?'

'Who's had twins?'

'Belinda's my old pony. I outgrew her years ago. She's a skewbald so she's not pure New Forest. I don't know what we're going to do with the foals.'

'Then why does your mother breed from her?'

'She's sentimental.'

'And you're not?'

'Never.'

'Eat them then.'

'No meat on a foal.'

Mrs Laing's voice was penetrating, tuned to carry from hilltop to hilltop, calling in the acquiescent herds. 'There you are, at last. Good. I need some extra hands with these haynets. The grass is slow this year, as you can see. Take this, would you, young man – how do you do, by the way – and fix it up for Mirabelle in that box at the end. Eleanor dear, come and see your twins. Both bays. We may get away with it.'

EL removed her arm, leaped after her mother, paused to laugh out loud as I stood with the bulging haynet in my hands, and pointed down a path. 'Mirabelle is small and fat and very bad-tempered. She won't be a good introduction to the species. Leave the haynet outside the door and I'll do it when I come back.'

Mother and daughter set off the other way. I followed them. EL was slim-backed and leggy in her beige pleated skirt. There was nothing to suggest she could ever develop the tailored shoulders and solid waist that must lie under Mrs Laing's herring-bone jacket with its single vent. In the sun EL's hair was new copper; Mrs Laing's, all white, gleamed like a silver plate, obedient in its restraining net.

A barbed-wire fence ran along the garden. In the field beyond, a group of ponies stood heads down in the slow grass. There was a paved yard behind the house and on the other side six pony heads poked above the tops of six black wooden doors, chest high.

EL and her mother made for a small brown and white head. 'Who's a clever girl, then? Come on, Belinda, show Eleanor your babies.'

I propped the haynet against a wall and looked over EL's shoulder. The brown and white pony nodded its head repeatedly and EL blew into its hairy nostrils. The pony curled its lips back and displayed fierce yellowed teeth.

'Oh, all right. Just this once.' Mrs Laing pulled some brown nuggets from her pocket. The lips took the nuggets and the head-nodding began again. Two flat heaps lay in the straw behind. Without meat. Disturbed by their mother's excitement the foals struggled to sit up, then to stand on swollen jointed spindles, flapping their short face-flannel tails for support. Their noses were charcoal grey, their foreheads round. As one they dipped their muzzles under their mother's still distended belly and between her hind legs. She batted her neck round, once in each direction, nosed them into position and peeled her lips back again. 'No, you've had enough, you greedy thing. You're not the only one. Where've you put that haynet, young man? Here. Let me take it. Mirabelle's a nasty little thing.'

'EL . . . Eleanor told me.'

'Yes. No way to treat a guest on his first visit.' Mrs Laing seemed to be talking to herself. 'Now, budge over there. Gerrover.' She unbolted the door and biffed the black nose as it darted at her. 'Budge over, I said.' She leaned on the pony's rump with her own and Mirabelle budged over, already crunching her hay like a mouthful of pills. 'Any minute now. Maybe while we're having lunch, what d'you think? Speaking as a doctor?' She pointed to the pony's pendulous, triangular stomach. 'Already dripping too, do you see?' Swollen black udders. Did ponies have udders? Were they breasts?

Next to me EL was watching the bad-tempered pony with affection and her small breasts shook slightly as she laughed. I shivered, embarrassed on Mirabelle's behalf. The Laings were pony breeders so the pony had been deliberately impregnated and now her functions were the subject of amused discussion.

'Were you thinking of obstetrics? We might need you.' Mrs Laing bolted Mirabelle's door behind her.

I retreated. 'I'm a long way from that. I'm only in my first year.'

'It wouldn't matter if you were in your tenth. I've yet to meet a doctor who wants to go elbow deep into a mare to get those forelegs out. People like me do that, if the vet's not about. Lunchtime.'

Mrs Laing brushed aside the papers on the kitchen table, in that single unconcerned movement destroying her morning's work. She dealt out the plates, variously patterned, differently chipped.

'We have got a proper dinner set in a box in the dresser. But you're a student so you won't mind eating with us the way we do. Please help yourself. Young people are always hungry.'

Meat. Potatoes. Carrots. Steaming mounds of hot colour. God save me from cooked food. I'm told the smell, the odour, the perfume – whatever it is – prepares the taste buds, kicks the appetite into action. Unprimed, my tongue is dry with apprehension at the trial before it and whatever small hunger there was before scuttles out of reach. I had not managed to mention my disability to EL. It was too late to do so now.

What was the smallest portion I could serve myself without

appearing to be critical, in advance, of Mrs Laing's efforts? She was as unlike my mother as it was possible to be but perhaps all women were the same if they suspected their food was rejected.

Three pairs of eyes followed the serving spoons from platters to plate, rested there and considered what I had taken.

'Thank you,' I said, to indicate that what I had was all I wanted and that the spoons were released for someone else's use. The eyes, however, remained on my plate where the expanse of empty china was greater than the islets of food.

'He never eats anything,' said EL dismissively, as if we dined together every day.

'You should build yourself up.' Mrs Laing passed the platters to her husband. Should I? What for?

I tried self-defence. 'EL . . . eanor is very . . . slim, too.'

'Different. The girl eats like a horse. Burns it off. Metabolism. Don't know where she gets it from.' She laughed and banged her tailored hips with her fists. 'I, on the other hand' – taking the platters back from her husband – 'eat half as much to be twice the size. If I thought it mattered I'd be very miserable, I expect.'

I prepared to murmur that she was not so very large, which in fact she was not, but bit back the comment, fearing that it would sound polite and, therefore, untrue; fearing too that it might be thought none of my business to make any comment whatsoever.

'In which case,' said EL, already halfway through an awesome helping, 'there's no "should" about it. If you don't eat but grow all the same and he doesn't eat and stays skinny, what's the odds?' Why are you so scrawny? she had whispered. 'Besides,' she added by way of explanation, 'he writes poems.' She put her knife and fork together and sat back to watch the effect of this revelation on her parents.

'Never mind, dear,' observed Major Laing mildly. 'People do all sorts of odd things when they're young. He'll grow out of it.'

EL was disappointed. She tried again. 'A lot of poems, on scrolls, which no one can understand. Not even him. Actually, Daddy, he writes in G –'

'Jolly nice lunch,' I said. 'It was delicious.'

Mrs Laing was mollified. 'Well, we'll have to do something to get more down you. And, Eleanor, your father's right about the poems. Don't fret. There's a war on. You don't have time to write poems in the army, do you, dear?'

'I should hope not,' said the major. 'Have you had your papers yet?'

'I . . . no, I haven't.'

'He's not going to be called up, Daddy.'

'Isn't he? Why's that?'

'Well,' Mrs Laing stacked the plates. 'I should think we'll be needing every doctor we can get. I should think they'd leave the medical students alone, wouldn't you? Anyway' – she twinkled at me – 'he's far too thin. If he was asked to present arms you wouldn't know which was the rifle and which was the soldier, eh, Eleanor?'

So EL had to laugh, even though for the moment she had been deprived of her second disclosure.

'We'll take the dog out after, what do you say? Deserves his bit of fun too, give him the feeling he's still got it in him. He was the best gun dog I've ever had in his day, weren't you, you old Bounder?' Major Laing held the heavy muzzle in his hand, while the dog's greying tail whacked the table leg in metronomic agreement. 'Never left a mark. Mouth as gentle as a baby's. You'd have been amazed. I'll show you.' I stared across the table at EL, willing her to intercede with a tangible panic on my face. Was he offering me a gun? Was I to plunge in the undergrowth to frighten some overfed bird into the air, bang it down again and walk home head high, the red drops turning brown on my trouser leg? 'Or I would if I could. But we're out of season, of course. Leave the guns behind today. Take the binoculars instead. Eleanor says you're something of an ornithologist.' He looked up at the kitchen clock. 'I'll just listen to the wireless first. Will you join me? Don't worry about the washing-up. Eleanor will see to that today, won't you, dear?'

He led me through a door that seemed so low I ducked my head, unnecessarily, into a sitting-room of old armchairs, a low round table covered in magazines, rumpled rugs on the floor. The windows were low, latticed, small, so the room was in twilight despite the brightness outside.

The major pre-empted my thoughts. 'We're very cosy here in winter especially. The fire draws well.' Bounder had stretched himself out in front of the empty grate, waiting for winter. 'Sit yourself

90

down, young man. Take any seat except this one. This one's mine. That's Marjorie's but she won't be coming in now. Too much to be getting on with outside, ponies popping all over the place. Busy time of year for her, although, between you and me, she knows the war won't do the business any good. Mustn't complain, of course.'

I took Marjorie's chair. It faced the major's on the other side of the fireplace and I thought of the McKechnies in the gloaming of their basement, the McKechnies to whom I had yet to write. Mr McKechnie's ugly, sardonic face floated on to the major's shoulders and his thin voice winkled into my ear. *Settling yourself comfortably, are you, laddie?'*

'Comfortable, aren't they, even if they're not much to look at any more? A bit like all of us, really.' Major Laing laughed and patted his wooden leg and the arm of his chair simultaneously.

The chintz was murky, the fabric's pattern entirely worn away on the arms. My father would not have tolerated these chairs in his house. He would have had them seen to long before for professional reasons, my mother for social ones. These cushions, subject to neither demand, were simply sat on, the horsehair stuffing sighing into new positions over the years; shaped by so much sitting, they accommodated themselves to an unknown body and made me welcome. I leaned back and smiled my answer to EL's father, who couldn't see my expression in the half-light.

'This won't take long. I just want to catch up with the latest news.' Major Laing switched on the wireless. The set crackled momentarily and he sat forward, cupping both hands behind his ears.

The sound suddenly leapt out. '. . . and it's Cheddar Gorge coming up on the inside, there's no holding him now, it's Cheddar Gorge from Happy the Day, and, in third place but a length behind, Uncle Sam . . .'

Next to Marjorie's armchair the shelves across a small white-painted alcove offered me framed photographs of a girl with chubby pigtails astride a two-toned pony on whom the patches of dark and light met like a map.

The paddocks of the stud farm were separated from the land of their neighbours by a tiny river, a brown line of weed-strewn water so narrow in places we could almost have stepped across. Wearing borrowed boots I kept pace with the major as he strode over the fields, swinging his wooden leg out in a semicircle at each step with such force that his shoulder lurched upwards in sympathy. Bounder padded close by his side, his nose an inch behind the major's good leg, perhaps from habit or blank obedience or the fear that he might otherwise get lost in his dotage. Near the water the grass was coarse, yellow tussocks. The binoculars slung on a strap round my neck bumped my chest every time I put a foot down. The strap weighed on the back of my neck.

I saw birds I had never before noticed, whose names the major told me and I resolved to remember. I pledged to myself to become the ornithologist that he already believed me to be. Tight flurries in the uppermost twigs; fastidious stalkers shaking the water from their manicured feet, replacing them distastefully in the water between reeds; fat brown and yellow ducks, masked coots sniping at the ducks; a sparrow-hawk with folded wings which fell like a parcel thrown from an aeroplane, dead, rose again thwarted and veered out of view. When we sat by the water's edge at the rivulet's widest point I missed the kingfisher's blue flash entirely.

Major Laing had seen through me and commiserated. 'You'll learn to see things more quickly in time and with a bit of practice. Look.'

A blunt-nosed vole pushed out over the water as if something fearful were on its tail. A flat fan widened behind it and dissolved as the sleek wriggle vanished into the dark of the opposite bank.

'Neat,' said the major. 'No wasted movements. Built for the job. I like that.' I looked at his mild face and wondered how anyone could take such pleasure in the life of these things and want to kill them too.

I lay back in the grass and stared up at the sky through the oak leaves still in the emerald of their early summer growth. This gentle warmth, a tame sun, a silent companion with his silent black dog, green filigree embossed on the blue, deep blue and friendly. It was my size, this landscape with its limited vista. Nothing grandiose, but a domestic country quietly suggesting I make myself at home.

'Shouldn't do that if I were you. It rained last night and the ground's still damp. Marjorie would say we shouldn't be sitting here at all. You can get piles from damp ground. Can't say I ever have, but it warps the leg, the damp.' He knocked the wooden leg with a knuckle. 'Besides, we'd best be getting back. Marjorie's doing tea today, in your honour. She doesn't usually do tea. I'm looking forward to that. Maybe Eleanor will bake something. She used to like that when she was a little girl.' He was wistful.

I sat up, crossed my legs and stood in one movement.

The major levered himself up with the help of his stick. 'All very well for you, young, hale and hearty. Dear, dear. Never mind. It was all in a good cause but it'll be forgotten now we're having another go at them. You don't want to join up?'

'Oh, I do. Yes, I do. I'm not sure they'd have me.'

'What's that? Oh no. I'm sure they would. You mustn't pay attention to Marjorie. That's just her way, her tongue. Sharp-tongued, both of them, mother and daughter. Let's have a look at you. Not got flat feet? Eyesight all right?' We had taken off our jackets in the sun, holding them over our arms. The major tapped my timid biceps gently with his stick. 'You're not born with muscle. You build it. Use your arms, and you toughen up. Nothing to worry about once you're prepared to take the thing on. It's like the brain, as I tell my boys. You have to use it for it to work. But then you Oxford types, you know that already, don't you?'

We retraced our path over the rough meadowland, the sun behind us dancing the major's shadow grotesquely on the golden grass.

'Tell me,' he said as slowly as if he were about to solicit an awkward and intimate confidence, 'how's that girl of ours doing up there? Is she working? Can she manage the work? It's not our world, you can see that for yourself, but she was so keen to go. Restless here, there was no denying it, though we would have laid out on a thoroughbred if she'd wanted one. But she wanted a different life altogether, pavements and young people . . . if you'll forgive me, people like you. Not our sort, you understand what I mean, don't you? She came to us rather late in life, never knew me as a young father. Already had this thing.' He gave it a more vicious tap this time so that I doubted the nonchalance with which EL had said he regarded it. 'Perhaps we're just old-fashioned. Though there's nothing wrong with being old-fashioned. You'll be old-fashioned yourselves one of these days. But she's clearly taken to you, bringing you back to meet us. I'd never stand in the way of what she wanted, even if . . . Heel, Bounder!' The dog hadn't wavered from its posting behind the major's knee.

I couldn't locate a reply but sensed that the longer I said nothing the more Major Laing, whose affection I wanted to share, would feel he had offended his daughter's sweetheart. 'She's very clever,' I blurted.

'I don't need you to tell me that,' he said curtly, so that for the first time I was offended and definitively silenced.

'Don't mind the mud. The dog's never learned to wipe his paws.' Mrs Laing was buttering bread and my appetite whooped with expectation. EL was bending over a cookery book propped open on the kitchen table, her hair dusted with flour like a young actress playing a dowager.

'Here,' she said as I came in, treading off my boots outside, Mrs Laing's injunction notwithstanding. 'Read this to me. It's taking far too long like this. I used to be able to bake without a recipe.'

'I know,' I said, and received a quizzical look. 'How far have you got?' I picked up the book. EL swept a hand over the ingredients assembled on the table, measured quantities of flour, sugar, chocolate powder and nuts. 'Sift the flour into a bowl,' I intoned like the chaplain at evensong, and saw my mother shaking icing-sugar through a fine sieve on to the blue-veined marble slab she had kept for pastry. She would always be talking as she did it, her hands and eyes so practised they didn't need her attention.

EL shook the flour into the mixing bowl. 'Yes?'

'Cream the fat and the sugar together. Separate the egg and whisk whites and yolks separately. Fold egg whites into creamed fat and sugar . . .'

'Wait, ho! Whoa, there! Wait. You read, I'll do the thing, and you read again.'

'The *Gnädige Fräulein* vill pleeze to excuse zi ignorantz.' I laid it on so thick that Mrs Laing chuckled, unsuspecting. Only EL, taken aback, shot me a look of surprise.

She stirred slowly with a long wooden spoon and for a few moments the foaming egg whites, like shaving-cream, coated and slid around the sweetened margarine, unwilling to mix. Then all of a sudden the egg whites disappeared, absorbed into the solid yellow mixture. Bit by bit the flour went in, then the nuts, and I was looking out of the window at the sun, as flat as a copper-bottomed saucepan swinging on a hook beyond the trees.

This was the sun she had looked out on evening after evening, the little girl with the fat red pigtails, so confident on her brown and white pony. She had sat here, at this table, maroon head lying on her forearm as she wrote out her homework, shielding her exercise book from the greedy eyes of an imaginary classmate, her mother beside her shuffling through her book-keeping. From here she had set out, leaving behind her home and her doubtful parents, a safety she could afford to flout. It was like money: having it you could despise it.

'So you do have an appetite, after all.' I had cleared Mrs Laing's heaped platter of sandwiches, hungry after the walk, tempted by the soft bread. EL's cake emerged steaming and frothy – and, no doubt, fragrant. I swallowed a huge, weightless wedge and licked my fingers. They all watched me and seemed gratified.

'I suppose you don't play draughts, do you? They laugh at me' – a self-deprecating smile on the major's face – 'but I enjoy board games.'

'I do play. I like it.' I was enthusiastic, the invitation to aid him in his entertainment more appealing than the prospect of the game itself.

Major Laing reached down the box from a shelf above his arm-chair, offered me his wife's place again and laid out the board on a folding card-table between us.

He beat me, but only just, and his gentle eyes gleamed. The second time I beat him. 'That's more like it. To battle, then.' He laughed aloud when his black counters hopped and zigzagged over mine, and his pleasure was as obvious when my white counters massacred his.

He rubbed his hands. 'Pass me that pouch, would you?' Pressing tobacco into the bowl of his pipe, he looked at me over the flame as he sucked it down, released it, sucked it down. 'Smoke?'

'Cigarettes.'

He passed me his matches. 'Good game, draughts. Let them laugh, but it gives me pleasure. Who taught you?'

'There was an old lady in a family I stayed with once. She was bored so I used to play with her.'

'Humouring the old thing, were you? I hope you don't think you were humouring me . . .'

'Oh no, not at all. It was quite different. She and I weren't adequately matched.'

'Cocky young pup. Like all of them, all your generation. You think that with our receding hair and stiff backs and a bit of deafness we should all be put out to grass. Nothing more up here' – he tapped his forehead with his pipe – 'nothing more down here, either', and he patted his groin, laughing behind his hand like a girl. 'Marjorie wouldn't care for you to hear me say so, but it's only the words she doesn't like. Now, if you were anybody else, I'd say that a young man needs to experiment a little before he settles down, if he can find enough young ladies prepared to help him. And from what I hear there always seem to be plenty of those. But you're here with my daughter. Don't ever forget that. Don't think of trying any experimenting with her, do you hear? I won't have it and nor will my wife. I may have only the one leg but as you've seen it doesn't hold me up, and I'd catch up with you. Because, believe me, you'd be running. Don't even think of it.'

'I assure you, I wasn't.'

'What? Of course you were. Got to. No good to the girl if you're not even thinking of it. Don't act on it, that's what I mean.'

'I'm in no position to act on it. Eleanor hasn't led me to believe –'

'Now, you'll never get anywhere if you wait for the lady to lead you to believe, and if she does she's not the lady for you. No, no. You have to make the running. Always. Talk to your father about it, I'm sure he'll tell you the same.'

I thought of my father's eyes meeting mine as he presented a tissue-wrapped handbag to my mother. Perhaps these two fathers had very similar opinions. Yet my father preferred to hint, to demonstrate, and would not be drawn. I could not imagine Major Laing 'doing the dirty' on his wife as he would doubtless put it.

The major folded the draughtboard away into its box and

carefully piled the counters into their allotted crevices. 'Can you see in this light? The time?'

'It's nearly nine o'clock.'

'Time for the news. Would you call in the ladies? They'll be wanting to listen.'

Mrs Laing sat squarely in her armchair opposite the major, both feet planted on the ground, one hand in the small of her back. 'Eleanor, dear?'

'Of course.' EL picked up a small hard cushion from the window-seat and set it behind her mother.

'Thank you, dear.'

Stiff backs, the major had said. If my mother had had a stiff back she would have been sure to mention it to a guest at least three times before the evening was out. EL sat in the window-seat and with a foot hooked out an upright chair for me. I turned it towards the wireless as if doing so would make the newsreader's message clearer. EL snorted quietly, put her feet up on the cushions and leaned against the closed blackout curtains.

'This is the BBC Home Service. Here is the news. The King has sent a message to Lord Gort. The desperate battle on the northern front continues. The British Expeditionary Force has withdrawn intact towards the coast. Bombers of the Royal Air Force continue to give our troops all the support in their power. This evening a formation of fighters shot down twenty-two enemy aircraft without loss to themselves . . .' Major Laing applauded, clapping both hands on his leg. His Majesty the King had sent a message of support and gratitude to the soldiers of the British Expeditionary Force, thanking them for their gallantry. Their commander, Lord Gort, had replied that the army was doing all in its power to live up to its proud tradition. The members of the BEF were deeply encouraged by the King's telegram . . .

'It's still a retreat,' muttered the major. 'No question of it. And of course those French chappies can't be up to much. I've wished I was out there sometimes' – he was talking to me – 'but to be honest I can't say I'm really sorry I'm not. No fun. No fun at all.'

'Ssh!' said his wife.

The BEF was retreating but in perfect order. Dunkirk was in no immediate danger and Calais was still in Allied hands. The

Germans had been harrying the civilian population, low-flying aircraft had machine-gunned refugees on the roads and people had been deliberately crushed by tanks . . . EL's hands were over her eyes as if warding off the image the newsreader was sending her. How large is a tank as it is about to roll over you, its driver concealed from his chosen victim whom he can't hear, and whose splattered remains he won't see? Would it be different, I wondered, if there were less distance between the tank commander and the refugees on the road, if he could hear the high-pitched voices of the children, hear the slow heavy footsteps of tired people, smell their fear? Fear, apparently, had a scent all its own. Was it so distinctive that there could be no mistaking it? A sweet smell, an acrid one? Words without meaning – like my poems. Involuntarily I smiled, wiped the smile away but saw that the Laings were all engrossed by the newsreader and had noticed nothing ill-mannered.

Britain's war production was not to be held up by holidays. The seven-day week was to be continued but there were to be rest periods organised by the Labour Supply Board . . . I glanced over at EL and met her eyes. We were, in our way, on holiday now, producing nothing.

Mrs Laing knew her daughter. 'You're no use to anyone yet, dear. Finish your studies quickly and then you'll really have something to offer.' Then she added, 'But it should all be over before then.'

'Ssh!' said the major.

New taxes to prevent excess profit in wartime, a new budget . . .

EL's profile was softened by dim light. Her hair, which she had gathered in one hand, holding it against the crown of her head, was swept back from her forehead. I imagined it was my hand around the soft mass; I bent my face to it. Perhaps it was perfumed.

'. . . he suggested an excess income tax so that no one should have a better income than before the war. In the debate that followed . . .'

I wove a wide lock of it in between my fingers, made a fist and saw how the hair gleamed where it was stretched over my knuckles. I ran the other hand up the hair until it cupped EL's face.

'. . . New regulations for the control of all aliens over sixteen were announced today by the Home Secretary. From Monday next,

June the third, no alien may have or control a bicycle, motor vehicle, sea-going craft or aircraft without police permission. No alien living in the provinces may be absent from his residence between half past ten at night and six o'clock in the morning without a police permit. In London the prohibited hours are from midnight until six in the morning. Aliens with no settled residence must report to the police next Monday. If an alien stays a night in a private house the occupier must report in writing to the police at once.'

Major Laing switched off the wireless. 'Well,' he said. 'Well, well. It doesn't hurt to be careful in times like these. You have to know who's who and what they're all up to. Time for bed, what do you say, Marjorie?'

'Cocoa?'

'Leo will have some, I'm sure. But he has brandy in his.'

'EL!'

'Do you? Good heavens! You students are cosseted.'

'No, I don't. I did only once when I was ill. Eleanor's joking.'

'Is she? I suppose she is. Sometimes I can't tell with that girl of mine.'

It was understood I was staying the night. Mrs Laing had made me up a bed in the spare room, next to EL's. Earlier than was my habit I found myself on my way upstairs, urged to make use of the bathroom first, as the guest, aware that this family would not wish to see me communing with a candle in the hours before dawn.

Outside her room stood EL, straight and slim and cool. 'I hope you get some sleep. I slept in that bed once. It was awful. I apologise on behalf of us all, in advance.' Once again, I thought, that 'us' of which I was not yet a member. She slipped into her room and closed the door silently but so swiftly that I had no chance even to glimpse the childhood decorations.

Eight

EL's apology was well placed but unnecessary. Had the spare-room bed not, indeed, been as uncomfortable as she had said I should still not have slept. I was not yet tired and I didn't want to sleep. I lay in that bed as if it were a rigid hammock and listened to the house readjusting its joints. A light wind frittered in the poplars near the gate and I imagined I could hear the ponies shifting from foot to foot out in their paddock.

I wondered what it must be like to be Major Laing, to have been Major Laing at another time, in that earlier war in which he had been a participant rather than a bystander. By all accounts that war had been a failure – even for the victors; a blunder of dead bodies and obliterated biographies. None the less, Major Laing, with his wooden leg to prove it, might be chafing at ineptitudes I would never understand. 'Ask me,' he might be urging. 'Let me tell you how it ought to be done.' Men of his age directed the War Cabinet and all those other offices but would not think to ask his advice. Why should they? They also knew how it should be done.

How had he lost his leg? Would he come round to telling me? Would I, perhaps, ever come to know him so well that I might even ask? Would I tell this mild-mannered man who thought I was his daughter's chosen – and was confused by her choice – that conceivably my father had caused his wound?

How was it now, stumping off to the preparatory school to teach pink-faced boys who couldn't wait to be big enough to be soldiers too? Was he infected by their excitement, imagining himself a warrior again? I could understand that. I wanted him to tell me stories of his wartime; I wanted him to want to tell them to me. I could promise to be a good listener.

EL had been born in this house, an experienced midwife in

attendance, the major forking straw to give him something useful to do. A new life was produced while his back was turned and he was in that instant stripped of his ability to make decisions of which he could be certain. The red-headed baby had been in charge from her first puckered wail, in charge of her father, and of her high-bosomed mother in her hairnet. EL had learned to walk on the grass outside, then learned to ride her pony on it, lain in the sun with her father's gun dogs, combed out her ponies' manes, ridden to hounds (a new phrase), learned about the villainous Bob Bold and all his neighbours because they were her neighbours too. They were neighbours who had also been born in the houses where they still lived.

According to her father, EL had been restless. She had run away to the university and people like me. Then she had come home again, on a flying visit, they must understand, and brought me with her, sporting her curving smile of mischief. She had put her arm through mine and her head on my shoulder to introduce me to her father, who had left a leg behind on some desolate field in France, the casualty of a grenade or a sniper's aim, both of them German. She had told her parents I wrote poems, she had tried to tell them I was German. She seemed to want them to dislike me, for reasons I couldn't fathom. So far she seemed to be failing, for which I was thankful but as confused, it occurred to me, as her father was. Major Laing's daughter was playing games with us both.

The house sighed and creaked again as if, in the night's silence, footsteps were moving the floorboards.

Footsteps were moving the floorboards. I heard a whisper, like all whispers devoid of voice and impossible at first to attribute. 'Shh! Let him sleep.'

'He might want to come.'

'He might have just got to sleep. He won't want to have to do that twice.' That had to be EL.

'Don't be silly. He won't want to miss out on this. I know the young man, believe me.' Major Laing.

Someone tapped on my door so quietly that if I had been asleep and undisturbed by the whispers I should not have heard the summons.

'Yes?'

'Did we wake you?'

'No.'

Major Laing in full voice. 'Then get up, get yourself dressed and come down.'

They were all wearing wellingtons so I retrieved my borrowed pair. The major carried a bucket. EL and Mrs Laing had torches. Mrs Laing's hair lay quiescent under its net which, perhaps, had not been removed.

'All set, then.' Mrs Laing led us out of the house, walking to one side so that the light from her torch would guide us. 'She knows what she's doing. She'll be in charge, as always.'

I thought she was referring to EL but the major put me right. 'You'll have to watch out for those teeth.'

In her loose-box Mirabelle was moving round in a tight circle, flicking her nose up and down. Ears laid back, eyes wild and white, she looked more malevolent than ever.

'All right, then. All right, then.' Mrs Laing swept her torch over the straining, sweating mare.

Suddenly Mirabelle flopped down in the straw, still tossing her head, her neck curved and taut. She swung her muzzle round to her bulging flanks as if she were trying to urge the trouble out of her. Then she was struggling to her feet again and turning in her tight circle. I found I was shifting from foot to foot too, possessed by her distress that no position, no stance was comfortable. She seemed, in her pain, to be irritated in her skin, she seemed to be trying to slough herself off. Her breathing was raucous, splintered snorts squeezing between her teeth with every exhalation. I heard my own breath sharpen in rhythm with hers and nearly cried out with her.

I thought, if I touch her, if I reach out with my hands, perhaps she'll be eased. I must have moved forwards because the major restrained me. 'Keep well out of the way.'

'Here we go.' Mrs Laing, inside the loose-box, was rubbing Mirabelle's back. 'I need some light.' EL and the major shone the torches on the pony's tail. Something glistened in the weak light and Mrs Laing bent her head to inspect. 'We're all right,' she said and I heard relief. 'We can leave it to her.'

'But surely it's dead!' I put a hand over my mouth to keep the exclamation in. The forelegs hung down, as if welded together and wrapped in cellophane. There was silence. No movement from the mare, no movement from any of us. The pony stood, head down as if she had given up. Under her tail the two small legs hung motionless. Then all of a sudden Mirabelle grunted and her head jerked up as if someone had yanked it from above.

'Look!'

The forelegs reached towards the straw and behind them a foal's head, gleaming in its wrapping and with flattened ears, was being forced out by an unstoppable power over which neither the foal nor its mother had any control. All at once, with a squelching and a rustling, the foal fell on to the straw, an immobile wetness. Instantly Mirabelle turned, the cord trailing from her body which had closed again over it, and was licking at her child almost roughly. The foal's folded body jerked rhythmically under her insistent tongue. It raised its round head, put out one spidery foreleg, then the other, splayed apart, and began the frantic struggle to get to its feet.

At that moment I felt a terrible sorrow. It was not pity for this new creature because of its smallness, its vulnerability. It was a sorrow, a pity, a sense almost of horror for us all because of this foal's urgency to be on its feet. Something was making that foal struggle up, something beyond that individual animal's choosing, something it could neither ignore nor reject. Pushed to its feet, at the moment of birth, because it was a foal and that was what foals must do.

'Botheration. Another colt. Never mind. Well done, Bella, all the same. All nice and tidy. We can get to bed now, thank goodness. You know' – Mrs Laing turned to me – 'I ought to take these things in my stride by now, but you always worry a little. Things can go wrong. I didn't expect it, though. Not this time, not with Mirabelle. She's an old hand.' We followed Mrs Laing back to the house.

EL had said nothing but she took my arm again and I jumped in the dark, not expecting her touch. 'What were you thinking? You looked so glum. I thought you'd be excited.'

'I can't explain. Something to do with destiny.'

'Whose?'

'Anyone's. Everyone's. That foal's.'

'Well, I can tell you his destiny easily enough. With the parentage he's got, no one will want him at stud, so in a couple of years' time they'll geld him and he'll grow into a nice, quiet riding pony.'

I shuddered. 'Don't. That makes it worse.'

'Why? What does it make worse?'

'EL, I can't explain. It has to do with choices. That foal has no choices partly because he belongs to you because his mother belongs to you, so you decide what happens to him . . .'

'Well, of course. He's a foal, not a human being. He can't decide for himself. He can only live.'

'But that's what I mean. He can only do what foals do. He can't do otherwise. He's driven.'

'He won't mind that. He won't give it a thought. He hasn't got a thought to give it.'

I was growing desperate, wanting to explain to EL what was still unclear to me. 'You say that and you're right. But what about you, or me?'

'What about us?'

'Aren't we driven in the same way too?'

'Obviously not. Not like that foal anyway, because we're talking about it. I should think that makes a difference, doesn't it?'

'I suppose so.' I was tired now, unhappy with my unfocused thoughts and the inability to express my desolation at that moment after the birth. EL was right in her dismissive way. My inchoate notions were neither here nor there in the business of living; and yet it was precisely that which was so disturbing. Being alive was both the beginning and the end of it, there was neither point nor purpose that was not in life itself. The wave of pity for the newborn foal swept over me again, as I saw it dropping on to the straw, over and over again, instructed, willy-nilly, to live out its cycle.

I have always had a talent for sleep and could press it into service whenever being awake was uncomfortable. So I slept tranquilly that night in the Laings' spare room, undismayed by the vilified mattress, and woke, as I tend to, early. It was that moment before dawn when you sense that the dark is about to be peeled back, when all the birds of the vicinity are clamouring at once. Birdsong, we call it. The dawn chorus. But it is no chorus. It is a cacophony of expletives, a thugs' convention, each small feathered thing throwing down a foul-mouthed challenge to the next, daring him to approach at his peril.

I lay and I listened, and to my distress the notions of a few hours earlier returned as I pictured each bird, screaming from its tree every morning before sunrise to ward off intruders, unable to do otherwise. Entangled in my distress was the realisation that EL was clearly not similarly disturbed; that, lying in the bed where she had slept most nights of her life, she was sleeping content that a new foal had been born without mishap; that should she care to remember our conversation she would most likely toss it sensibly aside with ill-concealed irritation. EL had run away to people like me, her father had said. But he was wrong. She had not run away at all.

Asleep in her room, next to mine. How was she asleep? Curled on her side? Spread-eagled on her stomach with her arms flung out on either side, face buried in her pillow? On her back, one arm over her eyes as if to shut out the light that wasn't yet there? Was the maroon hair tucked to one side or floating as if in water all round her face? Where were her hands?

The birds resumed their night-time silence as suddenly as they had broken it and a line of grey nudged at the lower rim of night. Enough light to see her by. I put my jacket on over my pyjamas thinking that, should she wake, I would appear somehow more dressed and, therefore, less . . . what?

As I put my fingers out to turn the handle of her bedroom door another door opened and Major Laing stepped out in a thick tartan dressing-gown, his spectacles already around his neck on their string. 'Like me, eh? An early riser. That's good. Let's go down. It's all right, we don't need to whisper. Those two women would sleep through thunder.'

I followed him down. He made straight for the kitchen door and flung it wide open. 'Look. East.' He pointed over the barbed-wire fence of the paddock where the grazing ponies were still drained of colour. The line of trees at the far end was etched in apricot. 'Best time of day any season you care to name. I always like to see the dawn and, if you'll understand me, by myself. No, no. I'm glad you're watching it with me since you like it too. No one around. No one wanting to talk. And the smell.' He breathed in noisily and I copied him. 'There's something about this part of the world at dawn that smells unlike anywhere I've ever been. Doesn't smell the same later in the day, or at night. I've wondered about that for years. You might call it a waste of time, I dare say, but I can't put my finger on it. Perhaps you can help me. You're younger. Your faculties are sharper. What is it out there that smells so different from the same thing at another hour? What is it, eh?' He looked at me expectantly.

'I don't know about sharper faculties,' I said. 'But mine are untrained. I mean, I'm so used to the smells of town that the difference between them and the countryside is so great I can't yet make out variations here.'

'Ah, towns. Yes. Enough to make you forget what life smells of altogether. And it does, you know. Life smells more than it does anything else, but don't let Marjorie hear I said so, or she'd laugh me out of the house.'

'Eleanor too, maybe?'

'Eleanor? You never know with her. That girl.' He shook his head. 'Well now, what can I offer you? I'm a breakfast man myself, not much of a cook the rest of the time as they'll tell you, which is as it should be. But I make a better breakfast than the lot of them. So what's it to be? Eggs? Bacon? Good. We're still doing all right down here. We have it all.'

I ate the breakfast the major cooked for me sitting opposite him at the kitchen table, feeling honoured. Through the open door I saw the ponies regain their black and brown and chestnut as the sun came up, and the major toasted me with a large mug of tea.

'To a young man who knows the best time of day and the food that goes with it. If you had that appetite the rest of the day you'd be twice your size. Marjorie's right, as she usually is. You could do with more meat on you and there may come a time when you'll need it. I saw men like you, thin as rakes, dying of cold in the trenches. They'd be shaking and shivering and all of a sudden they'd stop and you'd know they'd gone. Just petered out. That seemed more of a waste than if they'd had a bullet between the eyes. No glory in dying like that. No glory in dying at all, really, even if you go bravely. I never thought much of posthumous awards. You can't do much with one of those when you're dead and I'm afraid I've never managed to believe in heaven. Go to church, of course. But that's what we do down here, especially at Christmas. I enjoy that but I can't say I believe in any of it, and if you ask me I'd say half the congregation think the same. But it doesn't do to ask. Shall we go out and see how that young colt is doing? You can put your boots on and we'll go straightaway.'

Mother and child were sleeping. The foal lay curled in the straw, propped on its soft muzzle. Mirabelle slept where she stood, her head drooping. There was no sign that the birth had taken place only a few hours earlier.

'Where's the . . . ?'

'The afterbirth? She'll have eaten that. Solid protein and she knows what's good for her. They all do it. Wonderful, isn't it, how they know without having to be told? Not like us. We have to learn everything so slowly, so painfully. They say it's because we have more to learn but, between you and me, we may know a lot more than they do' — he gestured towards the animals — 'but we don't seem to know what to do with any of it. Give me horses any day. No nonsense, no fuss, no waste. Not like us.'

Mirabelle opened her eyes, laid back her ears and moved purposefully towards her stable door. The major pulled me back.

'Keep away. She's got vicious teeth, that one, and with the foal now she's got the protective instinct. She'll be even nastier than usual. Watch out!'

I retreated just as Mirabelle swung her head over the door and lunged at me.

The major laughed. 'I've known some women like that, haven't you? Now Belinda's quite another kettle of fish. Sweetest-tempered little thing but getting on a bit for motherhood. She's a great-grandmother, in fact, aren't you?' The brown and white pony, suckling her bay twins, was, as we had seen her the day before, begging for titbits. The major pulled a wrinkled brown carrot from his dressing-gown pocket. 'Not fussy, are you? Not the least bit fussy.' Belinda vindicated him.

'Let's get back now and put that kettle on again. I always bring them a cup of tea in bed of a weekend. They like it, and for me, well, it starts the day, in its public sense, if you understand me.'

'Do you ride?' Mrs Laing sucked toast crumbs from her front teeth.

'I never had the . . . I've never tried.'

'Pity. I'd instruct you on another day but I'm behind with my paperwork. The book-keeping. As for Eleanor, you'd best not take lessons from her.'

'Mummy! Why not?'

'You're much too impatient, dear. You'd shout at him and women shouldn't shout, least of all at their . . . least of all at men.' By my side I saw the major's eyes crease into a smile of affection, but I thought, Mrs Laing doesn't shout; her voice is so strident she can't ever need to. 'You forget sometimes, you know. You've ridden since you could walk. Leo will be awkward and stiff with those bony legs of his.'

Under the table I rubbed the outside of my thighs towards my knees. My legs were bony. I changed the subject. 'Perhaps I can help with the book-keeping?'

'Do you have a head for figures?'

'As a matter of fact I do.' I was almost a brilliant mathematician but one mustn't say so. 'I've always rather enjoyed maths.'

'Good heavens! Well, in that case I shall make use of you and Eleanor can go riding by herself without having to worry about you falling off and injuring yourself.'

'I wouldn't have worried.'

'You see, dear? You've just proved my point.'

I stood by the barbed-wire fence watching EL select one of the grazing animals, slip a bridle over its head, cheat the bit into its mouth and lead it out through the gate. The other ponies raised their heads to watch too, followed her desultorily, changed their minds and fell back to their grazing.

'Hold him a minute. I need to get my saddle.'

The reins were in my hand and the pony, which I learned later was in fact a horse, was in my charge – or I in his. I felt my stomach tighten. Could the animal sense this, smell my uncertainty? 'Hallo,' I said and drew my fingertips experimentally along his arching neck. They came away covered in fine grease and a number of long dark-brown hairs.

'Mind your feet. He never minds his, the clumsy great thing.' I put a yard between us, holding the reins in my outstretched hand. 'It's all right. I'll take him now.' I wiped my hand on my trousers. 'He's moulting, isn't he? I ought to get the curry comb to him. It always makes me think moulting must be so itchy and anyway they look so much better afterwards, you'll see.' She had thrown the saddle over the horse's withers and was leaning against his flanks pulling the girth as tight as she could, giving me the terminology I have set down as she went along. She pulled down the stirrups and turned to me with that smile. 'I'm lazy. Give me a leg-up.'

'How? What do I do?'

'Clasp your hands together . . . like this . . . and I put my foot in and you just don't undo your hands.'

Her foot in a black leather boot was in my palms for an instant, then she was sitting up there looking down at me, her hair, copper again in the sun, coiled on top of her head.

'Have a lovely day with your sums. Mummy's hopeless. You may regret your offer. Bye.'

She communicated something to her horse, which leaped into a slow canter across the grass and off towards the road. The girl on its back seemed to grow out of its body. As I turned back to the house I saw Major Laing's face in the window watching his daughter depart.

'Marjorie's gone to her maternity ward but she's asked me to show you what needs doing here. I'm no mathematician either, I'm ashamed to say, but one can't know everything.' He laid out Mrs Laing's papers on the table as they had been the day before. 'This column is for the feed we buy in, the extra straw and so on, all the outgoings, the vet's bills which you can see are pretty steep, all that sort of thing. Then this is what Marjorie makes in sales, and her training fees, and her livery charges while she's training . . .'

I could see that Mrs Laing's dislike of figures had kept her away from her book-keeping for some time, but also that any effort she had made had been wasted. She could not add up. She could not subtract. 'Is there a pencil and a rubber? I think I'm going to need them.'

'There should be a pencil here. There was at breakfast. Now where is it? Oh no, oh damn that girl.'

'What's she done?'

'What she always does. She couldn't be bothered to go upstairs for her hairpin so she's fixed her hair round the pencil. I've got the rubber, here, you see? But that's no good to you without the pencil. And I've got a pen, but a pen's a pen. You want it for neat work not for rough work.' He was addressing his class. 'You do rough work in pencil.' He was distraught, embarrassed that his daughter's waywardness was causing inconvenience. 'When will she ever . . . ?'

'It doesn't matter. I'll do it in my head.'

'Can you?'

'I can try.'

'Well, if you're sure. I'll keep out of your way and read the paper.'

We sat in silence at that kitchen table, the major with his newspaper, I with his wife's neglected book-keeping, and I was content. I picked up the pen, turned back the pages and began my calculations. The numbers arranged themselves in my head in rhythm with the ticking of the clock on the wall. Column by column I entered my corrections over Mrs Laing's haphazard guesswork, delighting in the ease with which I could repay this family's welcome.

'Don't move!'

'Pardon?'

Major Laing was no longer in his chair but in a corner of the kitchen pointing his shotgun at me. 'You will stay exactly where you are and when Marjorie comes in she will telephone the police.'

The mild major's face was ashen. He seemed almost to be choking on a chestful of quiet fury. I pushed my chair back but he advanced one step and I froze, still half leaning on the table. I had never seen such hatred in any man's features. I had never before been so frightened.

'What have I done?'

'Given yourself away, *Mein Herr*. My God, and to think that my daughter . . .' He swallowed as if his mouth were filled with bile.

I held my position, my elbow beginning to tremble under the weight of my leaning body. A blemish on the surface of the table was biting into the bone. A wave of nausea made my head swim.

What had I done? I moved the other hand towards my elbow to ease it.

'I said, don't move!'

'I'm not. It's my elbow.'

'What about your elbow?'

'There's something on the table. It's digging into my elbow.'

'All right. Move your elbow. Although I don't see why I should . . . Oh, move your elbow, dammit.'

I drew my chair closer to the table again and laid both forearms down so that the major should be able to see them. In front of me Mrs Laing's ledger lay open, the left-hand page accounted for, the right-hand page still a nonsense. What had I done? My eye strayed down the entries on the right-hand page and automatically I began computing them in my head, under my breath, and nearly cried out. The rote learning of childhood had welled out of me. I had been counting in German.

'There you go again. And you thought I was deaf. Hard of hearing I may be, but the old ears can still hear when they need to. You people, you think you can get away with anything, coming here, pretending to be English, fooling us into thinking you're English. That's what they mean by the Fifth Column. People like you, not the ones with the accents. Oh no. It's people like you. Damned German. Damned Nazi!'

'I'm not a Nazi. I'm a refugee!' I was pleading with the wall opposite, not daring to turn my head to him.

'A refugee! Naturally. Marjorie! Marjorie! Marjorie, look what I've caught. Come and help me, Marjorie.'

'Please. I *am* a refugee.'

'And what sort of "refugee" might you be?'

I looked up at the ceiling and back down again. I took a breath. 'I'm a Jew.'

'Oh, a Jew!' It sounded worse than his 'damned Nazi'. 'Prove it.'

How does one prove something like that sitting in an English country kitchen? I put my head in my hands and instantly raised it again, in triumph. Slowly I turned my head until I gauged it presented the major with my profile. I ran my index finger down my nose to draw his attention to the proof.

'Yes. You've got an outsize nose. I noticed that straightaway, but it won't do you any good, my lad. I've known men with bigger noses than that, and from good families too. You'd better try again. Marjorie! Marjorie!' And Marjorie arrived.

'Good grief! Derek, what's going on? What are you doing with your gun?'

'Phone the police. I've caught a German. That young man thought he had us fooled, but he's a German all right, planted in the university like an English student, taking advantage of our daughter, of you and me, and who knows what he'd have done when he got his orders.'

'I'm not a German. I'm a refugee.'

'He says he's a Jew because he's got a nose. Well, of course he would, wouldn't he? Probably why they chose him for the job. Almost looks the part. Phone the police before I take a pot-shot at him.'

'Tell him to take off his trousers.'

'What?'

'Tell him to take off his trousers.'

'Why?'

'Oh, Derek, dear. Think. Do I have to . . . ?'

'Oh. Yes. I see. Of course. You, take off your trousers. Marjorie, turn round.'

Thank God my father's irreligion hadn't gone that far. I stood up reluctantly, however. If this was to be the only proof they would accept I had no choice, yet I would rather have been anywhere but in that kitchen to provide the evidence. I put my hands slowly on my belt.

'Of course' – Marjorie's voice came over her shoulder – 'it might not mean a thing. I mean, think of the Palmers. They've all been . . . you know. You said yourself that if Eleanor had been a boy you'd have considered it, for health reasons and all that.' My hands paused on my buckle.

'Maybe so, maybe so. It may not prove he *is* a Jew, but if it's all there at least we'll know he isn't.'

I unbuckled, unbuttoned and let my trousers fall to the floor, conscious above all of the white boniness of my legs.

'Come on, come on.'

I hooked my thumbs in my underpants.

'Daddy!' EL stood in the doorway, neat in her breeches.

'Eleanor. Stay where you are. Turn round.'

'Daddy, what are you doing? What's Leo doing?'

'Leo! I should have thought. And what's the surname? You never mentioned it, now I remember? Schmidt, is it? Or Schwarz, perhaps?'

'No, it isn't, Daddy. It's Beck. What *are* you all doing?'

'Why didn't you say what my name was, EL?'

'Don't you talk to my daughter like that, or at all. And keep going. Eleanor, have you turned round?'

'No, I haven't. I don't see why I should.' And to me, 'Because I didn't think you'd want me to, knowing you. Why are you undressing?'

'Eleanor, for once in your life, do as you're told and turn round. Your friend, you may not have realised, is a German. He says he's a refugee. A Jewish refugee. They all say that. But before we telephone the police, because I am a fair man, I am giving him the chance to prove he is what he says he is. Do you understand?'

'No. Yes. Oh, Daddy!' And she laughed. 'You didn't have to do that. I could have told you he's a Jew. I mean, he's German too, but he is a Jew.'

'How do you know?'

I knew how she knew. She must have been there when the medics bundled me into bed.

'Jeremy told me.'

'Who's Jeremy?'

'He's reading medicine with Leo. He's a friend of mine.'

'And how does this Jeremy know?'

'They were at school together. Everyone knows.'

Major Laing lowered the shotgun and turned round so that he stood in line with his wife facing the wall. 'I have a very small bottle of sherry in the cabinet next door,' he murmured. 'May I offer you a glass?'

I bent down to retrieve my trousers, avoiding EL's laughing face. My knees shook and I sat down heavily. 'If you don't mind, I'd prefer a glass of milk.'

Nine

Mrs Laing drew a dish from the oven. 'It's not pork, you'll be glad to know. It's chicken. One of our own.'

'I wouldn't have minded,' I said. All three Laings looked at me doubtfully, then with disappointment. 'I'm not observant. I don't keep the laws. In fact, I don't believe in any of it. It's just an accident of birth.' I would rather have been talking about something else.

'Then', said EL, 'you can't be a Jew. It's a religion, isn't it?'

'I don't know what it is. But somebody must think otherwise or I wouldn't be here.'

Major Laing was eating his chicken in small, neatly arranged forkfuls: a piece of chicken, a sliver of potato, a shred of greens. As soon as he had placed a fork of food in his mouth he prepared a second. They followed each other so smoothly there was no chance for speech to disrupt their passage. His wife had issued the invitation to stay for lunch. He had not expected me to accept. Like EL, but for different reasons, he would have preferred me to refuse. He seemed to find this wholesome meal as tasteless as I did.

Mrs Laing served bowls of apple pie, from last year's apples, she explained. Good keepers if you store them properly. She put a pot of tea on the table and we each drank a cup.

The major patted his mouth with his napkin. 'I have some marking to do this afternoon. You will excuse me, won't you?'

'Don't you want to go birdwatching again?'

'Eleanor,' I said. 'I think your father's busy. And I think I should be getting back.'

'Before he rings the police to say there's an alien in the house?'

Major Laing folded his napkin and rolled it into its silver holder, blackened from use and no one's anxiety to polish it. 'If you remember,' he said heavily, 'there's no requirement to do so until tomorrow. And anyway.'

'Oh, Daddy! Thinking of breaking the rules?'

Stop it, I thought. Leave him alone.

'There are aliens and aliens, dear.' Mrs Laing collected the cups. 'Leo has some studying to be getting on with, I'm sure. And you must have too.'

'Term's nearly over.'

'I know, my girl. You'll be home again in a fortnight. Now go along and see that Mirabelle and Belinda have enough water and I'll check the train timetable.'

'I know the times,' retorted EL and swung out of the house, an insolent child.

Major Laing watched her departure and sighed, stood up and looked out of the window as if there were something out there that had caught his attention. 'It's not far to the station. Well, of course you know that. I hope you succeed in your medical career. They say you . . . people like you make good doctors.' He did not suggest they might invite me again.

'Thank you so much for having me,' I said in the flat tone Elisabeth had taught me, and held out my hand.

'Don't mention it.' He brushed my hand with his fingertips, eyes still fixed on the view from the window, and backed out of the kitchen.

'You'd best be getting along now, young man. Look, here's Eleanor with your things.'

'Mrs Laing . . .'

'No, no. No need. It's been a pleasure.'

'May I "look in on the mothers and children"?' Trying to sound like a GP.

EL snorted, like one of her ponies. 'What d'you want to do that for? You're scared stiff of them.'

'I shall look at them, keeping their closed doors between us, if that's allowed.'

With EL behind me carrying our two small overnight bags, one in each hand like a bellboy, I strolled slowly round the house, down to the loose-boxes, only glancing at the two mares busy with their domesticity. Beyond the stables was the pathway leading down to the tussocked grass where the major and I had walked the afternoon before, when I had been merely an oddity, not yet an embarrassment. Something pushed against the back of my knee. Bounder stood by my side and gazed milkily out into the fields, waiting for us to set off. I bent down. 'Another time, maybe,' I whispered, then said aloud, 'I'd love to have grown up in a place like this, like you, like those oaks.'

'Never,' said EL. 'You go crazy down here. You only think it looks nice because the sun's shining and you've been visiting. Come on. We've got a train to catch.'

EL sat facing the engine because she preferred to see where she was going and I wanted to keep my eyes on where I'd been. The window was open and from time to time she brushed the smuts of the engine's smoke from her lap, leaving dark flecks on her skirt. Suddenly she leaned forwards and put her long hands on my knees. The fabric of my trousers evaporated under her touch and all my skin shivered. I closed my eyes, annoyed at myself, willing her not to move her hands away.

'Leo.' I opened my eyes to meet hers, deep mauve in the afternoon light. 'Will you be going home to London for the summer?'

'Yes, of course. My parents are expecting me.'

'Can I meet them? Will you ask me down?' Her fingers tightened slightly on my naked knees and I held her eyes to keep them away from my rising crotch.

My mother would spring-clean the house in expectation of such a visit; the cut-glass would sparkle, the angel chimes would be singing, there would be cakes and coffee on the tablecloth, blazing white and ironed with crisp corners. There would be questions about fathers and mothers, grandparents, aunts and siblings, about houses and schools and ambitions, skills and, even, love. With her pitiful English no barrier to her curiosity my squat mother would shout her requests for information, toddling in her high heels from room to room, leading EL, who would be smiling inwardly, on a tour of our polished furniture planted in its new premises. My father would follow behind, appraising EL's tall slenderness and thinking his own thoughts.

'There's nothing I'd like more,' I said, 'but my parents are very shy and the house is awfully small. You wouldn't be comfortable.'

'Do I need comfort so much?' She sat back, taking her hands with her. My body subsided. As one we turned our heads to look out at the passing countryside. Quizzing her future she said, 'What are they like?'

Surveying my past I answered, using her words, 'Ordinary. Like other people's parents.'

'Oh, don't be silly. They can't be!'

'Why can't they?'

'They're not like my parents, I bet.'

'That's true. But they're just like other people's parents all the same.'

'Then I don't know those other people.'

'No, you don't. Be grateful.'

'I'm not grateful. I want to know. Why won't you tell me?'

'Because there's nothing to tell.'

'There's always something to tell. Tell me about your house, the one you grew up in.' Which one? 'Tell me about your house in Germany.' Tell me a story.

'It was a flat.'

'The flat, then.'

'It was ordinary. Like other people's. Over-furnished. Tidy. Lots of objects.'

'That need dusting.'

'That's right.'

'I see.' She didn't see. 'And your mother dusts them?'

'Yes. Mothers do.'

'Mine doesn't.'

'No. Yours doesn't.' Mrs Laing wore wellington boots. 'I like your mother.'

'Oh God.' She twirled a handful of flaming hair. 'I might like yours.' I almost laughed. 'She might like me too.' My mother wouldn't be able to help it.

The train slowed as it rattled into the outskirts of Oxford and my spirits slowed with it. Medicine waited for me there, bones and bodies, diagrams and chemical charts. A summer job, if I could find one, would be my digression but only a digression. Then I would have to return, a fortunate student, occupying a place that

117

another might have had and wished for more. It was not enough to console myself with my poems, or even those of better poets. I want to be a doctor, I had said, and so here I was. Was there to be no way out?

Perhaps they would let me sign up after all. They would cut my hair, make me polish my boots and learn to strip a gun. We would all go out and fight for Major Laing, and win him back his leg. We might come face to face with the enemy, as he had done, and among them I would recognise the children with whom I had been at school, and I would say to them, triumphant but also by way of apology, 'You see, I'm English now. I didn't have the choice but now I do.' They would be astounded, disconcerted at first by the alien uniform, more by my words, but we would fall back, they called by their duty and I by mine. Perhaps we would kill one another before there was time to explain properly what it was we thought we meant. They would have more explaining to do than I, but I would understand them better having been at least briefly a part of them. Or so it had seemed. Would their deaths be on my conscience? Under the circumstances, I thought, it was perhaps a luxury even to wonder. Would mine be on theirs? It was possible. Would anyone be grateful to me for my sacrifice? My father, who had fought for the Germans last time around, and Major Laing? How would EL receive the news, and from whom? Jeremy, an uninspired officer, would return from some sortie, always un-scathed, invincibly alive but without honour, bringing the infor-mation that whatever it was I had done had saved a regiment. That would be a fine story, with a posthumous ending. Then I remembered that Major Laing hadn't thought there was much glory in being dead. Maybe, though, wars were not fought like that any more. Our forces were in trouble in France, withdrawing in an orderly fashion, which in the major's interpretation meant retreat. It meant nothing whatsoever to me. It must be deafening. It must be terrifying. It was real. It was happening a short distance away but I could not imagine what it was. Nor could anyone, surely, before they had been propelled into it.

EL came with me to my rooms, although I had thought we might go our separate ways at the station. As we passed into the quad the porter called out to me. 'There's a gentleman been waiting for you all day, sir.'

'Did he say who he was?'

'Not a word. I been up once or twice but he was sat in your chair reading. Made himself a cup of tea, happy as could be.'

EL took my arm as she had the day before. 'Let's go and confront your mysterious visitor.'

He had turned my chair so that the last of the evening light fell on to the pages of his book, but even with his back to the door I knew him instantly. 'Mr McKechnie!' I could think of nothing else to say.

'Ah! At last.' He jumped up and turned to us. 'Ah, well now I see why you've not written. You've had better things to do. Bob McKechnie.'

'Eleanor Laing.'

'Another Scot!'

'A very long time ago, possibly, but not that I know.'

'Will you have tea? I can see you've been travelling. Now put those bags away and sit yourselves down. That kettle boiled not so long ago, I'm all awash with tea, with the waiting for you.' He pulled out two cups and the tea caddy as if he were the resident and we the visitors. EL put down her bag and sat obediently in the chair he had indicated, folding her hands in her lap with exaggerated demureness. Stirring the tea leaves, Mr McKechnie appeared not to notice. 'I've wondered', he said, 'whether I might have been getting the address wrong, whether you've received any of my communications.'

I muttered that I had.

'And did you have any particular reason for not replying?'

I said I was a bad correspondent. This was true, but Mr McKechnie's few enquiring, sardonic letters had remained unanswered because I had not known how to reply. I had not wanted to concede to him, of all people, that taking medicine had been a mistake.

'You're wanting in manners, laddie. I'd thought better of you.'

I apologised.

'And Jean and Lucy have been thinking you've forgotten all about them.'

'Oh, they mustn't think that.'

'Ah well, as I say' – nodding towards EL, who was sitting bolt upright, eyes gleaming as I was being ticked off – 'you've had other things on your mind. I notice you seem to read an awful lot of poetry for a would-be doctor.'

'Doctors have been known to be literate too.' Dr Meissner thumbing Goethe; Dr Hoop bit the dust.

'Maybe so, but they usually, at least while they're studying, display some medical textbooks on their shelves. They are usually, I think, kept rather busy. Too busy to be writing poems of their own, or at least not so many.' He opened the cupboard where I had stuffed my scrolls. 'Maybe', he went on, 'if you wrote fewer they might be better. However,' and he put up a hand just as I was about to defend my privacy, 'that's not why I'm here. I happened to be passing', but waiting all day, 'and it crossed my mind that, if you're still the lad you once were, you will not have been reading the newspapers.' I stared at him. I had not been reading the newspapers. 'In your shoes I would go out and buy myself a stack of the drivel with which Lord Rother- mere and his friends line their pockets. Even you should be able to understand the message. In your shoes, I would also get my- self home to my parents before too long. It could be that they will be needing you again.'

His admonition frightened me. What was it that I was supposed to know? But it also irritated me that for a second time this school- teacher should presume to instruct me on matters concerning my life. I bridled. 'The term's nearly over. Naturally I will be going home.'

'Now look, Beck, there's no need to get prickly. I know you. I've known you a long while, don't forget that. You with your head in the air, you don't see, or you don't want to see, what's right in front of you. I'm sure Miss Laing would agree.'

EL was startled at her sudden inclusion. 'Me?'

'Aye, you. Would you not say your young man is a bit of a dreamer?'

EL laughed. 'Just a bit.'

'Well, maybe you can get him off his backside and out into the real world. Buy him a newspaper to read with the breakfast they serve him here. I would recommend the *Daily Sketch*, or the *Sunday Express*, or even the *Daily Mail*.'

'*The Daily Sketch!*' EL was indignant. 'I don't read that.'

'I'm sure you don't, lassie. But a heck of a lot of people do. That's my point.' He got to his feet. 'Well, I'll be on my way now and, if I may, I'll tell Jean and Lucy that you'll be sure to call in once you're back in town. It was a pleasure to meet you, Miss Laing. Goodbye, Beck. A little less poetry for the time being, please. Never mind about the medicine. I never thought you were cut out for it. Stick with your friend the chameleon. On second thoughts, I'll make it easy for you.' He took a newspaper out of his pocket and laid it on the table. 'I trust that will be all right, sir.' Then he put an ironic finger to his hat and closed the door gently behind him.

We sat holding the cups of tea which neither of us had touched. When she spoke EL's voice was sharp in the silence. 'Who's your friend the chameleon?'

'That's nothing, really. When I was at school I used to go to the zoo and watch a chameleon.'

'You watched a chameleon?'

'Yes.'

'What did it do?'

'Nothing. It just sat.'

'So why did you watch it?'

I shrugged. 'It made me think, that's all.'

'I know.' She was almost dismissive. 'Destiny and choices, is that it?'

'I'd better look at that paper, hadn't I?'

'Do you always do as you're told?' But she unfolded the *Daily Mail*. It was over a week old.

Act! Act! Act! Do it Now.

The rounding-up of enemy agents must be taken out of the fumbling hands of local tribunals. All refugees from Austria, Germany and Czechoslovakia, men and women alike, should be drafted without delay to a remote part of the country and kept under strict supervision . . . As the head of a Balkan state said to me last month: 'In Britain you fail to realise that *every* German is an agent. All of them have both the duty and the means to communicate information to Berlin.' Certain 'diplomatic bags' leaving this country are at the disposition both of such people and also of disaffected Britons.

'Daddy reads the *Daily Mail*.'

I put the newspaper down, moved over to the window and looked down on to the striped baize of the quad. I thought of my father sitting in Henry's chair, his hands folded like empty gloves in his lap, my mother with her yellow curls and her cheeping cherry mouth. Who could imagine they thought it their duty to communicate information to the very people from whom they had fled? Did someone really mean to lock them away and thereby preserve England? As he had done before, Mr McKechnie was calling me to action for which I was not prepared. Help your parents, he commanded. But how? They were at risk, or likely soon to be. I had just learned that and was therefore wiser than a few moments before but no more capable. Somebody would make a decision, somebody in the government, and they would come to take my parents away. I was supposed to prevent it. Mr McKechnie believed I could, had said I should. If I knew who that somebody might be perhaps I could go to him and plead for my father, a furniture salesman, and my mother, his wife, a domestic woman whose expertise was in icing-sugar and paper-thin pastry but whose understanding of events around her went little further. No one would think of asking her to convey anything more than a recipe. People like these could be safely overlooked. Their English was halting and childlike, they were conspicuous; their hats gave them away, so did their demeanour in the street. They could do nothing without being noticed. My mother had only recently finished having locks fitted to all her doors and cupboards so that my father, barred entry, might again stand roaring outside the unoccupied lavatory.

'Will you make love to me?'

My parents vanished. EL materialised between me and the glass. She laid both hands on my shoulders and her thumbs brushed against my neck. I heard my own indrawn breath like a rustle of paper.

'What?'

'Now. I want you to make love to me now.'

Her fingertips were on my face. My mouth was dry. Prickling electricity flew along fine wires from the bridge of my nose, through my body to the tips of every periphery and out into the space around us. Tall as she was, I looked down only slightly into the dark pupils flowing into the mauve. She was not laughing. She was not asking. She was waiting, growing impatient.

'Oh, come on.' She put one cool hand behind my neck and the hairs rose in concert with my groin. My face tipped forwards on to hers and to her lips which touched my jaw with the same soft touch as her fingertips.

How do I say this? I couldn't recall ever having put my arms round anyone before, wishing to, unable to prevent myself. I remembered my mother's confining arms, but no arms that I had sought, no other body that I wanted close to mine. I wrapped myself around her, and again around her. You could not have slipped a sheet of paper between us. She seemed insubstantial, pressed into a two-dimensional reflection of myself as if I had peeled my shadow from the ground and pasted it to me, head to toe. But this shadow was warm, stirring slightly in my embrace, worming itself closer to me than could be possible. My cool girl was warm, and her arms were around me.

'Now,' she insisted, but quietly, and led me to my bedroom beyond the prying slant of the setting sun in whose rising light I had stood with the major, watching the ponies drift into full colour. We had breakfasted together, at ease in one another's silence before he ordered my trousers off at gunpoint. As I remembered the trembling of my bared knees and EL's incredulous laughter, the passion drained out of me, leaving me longing but helpless.

'I can't. I'm sorry.' She would never know how sorry.

'What's the matter?' Her voice was gentle.

'Nothing. It's your father.'

'My father?' In the sharper tones of daytime.

I lied, but not entirely untruthfully. 'I feel . . . I would be letting him down, abusing his trust.'

'Leo. I wanted you to make love to me, not to my father.'

So the moment had passed. Hearing myself speak, I believed

what I had said. Major Laing had not asked what I did with his daughter, he had not needed to because his manner implied the expectation of correct behaviour.

'The trouble is, my father thinks I'm the virgin I dare say I ought to be and which, if you don't mind my saying so, I think you are.' I blushed until my palms grew moist, not knowing which of the two statements she had made was the cause. 'So it wouldn't be you who was abusing his trust because, if that's what's worrying you, someone else already has.'

'Who?'

But of course I knew, and did not want to hear her tell me. So EL went away leaving me to nurse my virginity, kicking the skirting-board until my toes were bruised.

That night I lay awake and stared through the dark to the ceiling. Major Laing should be grateful to me, I thought bitterly. I had not sullied his daughter. I hadn't managed. I heard again her light laughter as she came upon the scene in her mother's kitchen. The same laughter would accompany her narration of our love-making, and Jeremy's shoulders would shake with merriment. Mr McKechnie had as good as ordered me to London to keep watch over my parents, whose liberty was suddenly at risk. But there were still eighteen days to go before the end of term and the end of my first unfortunate year. I did not want to leap so meekly to Mr McKechnie's command. I wanted even less to stay where I was, Jeremy in the next room, Jeremy in the lecture hall, EL's swinging skirt jaunty in the street, her bright hair catching the summer. But departure would be defeat. Somehow I would have to trudge through the remaining days, trying to become the doctor of my mother's aspirations, avoiding the company of the man I detested and the woman I suspected I loved.

When I woke, thinking I had not slept, there was a cup of tea by my bedside, a folded piece of paper propped against it. 'Hope you had a good weekend. Must get together before I leave. I've been called up. J.' As I poured the tea away I wondered how long it had taken Jeremy's dull mind to concoct a note which enabled him to gloat twice in three short sentences.

I sat by the river with my books, which rejected the reading of them. I lay in the grass and Major Laing's gentle admonition brought me to my feet. I took off all my clothes and swam where I had almost drowned, waiting to be reproved by an authority that failed to arrive.

I left my rooms early in the mornings, returning only after dark, spending the hours in between at a table in a far corner of the library. There I tried to commit to memory the sinews and ligaments of anatomy someone was going to require me to know. I spread my left hand out on the wooden surface, flayed it in my mind and with my right drew the fibrous and glistening muscles; wasted the tissue away, let it decay until only the sad, rattling skeleton clawed the table-top. But it was my right hand that intrigued me, so blithely manipulating the pencil, so unwittingly capable. How had I come to own such an elegant tool? I pounced on the question with eager relief but it slithered from me as, before my eyes, another hand with cool, slender fingers seemed to cover mine.

The long days replaced one another and methodically I ticked them off. I would have departed with some vestiges of dignity had not Jeremy waylaid me on the stairs.

'You're never in. Been knocking. Leaving you notes you don't answer.'

'No.'

'Something wrong?'

'What should be wrong?'

Jeremy shrugged, and put a hand on my arm, the heavy, warm hand of a man ponderous with advice. 'You haven't seemed yourself since you came back.'

'Came back?'

'From Eleanor's people. Didn't it go well?'

'Don't patronise me, Jeremy,' I said venomously. 'I dare say it went every bit as well as you might have hoped.'

I closed the door quietly in his face as he seemed to be about to follow me into my rooms. Then I packed my suitcase, gritting my teeth as I observed myself rolling my shoes in newspaper to protect the clothes the way my mother always did. Odd, I thought, as I turned out the light. Jeremy's expression had been a mixture of bewilderment and elation.

Part II

Ten

The closer my train got to London the more I was aware of the same lassitude of spirit that had troubled me almost three weeks before as we had approached Oxford. I did not want to go home, I did not want to sit with my parents while my mother poured her dark coffee into her tiny cups and my father told me tales of business. I did not want to be conscious of my shadowy reflection in the heavy shining sentries of furniture, nor to see the pink sateen coverlet on my parents' bed and the rows of labelled jars in the larder which housed my mother's threatening ingredients. I did not want to be made to watch my father's confidence in his suburban fortress fracture into hesitancy as he opened the front door. I did not want my mother's little arms raised in readiness to encircle my neck. I wanted only the body of the cool, disappointed girl I had left behind.

I stood on the platform with my suitcase and didn't move. Perhaps I might visit Henry and Elisabeth first, a compensatory call, an apology because in all that time I had not written. I could leave my suitcase in the hall and take Jason out for the slow shambling walk that was all he could manage in his old age. I could eat rock cakes again. I might ask to stay the night and lie upstairs in the nursery bedroom, on my back, with my hands behind my head, counting the fine cracks in the ceiling, deferring tomorrow. Henry and Elisabeth would be surprised but too diffident to enquire, and also gratified that I should have chosen to return first to them. Not so Marrrm. I saw her pencilled eyebrows artificially arched, those sardonic lips twitching as she asked me to what they owed the honour.

Motionless on the platform with my suitcase, I must have looked as much in need of direction as I felt, because a young policeman approached me. 'Can I help you, sir?'

I fought a sudden urge to clutch my case to my chest and wail at him in German: Help me, I'm lost, I don't know where to go! 'Thank you,' I said, 'I'm quite all right', and strode vigorously out of the station.

I would walk, I thought, wherever my feet would take me and for as long as I could carry the case, and then I'd go home. For a while I watched my feet as they took me, the left and the right; I watched the toe of my shoe rise as the heel struck the pavement and bend again as the heel lifted, and I saw the paving stones slide evenly away, noticed in my periphery the occasional trunk of a passing tree. What an odd word that was, 'home'. What was it supposed to mean? Somewhere one wanted to be and thought of sentimentally on being deprived of it, or the place where one was deemed to belong, irrespective of commitment? Home had been Berlin, which I could barely remember; it had been Henry and Elisabeth's; now it was supposed to be the house in Cricklewood; in Oxford it was my rooms. What would the word mean to me if it described the house with the breeding ponies and the ancient, waddling gun dog, and had always done so? Would I, like EL, strain to be away from it as quickly as I could? It seemed inconceivable. How could she? Why had she?

I followed my feet off kerbs and round corners, recognising that they had, indeed, selected a destination, meekly accepting their choice, until they brought me to Tolini's, with an appetite. I pushed into the door with relief and was bounced back. The door was locked, its glass rain-spattered. I put down the case I had been switching from hand to hand, my arms rebelling at their release, and blinkered my eyes to see inside. The restaurant was empty, silenced even through the glass by absence. The chairs were tucked in place, the red cloths expectant. Its emptiness slouched over the room and I thought I could see dust at the corners of the tables and on the tops of the chairs. The Tolinis were taking their summer vacation early, perhaps visiting that old grandmother for the last time.

Now that I was standing still the soles of my feet burned with walking and I sat down on my suitcase like a disconsolate traveller whose train has been cancelled and no further one announced. My mother's manicured fingers on her coffee-pot seemed too distant.

*   *   *

Opening our front door I bumped into something soft and shouted in shock.

'Leo, shhhh.' My mother's whisper recalled childhood fevers. I switched on the light. She was sitting on a low stool behind the door like a woman in mourning. Wearing her coat and a hat, she held her gloves in the hands folded on her lap, like someone waiting for a taxi. Next to her, also waiting, stood a suitcase, strapped and labelled.

'What are you doing? What's going on?'

'I'm waiting for them. They're late, but I suppose they're very busy.'

'Who is? Who are you waiting for?'

'The policemen who came this afternoon. They took Pappi and they said they'd come back to fetch me so that we could go together.'

'Go where?'

'I don't know.'

'Didn't you ask?'

'Pappi asked but they said they didn't know.' My mother looked up at me soberly. 'I think they didn't know, actually' – puncturing the bubble of irritation on my lips. 'They were very polite. Said they were sorry. They said excuse me and asked Pappi to pack.'

'How do you know?' I asked, almost viciously.

My mother looked at me with a flicker of weariness. 'Do you think I haven't learned any English at all, *Kleiner*?' I was rebuked.

'Was Pappi angry?'

'No. Why should he be angry? And who with, anyway? He left you a note. It says you should go back to Oxford and stay there. Finish your studies and keep away from London. And now you'd better go out again.'

'What for, for heaven's sake?'

My mother considered me for a moment. 'Because they don't come at midnight because they're English, and they don't come before seven in the morning because they haven't had breakfast, so if you stay out between seven and midnight every day they'll leave you alone.'

'How do you know?'

'Everybody knows.'

'I didn't.'

'No.' My mother fingered her gloves. 'But our friends, Pappi's and mine, are different from the people you know.'

I acknowledged that and ignored it. 'If you knew, why didn't Pappi stay out? Why didn't you?'

'Because', said my mother, patiently explaining the self-evident, 'he wanted to go. He said that the English are fighting alone now, and that Mr Churchill said there's going to be a Battle of Britain, so Pappi says we should do whatever the British want to help them. He said he'd heard they're sending our people to the Isle of Man, by the sea. He said, if he were Hitler, he'd put spies among people like us.'

'No, he wouldn't. Not among people like you. You look so . . . Anyway, they don't have to think everyone is dangerous. It can't be hard to find out. They must know about you and Pappi and hundreds of other people like you. They already decided that before, remember?'

My mother nearly unpinned her hat. 'That man. That man you worked for.' She hung on my arm. 'He's an important man, isn't he? He could help us. He could explain. Go to him and ask him to help us.'

But the Magistrate had kept his name from his interpreter too.

I left my mother where she was and tailed the elderly couples in Gladstone Park who walked, shoulders touching, arms about each other, each with another, insouciant of the shadow padding behind them and grinding his teeth. My father was not in my mind. Nor my mother with her suitcase, gloves and hatpin. All I could think of was EL's disconcerted expression as I failed her, her fingers kneading a fistful of hair. *You shouldn't worry so much*, she said, and ran her fingertips down either side of my face so that I closed my eyes to keep her from seeing the desire behind them. I put my arms around her again, and kissed her this time, again and again until I was throbbing with longing for her. *Yes*, she was saying, *so do I*, and for a moment I thought, I don't know how to begin, remembered that she knew that, and also that she did know how to begin because she had done it before. And then, under a tree in the park, I opened my eyes and felt the tightness of my jaw. EL's image turned away from me, her hair loose. All she left me was an irritated smile as she lifted her arms and wound them around Jeremy's neck. His clothes melted away and there under the tree, where I glimpsed them, her legs glowed pale, tangled among Jeremy's. Her face glowed pale over his muscled shoulder but her glazed eyes stared back as if I was not there. *I've been called up. Did I say?* And Jeremy's naked body, its rhythm unaltered, sprouted a uniform. *Was there something you wanted?*

When it was dark I crept home and let myself in. My mother was where I had left her. I sat myself down on the floor next to her chair and we waited in silence until midnight. Then she took off her coat, slipped it on to its satin-covered hanger and put it away. She unpinned her hat and put that away. She laid her gloves on the hall table, patted her suitcase briefly as if reminding it not to stray and went upstairs to bed.

The following morning she tapped on my door at half past six to tell me that my breakfast was ready. We ate together, in some hurry, and by seven o'clock the kitchen was cleared and cleaned, ready for inspection had there been anyone interested to do it.

'Now, off you go,' she said.

'I'm not going anywhere.'

'But Pappi asked –'

'I know he did. I'm sorry, but I live here. This is my home. I'm not going to scurry from one place to another between seven and midnight hiding from your nice policemen. If you're staying here, then so am I.' I added with a touch of cunning – and melodrama – 'I'm sure Pappi would prefer me to be around to look after you.'

That first day she resumed her vigil at the door, leaving it only to cook me a three-course meal neither of us wanted. I saw her back growing stiff as she moved her weight from buttock to buttock, checking her watch, and her hands were impatient from inactivity. On the second day she waited in her hat and coat, but making forays to diverse corners of the house with her keys and her duster. On the third she pulled all her pans and dishes from the kitchen cupboards out on to the floor, and knelt on a folded towel, scrubbing the furthest corners of her pristine shelves. She seemed to be willing the authorities to arrive at the most inopportune moment, her earlier preparedness having apparently repelled them. No one came.

It took my mother five days to polish her house, during which time she grew noticeably thinner, her appetite as puny as mine, so that she refrained from cooking, without regrets, and we nibbled on bread and sausage. When there was nothing left to clean, she could no longer contain her impatience.

She put on her coat and hat, pulled on her gloves and instructed me. 'I'm going to find out what's gone wrong. If anybody comes, ask them to wait. I'll be back in two hours, I'm sure.'

'Where are you going?'

'To the people I've been waiting for, the police, of course. They must know why they haven't arrived yet.'

She left me surrounded by polished surfaces and flawless mirrors, and in a space stripped of the sounds of her industry, silenced and alone. I took books from my shelves, settled myself into the deep armchair my father had chosen for me, placed books within reach all round me, opened one and closed it almost immediately.

Outside the sky was limitless, the sun unhindered. My mother must be hot in her careful garb, pestering the polite police. I crossed and uncrossed my legs, stretched them out one by one until my knees clicked, as edgy as an unexercised puppy. I could take them for another stroll in the park and pretend that its immaculate lawns were, instead, spongy and tussocked, leading to a rivulet narrow enough to leap across, imagine the weight on my neck of borrowed binoculars, at my heels a rheumatic black gun dog. But I must stay at home to receive the callers my mother expected, detain them, maybe, with coffee and stale Sachertorte, lest they hurry after other duties leaving my eager mother unarrested.

I went into the back garden and ate redcurrants, singly, from the bushes that the previous occupants, whoever they were, had nurtured. The acid juice brought a rush of protesting saliva to my mouth. I could pick a bowlful and douse the fruit in my mother's icing-sugar, but even sweetened I didn't like redcurrants. I moved among the bushes nevertheless, obstinately plucking the translucent crimson orbs. Then I sat on the warm stones of the path someone had laid from the back door to the dead end of the back fence, brought my knees up to my chin, clasped my arms round them and rocked on my buttocks further and further until I tipped over backwards and lay, still curled, looking into the sky. From the upstairs window of a neighbouring house an astonished woman with a hairbrush gazed down on me. I waved and she retreated.

I spread out my arms, lowered my legs, locked my hands behind my head and slept.

The doorbell rang long and repeatedly. I must have been in a heavy sleep. The neighbours knew I was in. Bleary, slightly dizzy from napping in the sun, I ran unsteadily to the front door, brushing my hair with my fingers.

'Mr Beck?' A uniformed constable with a clipboard and a tired temper.

'Yes.'

'Mr . . .' He consulted the clipboard. '. . . Leo Beck?'

'Yes.'

The policeman smiled. One of his teeth was chipped. 'Well, and I wasn't sure. I'm very much afraid, sir, I'm going to have to ask you –'

'I know,' I said, 'I've been expecting you. But my mother's not back yet.'

'Your mother, sir?' His smile broadened, beating his effort to restrain it.

'Yes. She said to ask you to wait. She said she'd be back in . . . oh, my goodness. She's late.'

'Why would she be wanting me to wait? I can't be waiting for gentlemen's mothers.' He was nearly laughing. 'I can see you're all ready.' He touched the suitcase in the hall appreciatively with the toe of his boot. 'So, if you don't mind, I've a lot more to get round.'

'But that's not mine. That's my mother's.'

'Your mother's?'

'She's all ready to go. She's been waiting nearly a week. You've left it very late.'

'Your mother, sir?' he said again. 'I've got nothing here about a mother. It's you we're wanting.'

'Me?' As if I had not known it all along. But you can't think ... 'I see. Please wait inside. I won't be long. What do I need?'

'Whatever you can pack into a suitcase, sir. Clothes, you know, shaving things. Well, perhaps not in your case.' He fingered his own smooth chin round the strap of his helmet. 'I'll just wait here, if that's all right. You won't be too long, will you?'

'You could come back later.'

He smiled and shook his head. Good try, but it won't wash, sir.

My vests and underpants were ironed and folded in the chest of drawers, I had only four shirts anyway and a fistful of socks . . . would I find my father to explain the misunderstanding? . . . trousers took up too much space, wear one, take one, carry my overcoat for protection against the wind from the sea at the Isle of Man, my mother would insist . . . where had she got to? . . . I ought to have stayed out, gone back to Oxford, hidden with Marrrm, with EL. Would Major Laing have turned me in? He would have felt bound to, his daughter shouting and crying, spitting contempt. How could I tell her, let her know? I needed an address to send her, but that constable wouldn't have one. Jeremy upstanding in his uniform, no longer a student but some sort of officer, surely, with EL on his arm, in his arms. The books on the floor by my armchair, all of them, no time to make a selection, anyway I liked them all, Eliot, Auden, Donne, de la Mare. Toothbrush, soap. There was only one cake of it in the bathroom. My mother would have to get more. Handkerchiefs. Shoe-cleaning materials. Packing for myself as once my mother had packed for me, packing for myself to leave the country my mother had packed for me to arrive in.

'Excuse me, sir. Do you expect to be much longer?' The constable was leaning up the stairs.

'I'll be right down.' The case was heavy. Evidently.

'Here, sir. Let me.' Constables have large hands, like porters.

'I need to leave my mother a note.'

'Certainly. That's all right.' I pulled a piece of paper from a notepad in my pocket and leaned on the hall table to let my mother know she might as well unpack her things, to let her know I would tell my father she was all right, to wish her well. In large round letters I wrote the Chapmans' address in case she had forgotten it or lost it, which was inconceivable.

136

The constable breathed by my shoulder. 'You're writing in English!'

'Of course,' I said triumphantly. 'It's the only language I know.'

Eleven

The constable ushered me out before him and fastidiously closed the garden gate behind us. Looking up to the window of my father's office, I glimpsed, in the window of the adjoining house, the woman with the hairbrush. She was standing very erect, with her hands on her hips, as if she had personally seen off a marauder. The constable slung my suitcase into the boot of his car and I was driven to Willesden Green police station, unloaded and seated on a chair in the corridor. They put my suitcase on my knees. The sergeant, leaning over the counter, beckoned.

I stood my suitcase on the floor, relieved. 'Hallo,' I said.

'Passport.'

'Is my mother still here?'

The constable was sitting behind the counter. I heard him laugh.

'Passport, please, sir.' The sergeant was offering me tested patience. I handed him my papers, which he opened, closed and handed back.

'Don't you remember me?'

The sergeant folded his arms, stepped back a pace and made a show of studying my features. He smiled, not at me but at the constable, who had got up to join him. He spoke to the constable. 'Some people don't know how busy a police station is, do they? If we was to remember all the people what come through here we'd be better at catching villains than we are, isn't that right?'

'This way, sir.' The constable ducked under the flap as he was lifting it. 'Don't forget your case.' He pointed down the corridor, indicating where I was supposed to go, and walked close behind me, almost touching me, as if he feared I might find some way of scuttling out of sight. I was taken downstairs and locked in a cell where five men sat in a row on the single bed, all with suitcases, all wearing hats and coats. They moved closer together and I sat too.

'Schönbach,' said my neighbour in a three-piece suit but walking-boots.

'Rosenthal.'

'Meyer.'

'Finkl.'

'Engel.' Engel was fat.

'Beck.'

We shook hands.

'Does anybody know what's going on?' I asked in English. The five men exchanged glances and smiled.

'How long you are here?' Meyer's grey hair was little more than stubble.

'About ten minutes.'

'And such pretty English.' They all laughed. I was providing amusement for everyone, it seemed.

'Oh, I see. Seven years.'

'In that case,' said Meyer in German, 'we don't need to speak English. Some of us haven't had your practice. What's going on in general you know as well as we do. What's going to happen specifically is anyone's guess. Are you hungry? Young men are always hungry.' I was hungry. It was mid-afternoon. 'Now I have had some practice, in some things, and one of them is being taken to places where people don't immediately think of offering three-course meals. I have a loaf of bread in my case and a sausage – and, because I know what's what, a knife, of a sort.' He opened his case and took out a bundle wrapped in newspaper. The paper was greasy from the sausage. 'The knife, I'm afraid, may not be very effective.' His hands were arthritic and the knife slipped awkwardly between his swollen fingers. We all watched. 'Or perhaps I should say that I am not adequately effective with the knife. Schönbach here is a butcher. Schönbach, would you please take over?'

So they had already had time to introduce themselves fully.

Schönbach, big as a butcher should be, weighed the knife in his paw. 'Call this a knife? I couldn't cut butter with this.'

'My apologies. I purloined it from my landlady's kitchen cabinet as I was leaving. A shameful thing to do because she is a nice woman and not unduly rich. But there was no time to hunt for a better one. I could ask the policeman if he could arrange for a car to take me back and choose something sharper.'

'He'll say he's too busy. That's the police all over,' said Schönbach, sawing at the sausage, the muscles of his forearm forcing the blunt blade through the meat. 'Wait a minute.' He handed the sausage to me, slid his case to the floor and climbed on to the end of the bed. There was a small window set in the rough brick high on the wall. Schönbach stropped the knife against the edge of the bricks, flicking his wrist with such speed that the blade became a blur of dull light. He tested it on the ball of his thumb and grunted. 'I wouldn't be seen dead with this, if you ask me. But it'll have to do.' He sat down again and retrieved the sausage. 'Are we all having some of this?'

Meyer spread his gnarled hands by way of invitation and slices of identical thickness fell from the sausage, rising in a pile on Schönbach's knees. He cut the bread.

The corridor outside the cell echoed with feet. The sausage and the bread disappeared. The door was opened and a tall man with glasses, the bones of his shoulders showing through his coat, joined us. We shifted closer together but there was only room for one of the tall man's scrawny buttocks.

I was the youngest and well brought up. I stood, offering my place and said, 'Beck.'

'Schönbach.'

'Rosenthal.'

'Meyer.'

'Finkl.'

'Engel.'

'Mandelbaum. Doctor.'

'Oh ho! The company is improving. Medicine? Music?'

'Physics.'

'Excellent.' Meyer rubbed his hands together as best he could. 'I, as the others already know, became a thief today. Schönbach is a magician. Beck is an Englishman. Engel is an engraver. Finkl really is a thief, he swears, and Rosenthal teaches geography. You're just in time for lunch.'

140

When we had eaten, Meyer smoothed the greasy newspaper, folded it carefully and closed it in his suitcase. The footsteps echoed in the corridor again.

Meyer wiped his mouth on a pristine handkerchief. 'Don't anybody say we've just had a meal. I should have thought to leave some over but maybe this one will be lucky enough to have had something before he came out for the day. If he hasn't, we mustn't make it worse by letting him know what he's missed.'

But the constable was alone. 'All right. Everybody this way.'

'Excellent,' said Meyer again. 'Every meal should be followed by exercise.' He made to get up, struggled, and was levered to his feet by Rosenthal and Engel. 'Thank you, gentlemen.'

Schönbach picked up his suitcase, then bent and lifted Meyer's as well. Meyer, already stooped by his disease, bowed further. We followed the constable back along the corridor, up the stairs and out through the police station. There was a bus parked outside, almost filled with men in hats and coats. We filed into it.

The constable tapped me on the shoulder. 'Your mother was here this morning. She left at about eleven o'clock. I made some enquiries. I thought you'd like to know.'

'Thank you very much, constable. How was she?'

'I don't know. Didn't see her myself, I'm sorry. Have a . . . a good trip, sir.'

Any mass of people is made of smaller groups and each of these is its own unit, sensing itself to be different from the others, as different as each of the individuals who have come together, or been made to come together. What was eventually to become three thousand men began for me with myself, and then my six companions from Willesden Green police station, then the forty-six on that bus. You could tell, I thought, who belonged with whom, the knots of knowing one another that little more than the others already tying us. Forty-six men had met in London police stations, but the way they sat in their seats, sometimes leaning over the back of the seat to say something to the man behind, leaning across the aisle to tap an arm, drew lines of connection and exclusion. Seven seats were empty, seven seats together, marked out by their emptiness as ours.

I let the others board ahead of me, held back momentarily,

creating a space of seconds, and spoke to the driver. 'Good after-noon,' I said in rounded tones. 'Full house today, haven't you?'

The driver was leaning back in his seat, hands behind his head, stretching his shoulders. He responded to my voice. 'You in charge, sir?' No one would call me that again for a long time.

I blushed. What did I think I was doing? Where should I let it lead me? 'Not exactly.'

The driver looked me over, filled his mouth with lazy saliva, rolled it in his cheeks – and swallowed, fixing his eyes on the floor between my feet so that I should know where the gob would have landed had he deigned to send it my way. Then he let the bus go with such force that I was jerked off my feet and flailed for a handle. Meyer had been watching me, smiling, shaking his head. He beckoned, pointed to the space next to him.

'You take the window seat,' he said kindly, as if I were a child, but added, 'I need to be able to stretch my legs into the aisle. They get stiff. I am stiff, like rusty old wire. Anyway, I haven't been here long enough and I don't want to fall in love with a countryside I'm about to leave. You can tell me about it. You can tell me where we're going.'

The bus trundled us through Kensington and Hammersmith.

'I can't tell where we're going,' I said. 'But I do know where we're not going. We're not going to Oxford.'

Meyer turned to look at me. 'Are you studying there?'

'Yes, I am. I was.'

He nuzzled my knee with a rigid claw. 'Poor kid. At least I had my student days to myself. *Ach* well.' He looked across me out of the window for a while at the white-porticoed urban villas. 'Elegant,' he murmured. 'What were you studying?'

'Medicine.'

'Mmm.' Appreciatively. 'Good for you, but it'll be hard to come back to. It takes such a long time, and who knows when you'll be home again? Were you enjoying it?'

'No. I hated it.'

'Ha ha! Then I'm not sorry for you any more. Consider yourself released. You have the perfect excuse. Now all you have to do is decide what you want to do instead . . . when the time comes.'

For me travelling by bus had been, above all, my journeys to and from school, where the commuters had kept their shoulders to themselves, indicating displeasure if others did not. They had kept their silence. This bus was noisy. Forty-six men with a great deal too much to say and not all of them inclined to listen. Only the driver, cocooned in his driver's space, his neck stiffening as the burble of German behind him grew louder, was alone.

We passed a road sign. 'This is Chiswick.'

Meyer chuckled. 'Yes. Even I can read road signs in English but thanks for the pronunciation. *Ja*, what a waste.' Was he thinking of my wasted youth? No. 'I should have learned English. There are things I should have liked to read in the original.'

'What things? Eliot? Donne? I've got them in my case, I think.'

'So that's your interest. No, young Mr Beck, I should have liked to read your Darwin. It's a sort of hobby with me. I feel sure that in his own language I might get closer to that man's excitement and his doubts. Maybe you can teach me, if we stay together. There'll be the time, make no mistake. And I'm no fool. I can learn something new, even at my age.' I could not imagine teaching anything to someone older than my father. He should be teaching me. Meyer seemed to sense my awkwardness. 'And I shall teach you that.'

'What?'

'That you can learn something new at any age, even though you are no age at all.'

Feeling again like a child I blurted a question like a child. 'Can I ask you something? Why is your hair so short?'

Meyer rubbed his pate with his wrist. 'Because they shaved it all off.'

'Who did?'

'Hitler's people. In the camp.'

'What camp?' Feigning ignorance, preferring ignorance.

Meyer screwed his grizzled head round to look at me once more. 'What's your first name?'

'Leo.'

'Little English Leo. You see, I've learned something new already, something which I suppose I should have known. That when you go through something unspeakable other people don't necessarily know. But somehow one always thinks they ought to know or,

143

rather, they ought to have bothered to find out, because knowledge, of course, isn't given, it's acquired. And one makes the mistake of thinking that people want to know about important things when of course it's the important things they want to know about least.'

It sounded like a rebuke and I bridled. 'Well, tell me then.'

'No. I said it was unspeakable.'

'That's not fair. I'm trying to acquire the knowledge, from a primary source, and the source won't let the knowledge go. How am I supposed to find out?'

'You'll find out, in time. You won't be able to avoid it.' The bus slowed to cross the Thames at Twickenham. Offended by his rebuttal I glared grimly at the quiet summer water. Meyer leaned forwards, also looking out but his eyes apparently unseeing. 'Don't be angry,' he murmured. 'Some things are not easy to talk about when one is trying to reassemble lost dignity.'

Someone shouted from the front, 'Home at last!', and people jostled, leaning on one another for a view. The sign was scalloped out of the sky in an arch. Kempton Park Racecourse was teeming with racegoers in hats and coats, all with suitcases, in an orderly queue that meandered but did not break, standing, waiting. An officer tapped us sharply out of the bus with his swagger-stick, one flick on the upper arm and another flick pointing to the tail of the queue.

The shadows lengthened in the mid-afternoon sun as we stood hugging the white barrier of the racecourse, fallen silent, listening, perhaps, to the drumming of the sometime hooves.

A forward pace, a wait of minutes, another forward pace. Behind me Meyer said quietly, 'The surroundings are perfect. But the catering's lousy.' He was grey. The standing was painful.

'Who knows, maybe there's something to eat here. Anybody mind horsemeat?' said Schönbach. 'Keep my place. I don't want to miss anything.'

'Don't be a fool.' But he was gone.

'They don't hurry in this country of yours, do they, Leo?' Another pace forward and Meyer was leaning heavily on the barrier.

'Why don't you sit down, on your case?'

'Because it's so difficult getting up.'

'But you could sit and wait here and we'd come and fetch you.'

'Maybe. Or somebody else will come and say, "You've got out of line, now you have to wait all over again." I don't think I want to take the risk.'

The sun was grazing the tops of the trees and the shadow of the queuing men loomed away from our feet, moving like dark breath on the grass.

'Look, it's Schönbach!' The butcher came pushing a wheel-barrow at a slow jog. 'What have you got there?'

'Transport for Herr Meyer.' The wheelbarrow was padded with sacks. 'Please sit.' Meyer shook his head, laughing, nervous. We took him under the arms and lowered him into the barrow. 'He needs a support for his back,' said Schönbach, looking around. '*Ach*, they won't miss this for a while.' He grasped a white-painted plank of the barrier, put one foot against the upright and yanked. He pulled out a second plank. 'Be careful! Here come the gee-gees!' The barrier was breached. Wrapping the planks in sacks, Schönbach eased them behind Meyer's back so that he was propped upright, his legs dangling over the end of the barrow. 'And one more here, so the legs don't go to sleep' – tucking more sacking under Meyer's knees – 'and off we go! Beck will be the porter.' The queue moved imperceptibly and Schönbach wheeled Meyer with it.

'How did you get this?' Meyer's colour was returning.

'Did you ever see stables without wheelbarrows? I'm afraid you're sitting on old shit but I covered it up.'

'Didn't they stop you?'

'Sure they stopped me.' Schönbach was swaggering with his triumph. 'But I told them why we needed it.'

'How? What did you say?'

'I said' – dropping into English and self-parody – ' "Vee haf old man. Wery old. Wery sick, you come, you see" ', and setting down the wheelbarrow Schönbach staggered with bent back and an imaginary stick. 'The English, of course, are decent. And this one was busy. So here we are.'

'I'm very grateful,' said Meyer drily. 'I think, if you don't mind, I'll go to sleep now.'

'Some people can sleep anywhere.'

'Some people have learned how to.'

It was dark by the time we reached the thing we had been queuing for – a small table, two officers and a box. One of the officers spoke without looking up. *'Der Name?'*

'My name is Leo Beck.'

'Der Vorname?'

'I told you. Leo. I should prefer you to speak English.'

'Die Adresse?'

'111 Melrose Avenue, Cricklewood, London NW2.'

'Und vorher?'

'43 Acacia Avenue.'

'Und vorher?'

'I can't for the life of me remember. It's too long ago.'

'Geld.'

'I've only got two pounds three and sixpence.' They took it and laboriously wrote out a receipt for me to sign.

'Dokumente.'

'I've hardly got any –'

'Just hand your papers over and stop holding things up. There are people behind you.' They riffled through my passport, barely scanning it, and dropped it into the box beside them. 'Suitcase' – indicating the table. 'Open it.' They stood to examine my things, leafed through my books, coughing, 'haw, haw', then left me to repack and close the case. 'What's this man doing?' Meyer was snoring gently, his twisted arms aping relaxation.

'He's disabled. He can hardly walk. I'll wake him, shall I?'

'What sort of riff-raff are they sending us? Yes, wake him.'

'Herr Meyer. Herr Meyer!' Meyer slept on.

Schönbach bent down. 'Breakfast!' he shouted, and Meyer woke.

'Put your things on me.' Meyer offered his lap. We each laid the issued blanket on top of his and wedged round him our tin mugs, our plates, our spoons. 'Crockery and cutlery are always a hopeful sign.' We queued again. Tea was poured into each mug, thick as beer. We drank it where we stood, and ate the slice of bread and the piece of cheese. Schönbach had scoffed at the knife Meyer had stolen from his landlady; but Meyer no longer had it and we spread the ration of margarine with our spoons.

Schönbach wheeled the barrow to the restaurant, where we were to sleep. At the door a soldier with a gun ordered Meyer out. The restaurant floor was laid end to end with mattresses, heaving with the bodies of men, turning, complaining, laughing. No one was to leave, no one was to make a move outside. All through the night the muttering and murmuring of two hundred and fifty men was punctuated by the rattle of gunfire, and I expected bodies. The air grew heavy and lay on our faces. At dawn when they called us out to the first roll-call of the day, spent cartridges crunched underfoot like cockroaches. The breeze in the branches had ignited the guards, who had promised to shoot anything that moved. Tea, a slice of bread, plum jam to cover a thumbnail. The sun on the trees, the grass under my hands and my neck, lying in the sun. Slender potato soup. Swifts riding roller-coasters in the high sky. May I have paper to write to my mother? No one writes letters from Kempton Park Racecourse. Whatever had made me suppose otherwise? Spread-eagled on my stomach, the sun on my back, I pressed my stomach into the ground to still the hunger. I had never thought about food before but now, listening to Schönbach torturing Engel with recipes, I felt aggrieved that words could make Engel salivate, his memory singing him songs of fragrance and taste. Though his cheeks were hollow Meyer said the country air was doing him good but sea air would have been better. Everywhere in England was near the sea, said Rosenthal the geographer. Maybe, I thought, on the Isle of Man, some elasticity might return to Meyer's riveted joints. When would we go? Why weren't we going? Until all of a sudden we went, we were on our way, leaving the mattresses in their stale air for the people coming behind us, thinking nothing of the people coming behind us.

Meyer put his hands together and saluted the wheelbarrow. 'Faithful friend, loyal friend, you who have carried me these last days . . . I will not forget you.'

'Give over,' said Schönbach. 'Who did all the pushing?'

'But we're not being separated, you and I. This fine barrow, on the other hand . . .'

They lined us up and locked us in the waiting train, which travelled, said Rosenthal, due north. I slept, the train rocking the ball of hunger rolling in me. When I woke the train was stationary. 'Where are we?'

Meyer pointed out of the window. 'We must be a dangerous bunch. It makes me feel quite proud.' The station sign had been blacked out. For the rest of the day the train trudged through an unlabelled land. And stopped.

The doors were opened from the outside by soldiers who called us out on to a platform cleared of travellers. They lined us up. They marched us out, left, right, along domestic pavements silent as Sunday. Hats, coats and suitcases, a crocodile of grown men, grumbling, shuffling hungry past shops forewarned and briefly shuttered. Murphy's, D. A. Jones and Son, Purveyors of Top Class Meats, Suzanne's Hair Salon, The King's Arms – nothing gave away location. A file of men walks slowly; a long file of men sways in slow motion. In that twilight and with our hunger we seemed to shamble forward for hours, flat-footed and muttering.

Somewhere ahead they must have halted because we began to bunch up against one another, feet still marching on the spot, unable to stop, uncertain whether we should. The news came whispering back, 'We've arrived.' Where? Somewhere.

The pavement gave way to the ridges of once churned mud, pieces of brick to twist the ankles, shoe-worn paths. In the dimmed street-lighting I could make out a gloom of houses, a high fence, a stretch of space, a field maybe, and small triangular outgrowths on the land. A few windows lit up in the houses, spots of torches wavered over the rough ground, torchlight flickered into our faces, a stab of light in the eyes, and a uniformed arm pulled me out of the file. I looked round, fearful of being alone, and saw Meyer pulled to the other side, Schönbach and Rosenthal with me, Engel and Mandelbaum with Meyer. Where was Finkl, small as a child? There, ahead.

'All right. This way. No talking.' The file flowed momentarily back together like a school of tiny fish, then broke apart. I saw Schönbach in front of me and stumbled to keep up with him, bumped into him.

'Watch it!'

'Why have we stopped? Can you see anything?'

'Not a damn thing . . . Yes, look.'

The black silhouette of a man, bulky with his arms full, another behind him, and another, following a line of torches shining a diagonal, from a fence of soldiers' hands to the ground, commanding, 'This way! Go this way!'

A blanket, a tin plate, a mug, a spoon and a knife.

Schönbach tapped his knife against his mug. 'If they give you a knife, will they give you something that needs cutting to go with it?'

Where was Meyer? How would he carry his things? Someone tipped tea into my mug, a slice of bread for my plate and a square of cheese. Carrying them, my blanket, my suitcase, I followed the torches. Come with me, Schönbach. He was there, behind me, cursing under his breath as he kicked against a clod of earth and some of his tea spilt on to his hand.

The last of the torches sent us into a tent – one, two, three, four – and instantly flickered back to the men still to come. In the darkness we groped for the limits of our confines. A tent for four. In it the four of us. We sat on the ground and ate our meal, relieved to be together but not saying so.

'I could do with a piss.' Schönbach put his head out of the tent. The line of torches had evaporated. 'Okay.' He opened his case, feeling and fumbling, brought out a small hand torch and slipped out of the tent. Holding the flaps around my ears like a protective hood I peered after him to see where he would go. He was standing, flashing his little stripe of light from side to side, apprehensive as an antelope at a water hole. He seemed to conclude there was nothing for it, and stood where he was, urinating on the ground. As he switched off his torch he was caught in the slash of a floodlight, scuttled out of it and fell, swearing. There was a burst of laughter from somewhere above and the floodlight blanked out, leaving its blaze in the back of my eyes.

We slept on our coats, rolled in our blankets.

A megaphone barked us out at dawn. I looked out into a vast field of tents, planted in drawn rows, line upon line of brown triangles, men crawling out on all fours. At the back stood a huge marquee. Men were crawling from that too, streams of dark, two-dimensional figures. A barbed-wire fence high as a house ran around the field, and beyond it I saw the houses of the night before, strange bare houses with new bricks stacked between them. How

149

many thousands of us were here? Was my father among them? Where had they put Meyer?

Schönbach had large receptive ears. 'This is Huyton.'

'What's Huyton?'

'You should know better than me. Near Liverpool, they're saying.' He nodded towards the houses beyond the barbed-wire. 'That's where Meyer's gone, and the others. Because they're older. It's going to be a housing estate, when they finish building it, when we've gone.'

'Where are we going to? Have you found that out too?' asked Finkl.

'From Liverpool,' said Rosenthal, 'it's the Isle of Man, Ireland, America or Canada.'

Schönbach licked his morning jam off his fingers. We had had porridge too. 'There's going to be a meeting.'

'Where?'

'We'll find out when we see everybody going to it.'

'What's it going to be about?'

'We'll find out when we get there.'

'How did you find out about Meyer?'

'I asked around.' Could he ask around for my father too?

The field streamed with men moving in a mass towards a hut by the barbed-wire fence. Sharing a direction, sharing a purpose, but not enough purpose, they drew us along with them. Guards with rifles stood in a line in front of the hut from which an officer emerged, carrying a wooden box and a megaphone. He climbed on to his box. The megaphone clamped itself on to his face and gobbled his words.

'What's he saying?' Schönbach was bending forward from the waist, his face a tangle of lines as he struggled to understand.

'Something about digging ditches.'

'Digging ditches? Where? When?'

'Ssh. Wait, let me listen . . . Storm trenches round the tents in case it rains.'

'Of course it'll rain. This is England, isn't it?'

Detached from the officer's face the megaphone hung, emptied, from his hand, and the officer dismounted from the box. The meeting was over. Was that it? The men stood for a moment, motionless, still staring at the box as if expecting it to tell them something more. The officer turned away to go back into his hut.

'Excuse me!' The officer paused, frozen, one arm forwards, the other back. 'Can you help me, please?' A voice from the front, high-pitched with urgency, needing no megaphone. The officer swung round, bland-faced. 'Here should be my brother. I am here already one week but nobody will tell me. He is ill. The name is Selig. S.E.L.I.G.'

'Names,' said the officer wearily. 'Don't give me names. I've got three thousand of you here. How am I supposed to know who any of you are?'

The man persisted, his fists hammering the air down lower towards the ground with every word. 'My papers. You have my papers. You have my money. You have my brother. I want to know.'

The officer rubbed his face and stared helplessly at the crowd, hushed before him. I sensed a bubble of menace in the mass of men and the officer retreated a pace. The guards fingered their rifles. Remembering his role, the officer squared his shoulders. 'Prisoners of war have no right to information. I wouldn't give it – even if I had it. And I have none.'

The crowd exhaled through its teeth. Selig lost all caution. 'I am not a prisoner of war. No one here is a prisoner of war. I am loyal to England, I demand –' The guards raised their rifles but the officer gestured them down again and Selig was swallowed back into the crowd.

I was queuing for the toilet under an overcast sky gravid with rain. There were still some fifty men ahead of me, how many behind I couldn't estimate. In the waiting I had tasselled the sides of the piece of toilet paper they had given me four days previously and which I had torn into four to make it last.

Schönbach, queue-jumping, appeared at my side, and the queue hissed. But Schönbach had a talisman. He held it up. 'A spade, gentlemen. I've found a spade. We are tent number five hundred and forty three. In two hours we'll be ready to pass it on.' Then he said to me, 'The builders left it behind. Cement, see?' The spade was encrusted. 'Engel gave it to me through the fence. Meyer's sick but there isn't a doctor anywhere. He needs aspirin for the pain. You got any aspirin? They've got a toilet in the house but no furniture. Meyer's stiff from sleeping on the floor. Find someone with aspirin. I'm going to do some digging. I said two hours so it had better be two hours, and anyway I don't want to sleep in a lake.'

I sent the request along the queue in both directions: pass it on, pass it on. Two men only in front of me and my bowels bursting. I came out with excrement on my hand but nowhere to wash. They had said we could shower some time in the week, and the week was passing.

'Are you the one who wanted the aspirin?' A tall man, thick-set, clutching his stomach.

'Yes.'

'Then for God's sake take it.' He pushed a screw of paper into my hand and threw himself through the lavatory door.

'Thanks,' I shouted through the closed door. 'Who shall I say it's from?'

There was a silence, then the spattering of diarrhoea, and a further silence. Finally, 'I don't know who it's from. It came up the line.'

I opened the twist of paper. Inside were three white pills.

Schönbach was sweating, his jacket and shirt draped over the tent. 'You sure enjoy a shit, don't you? Took your time. No, all right, only kidding. Here, you do a bit. I've done the hard part, all you need to do is carry on round. Give me the aspirin.'

'How did you know I'd got some?'

'You were bound to. See you later.'

He left me struggling with the spade, unhandy, unused, trying to keep the sides of the trench as sheer as in his digging. By the following night the neighbouring tents stood like ours, moated, islanded, as if each one was proclaiming itself an independent state. When the skies opened, the trenches filled and Finkl's deft fingers built a flotilla of tiny rafts of twigs and couch grass.

'If that's the best they can come up with for us, I'm staying here,' growled Schönbach, back from the fence where the rumours grew like weeds.

Hitler was poised to invade Britain, was already on his way.

Ships had been sighted and the War Cabinet was packing its bags to leave London and decamp to . . . where was furthest west? They were bombing London. London had been flattened. They had taken over the railways. A ship of men they'd taken away a week before had been torpedoed and gone down without a life saved. No one had known where the ship was heading, except, presumably, the captain of the submarine that sunk her. Where was the truth? Why wouldn't they let us have newspapers or listen to the wireless? Someone asked. The answer came back, 'Information is not the property of prisoners of war, internees, refugees or whatever you want to call yourselves. We'll tell you all you need to know.'

Somebody was dead, in the marquee where they'd put five hundred men. An old fellow, they said, hanging in the cloakroom empty as a discarded coat. He'd been two years in one of Hitler's camps. When the wind whipped the roof of the tent in the night and anti-aircraft fire clattered in the distance he'd run out into the dark, stumbling among the mattresses, holding his head. It wasn't Meyer. It couldn't be Meyer. Meyer was on the other side of the fence, grating flakes off his aspirins.

They were asking for volunteers to board another ship for the Isle of Man, some said Canada, where everyone would be released, and the wives and children would be sent out to join them. We had to hurry. They weren't going to wait for ever while people made up their minds. Choose the sea and its shoal of cruising U-boats, or the naked camp, exposed to the V-formations of the night. If Hitler arrived he would know where to look first. But what about the ones left behind, what about Schönbach's wife and their small daughters, last seen in a Stockwell vicarage? Finkl's sister and his grandmother? Rosenthal's wife who was in another camp somewhere, he thought? What about my mother? Ten days at Huyton and we had not been allowed to write. We had received nothing. 'What d'you expect?' said Schönbach. 'Nobody knows where we damn well are.'

My father was not a tent-dweller. I had established that. Nor, according to word from the other side of the fence, was he in the half-finished houses. They must have moved him on. He must already be on the Isle of Man as he had expected. I thought of the Canadian forests with trees so tall you had to lean back to follow the soaring trunks, trees so dense you could hear, if you were attentive, if you knew what to listen for, the loose-shouldered prowling bear. Trappers, Old Surehand and Old Shatterhand, flitted across the unbroken snow without snapping a twig. Take the ship.

I did not want to go alone among the hundreds they were asking for. Schönbach, are you coming? Rosenthal, Finkl? And Meyer? I went with Schönbach to the fence, tagging along behind him, the man who knew his way about, while I had lingered 'at home' in the field of tents. From a distance the separating line of barbed-wire might have been a trail of treacle to which ants were glued, milling, sucking, carrying away. Half the camp was there, drawn to the fence by its very existence, each side convinced the other was better informed. So many men on our side, so many on theirs, we would never find Engel or Meyer or Mandelbaum. Schönbach, however, strode through, pulling me after him, 'Come along, come along', steering with his shoulders through the hatted crowd from which came the ceaseless murmuring of words passed from one man to the next. As we progressed, Schönbach dispensed greetings with such speed that the replies floated behind us like the tail of a kite.

'Who are all these people? Do you know them all?'

'Of course. That's Klein's group, those are Müller's, those there are Fried's people. You're one of mine, only you haven't noticed. Look. There's Engel, and Meyer taking the sun.'

Meyer sat on a pile of bricks with his hands resting palm upwards on his knees, fingers clawed, gathering warmth. His eyes were closed and his face was immobile with impenetrable calm.

'Meyer! Hey, Meyer, you idle good-for-nothing. I've brought you a visitor. Get over here.'

Meyer's eyelids rolled up. 'Little Leo. Finally.' He hunched over his knees, and hands appeared on either side to lift him to his feet. 'I've had open house all this time and you never came to visit. How do you find camping? Suit you, does it? You don't look so bad but you ought to eat more. Your mother will never forgive me if I return you to her looking like a piece of string.' He was smiling, with decision I thought, for me. Engel, slimmer, guided Meyer under the elbow, step by step, to the fence. 'So, Leo. And are you going sailing too?'

Twelve

'E 76431.' A baptism at the camp gate, stamped on to me almost as if the number were in indelible blue figures on my forehead. I mustn't forget E 76431.

Meyer, E 76430, had managed somehow to smooth the creases from his suit. 'Upbringing,' he explained. 'It gets you like that. I always travel well turned out. I would never begin a trip untidy. How I end, of course, is another matter.' Behind me, Schönbach, E 76432, was once again Meyer's porter.

They marched us in single file back through the streets of Huyton, whose inhabitants now knew where their duty lay. From their small fenced front gardens women with flowered scarves tied over the early-morning rollers in their hair pelted us with potato peelings and fish-heads, reaching at random for handfuls of wet detritus from basins prepared for the purpose and propped on their hips. 'Nazis!' they screamed, and their voices, strangled with hatred, were reedy. 'Bloody Nazis!' Some of their menfolk, fathers, fathers-in-law, looked down from the upstairs windows, gesticulating obscenely. Others lingered in the open doorways; a few had broached their harbouring fences and, rooted in the pavement, sniffed us as we passed by.

In front of me Meyer was shuffling bolt upright, his neck cemented on to his twisted shoulders.

At Huyton station a waiting train exhaled a steady rhythm. Troops lined the platform, eyeing the slow men with the suitcases, restive as police dogs on the leash. I was impatient too, for the sea, for the space of it. Seated between Schönbach and Meyer, I pulled my thighs together lest any pressure on Meyer hurt his stiffened legs. The windows had been blackened for the short ride to Liverpool.

Standing on the quay, Schönbach whistled. 'That's a big ship and no mistake.' She was long, grey as dawn, with a single funnel set between two masts. '*Dunera*,' said Schönbach. 'See?' Six neatly blocked letters on the prow. She was *Dunera*. I was E 76431.

The sides of the ship bulged skywards, studded from prow to stern with three tiers of portholes. Craning up I saw, high on the top deck, *Dunera*'s crew gathered along the railing, dipping and pecking like birds on a wire. Among the grey caps bobbed the smaller, darker heads of the Indian sailors, the lascars. An arm went up in greeting. It was impossible to say whose.

'Drop your cases!' Soldiers stepped into the light from the shadow of the harbour wall, casual as kids on a street corner. An officer lounged behind them, watching and smiling. 'Put 'em down! There. Right there!' The first few cases were placed neatly in a line but the soldiers grew impatient. 'Quicker. Get on with it. Throw 'em down!' And the suitcases piled together as if they had been discarded. 'Everyone on board. That way.' The gangplank had been lowered and a corridor of soldiers sprouted on the quay, so narrow that a man could only just walk between its human walls. 'Okay. Who's first? You, come on.' Someone was pulled out. His body disappeared, jostled along between the soldiers, who rolled him forwards, knees and fists in his back.

'Hey! What are you doing?' The man's protest was shrilly ineffectual.

Then we were drawn, one after the other, as if roped together, through the corridor, Meyer in front of me, his feet slipping and stumbling and his arms wrapped around himself like a man in midnight frost. My neck jerked as a pair of hands swung me round and held my shoulders. The soldier I was facing pulled my coat from my arm, held it upside-down and shook it. A ten-shilling note floated down and he pocketed it. 'Yours,' he said, crossed his hands, locked his fingers on my shoulders and spun me round to face the other way. The soldier who had been behind me now pulled my jacket open, wrenching off the buttons. 'What you got? What you got?' His hands were in my pockets, he was slapping at my legs, but time was pressing. Schönbach on the conveyor belt, pushed from behind, was squeezing me onwards, and my two soldiers had to release me as he was extruded into their hands. The corridor ran along the quay and up the gangplank, on to the top deck. The ground might have been moving under my feet. I was carried on, unable to stop, but turned to see Schönbach flailing with his big arms and someone bringing a rifle butt into his face.

'You! Officer!' he shouted, able still to bellow. The officer under the harbour wall raised a hand to acknowledge the call, crossed his legs and lit a cigarette.

There was a scuffle on deck. Someone was being dragged between two soldiers, his feet trailing behind him, the toes of his boots scrabbling for purchase on the boards as if he hoped to anchor himself and prevent the onward motion. The soldiers trudged forward, heads down, lugging only a weight, making for the stern and a wall, house-high, of coiled barbed-wire, the men beyond pacing its length almost at a run. For a moment the corridor of soldiers fragmented as their attention was caught by the scene behind them, and through the space between them I caught a glimpse of familiar features on the other side of the wire. The man's face, drawn and tight, burst open with incredulity. 'Doctor,' he yelled. 'Hey, Doctor! Fuckin' Leo!'

'Oh no, you don't.' The corridor reached out its arms and yanked me back into line leaving me with the image of Giusè Tolini's ravaged expression.

Like a bag of boiled sweets emptied into a jar we were poured through a narrow hatch, bouncing down the walls of a steep stairway to a lower deck, an underground cavern pulsing in a dim light. As the bodies tumbled in I sensed that the space around me was already filled and heaving with people.

'Move. Get out of the way.' Schönbach scooped me ahead of him out of the path of the still descending men. 'Where's Meyer? For Christ's sake, is he still on his feet?' His shirt-tails flapped from his trousers and I saw the ribbed pattern of the sole of a boot imprinted in dust on one of his shoulders. In the twilight, under a ceiling so low I could scrape it with my fingertips, the voices, explosive with indignation as people landed at the foot of the stairway, were suddenly muted, muffled by astonishment and the weight of the air. Schönbach filled his lungs. 'Meyer! Klaus Meyer! Where the hell are you?'

'I'm above it all.' Over our heads Meyer's quiet voice sliced through the subdued hubbub. 'I thought I'd have a little nap. Why don't you join me?' He was swinging in a hammock from a butcher's hook in the ceiling. Over the edge his eyes were blazing and his marbled knuckles belied his calm.

'How did you get up there?'

'I didn't get up here. I fell in.' Fearful of being knocked off balance by the struggle of blundering men, he had eased himself on to a table, stood up to get a better view, cracked his head on the ceiling and toppled into the hammock where he now lay trapped, and parcelled like a joint prepared for roasting. 'And under the circumstances I think I'll stay where I am.'

The room had grown brighter as my eyes accepted the lack of light. Trestle tables stood in rows with benches on either side. Above them at regular intervals the butcher's hooks poked like beckoning claws from the ceiling, suspending hammocks.

'If you count, and I have counted,' said Meyer drily, 'you will notice that the number of hammocks and the number of people so far in here do not match. The people are increasing. The hammocks apparently not. This one, therefore, is mine. I may have to label it. What do you think?'

'Stick with your hammock,' said Schönbach, jealous and surly. 'All that swinging would make me throw up. I can sleep on a table for a night. All I need now is a meal, a bit of peace and some fresh air. Leo, you're nearer. Open a porthole, there's the lad.'

By now it was almost impossible to move except along the table-tops where people were already squatting. Hunching to protect my head I edged to the side and pulled at a porthole. It was jammed. I skirted to a neighbouring table and tried the porthole there. I couldn't open it.

Almost a shadow in his dark hat and coat, a small bearded man tapped my arm. 'None of them open. They're all locked. I think it's deliberate.'

'But we'll suffocate if there isn't more air.'

'Then we just have to breathe less.'

'Oh, for goodness' sake!'

'Calm down, child. Excitement consumes a lot of oxygen. Go and find yourself a quiet corner, take out a book and read it. Above all, don't talk too much.'

He nodded emphatically after each instruction, his beard sliding softly up and down his chest, and laid one finger on my arm again as if to say, watch me. Then, gathering his coat about him like a lady protecting her skirts, he edged his way into a corner where a copse of dark coats waited for him. Silently they seated themselves along the benches of the furthermost table and, exchanging significant glances, each opened the tome that had appeared from his pocket, laid it in front of him on the table and bent his head.

'We have full house,' said Meyer from his vantage point when I found them again. 'No more arrivals. Look, they've stopped sending people in.'

'Maybe so.' Schönbach had made a tour of our surroundings. 'But nobody's going to be getting out in a hurry either.' He led me to the foot of the stairway and pointed up. The only exit was a wooden-framed door lashed across with barbed-wire as if a demented spider had been at work. A single soldier stood guard on the other side, leaning against the wall, his rifle propped between his legs.

Dunera belched, all her juices running through her as she considered the meal she had ingested. Meyer's hammock swung and stilled. A cheer went up. The sooner this ship left port the sooner we'd be off her again. Lights all along the walls flickered and came on, momentarily freezing the men with surprise. The benches were full, men leaning on the tables, some caught in a gesticulation, elbow to elbow as if they were arm-wrestling, the accompanying words congealed on their lips. In the corner the rabbi and his students, immobilised by the lights, paused in their reading, each torso at a different angle. Although the distances between the tables was unvarying there seemed to be a ring of space round this one separating it from the rest. And up at shoulder height the bloated hammocks hung like flies wrapped in the spider's larder.

'Out of them hammocks!' Soldiers clattered down the stairway from the hatch and jabbed into the hammocks with bayonets. 'Out! Out! Get out!' The men squawked and tussled with the entangling netting, squirming to pull their defenceless bodies away from the dancing spikes that were seeking out soft places. Meyer, twisting and struggling, seemed helplessly enmeshed. 'Need a little help, do you?' A couple of soldiers grasped the hammock on one side and upended it. Meyer fell heavily on to the table below, his swollen hands still clutching the netting because he either couldn't let go or hoped to break his fall. He lay unmoving and there was a sudden silence.

Schönbach bent over the table. 'Meyer!'

'Sssh,' Meyer whispered, eyes closed, and Schönbach stood up.

The soldiers unhooked the hammocks with their bayonets and dragged them away up the hatch stairs. The dispossessed men crowded on to the benches, but some had to stand.

In a moment the soldiers returned and positioned themselves at the nearest table, standing behind the benches with their bayonets. 'Empty your pockets. Everything on the table.'

Hands in slow motion, prevaricating, brought out loose change, handkerchiefs, watches, photographs, documents. Heaped together, the pocket-stained objects, separated from their owners, were divested of identity. The soldiers picked out the documents and the photographs, held them up to the light, made ostentatious reading motions with their heads and tore them slowly across, once, doubled the pieces together and tore them again, dropped them on to the table and, as hands reached out, gathered them up and swept them off the table into a bag. The watches and the money went into another bag. The handkerchiefs joined the ripped papers. A toothbrush with splayed bristles lay alone, everyone looking at it, all the faces impassive.

A soldier waved his hand over it, hovering as if the thing might move, and pounced. 'Aha! Gotcha!' He held it up. 'And what might you be?' He brought it closer and closer to his eyes until he was squinting and his comrades laughed. 'What is this? Now, what is this? P'raps it's a violin.' He held it under his chin and bowed at it with a finger. 'Nah. Not a violin. Well, I dunno.' He shook his head, drooping his mouth in a caricature of bewilderment. 'Can anybody help me? I've got a little problem, you see, 'cos I got this thing and I don't know what it is. It ain't a violin 'cos I played it but it didn't come out wiv no music. Now it could be a broom, yeah, hadn't thought of that. Less give it a try, shall we?' He leant his bayonet against one of the seated men and the man stiffened, then he bent and scrubbed at the floor with the toothbrush, paused and straightened. 'No. Too small. I know' – his face cleared with mock enlightenment – 'it's for the boots.' He rubbed the toothbrush along the crevice at the sole of his boot, and scraped some dirt from its heel. 'Oh dear, not much good, is it?'

'I reckon it's a toothbrush.'

The soldier turned to his mate. 'Genius. You're a real genius. Now why didn't I think of that? Now we gotta find out whose toothbrush it is and get it back to its rightful owner, 'cos he'll be missing it. Is it yours?' He held it under the nose of the man whose back still supported the bayonet. The man shook his head, his body rigid. 'You sure?' The man shook his head again. 'Well, if it's not yours, it must be somebody else's.' The soldiers passed the toothbrush between them, offering it round the table. No one claimed ownership. 'This is very strange. We got a toothbrush and it don't belong to nobody. It just appeared on the table by magic but it don't belong to nobody. You know what that means?' The triumph in his voice was for his companions. 'That means none of that other stuff ain't nobody's neither. So wasn't it lucky we come along to do a bit of tidying up? Wouldn't want this place to get in a mess, now would we? Germans being such tidy people.'

An indistinct bellowing came from the top deck, instructions to the crew, and further feet clattered down the stairway. It was the officer who had monitored our boarding.

'Everything in order?'

'Yes, sir.'

'Excuse, please.' One of the men at the plundered table twisted in his seat to appeal to the officer, his cheeks flabby and grey. 'We have been robbed. I had here my watch, my passport, my visa for America. They have taken it, everything, these soldiers, these troops.'

The officer raised his eyebrows in astonishment. 'Are you saying that my men are thieves? I can promise you that the British army has certain standards of behaviour, you can count yourselves lucky, and theft is not among them. However, all complaints will be investigated. All right, men.' He bent, picked up the two bags the soldiers had filled, turned smartly and ran up the steep stairs, followed by the soldiers. The door was locked and we heard the hatch being battened down. Someone had shuttered the locked portholes because we were out at sea.

There was a moment's total silence and then from the seated men a hissing exhalation seeped throughout the imprisoned lower deck. Three hundred and eighty-four men relaxed their shoulders.

Meyer lay curled awkwardly where he had fallen. 'This I cannot believe,' he said. 'Who are these people? This is England? These are the English? Leo?'

'Cut it out,' said Schönbach. 'Leave the kid alone.'

But Meyer's face was lined with pain. 'He's so proud of being English. Let him answer. We sought sanctuary here – you, me, even him. So what's his answer?'

Schönbach ignored him. 'Come on, let's get him upright.'

'No. Leave me alone. I want to stay lying down.'

'You can't. You'll stiffen up.'

'I am stiffened up already. Let me be. I cracked something.'

'Then we've got to get you a doctor.'

'An English doctor? No thanks. Leo, how much did you learn? No, don't tell me. Nothing. You learned nothing at all, nothing at all about anything. Don't we have doctors here among us? We must have.'

'Any doctors here?' Schönbach yelled through megaphone palms.

'What sort of doctors you want?' came a voice.

'Medical, you fool. No lawyers, no astronomers, just a good down-to-earth doctor who's some use.' There was a silence. 'Pah! So what did you crack, Meyer?'

'I think, my ribs.'

'Yes? I cracked my ribs once when I slipped under a carcass. Boom! Half a cow came off the wall and I went down under it on to the floor like it ran me over. It was half an hour before anybody came and that was only because they were queuing outside and complaining. You don't do a thing with cracked ribs but bandage them up, maybe. I got a thin towel in my suitcase. We could cut that up for you.'

Meyer coughed, wincing. 'Thank you. But you haven't got your suitcase. Leo's friends and compatriots have it, remember?'

'Cut it out, I said, or I'll drop you on the floor. Ho, hallo!' Schönbach shouldered through the deck to the stairway. 'Hallo! We need here a doctor. Hallo-o! . . . Shit! They can't hear through

162

that closed thing. We'll have to wait. You want?' He took off his jacket and folded it for a pillow.

'Thanks. At least you won't be cold without it. Not in this fug.'

'Ungrateful bastard.'

'His ribs hurt.'

'Don't you be sorry for him, Leo. God, I'm hungry.'

'They're coming down again.' With a lot of clanging and noise.

'Catch!' The hammocks thudded on to the floor at the foot of the stairway and after them a dozen zinc buckets.

Schönbach leapt for a hammock and came back with it, grim-faced. 'Makes you ashamed, fighting over them like dogs over a bone. Can't they take a night on the floor?' He fastened the hammock to the ceiling hooks. 'What d'you say, Meyer? You want to sleep the night in this or are you better off on the flat?'

Meyer stirred and grimaced. 'I'll stay where I am, but thanks all the same.'

'I don't know why I bothered. I'm not sleeping in the damn thing like a bag of melons in the market. You want it, Leo?'

'I do. I was hoping you'd ask.'

Schönbach bowed and waved a frilly hand, gesturing me to my place. I stood on the table and tumbled into the hammock. The ceiling was directly over my eyes and the air was more oppressive at this slightly raised height. Perhaps the hammock was a mistake but I could not say so now.

'I like the look of those buckets,' said Schönbach, 'but if you fill them up the food won't go round us all with so few of them, wherever it is we fill them from.'

Meyer chuckled. 'Don't get so excited. The buckets are not for food, Schönbach. I don't think there's going to be any food tonight, and they're not going to be opening the door again either. Get one of them over here all the same, if you can. I'll have to aim as best I can.'

Aim? It wasn't a question of aim. As *Dunera* shifted her weight the bucket skittered away from Meyer's table and back again. All over our deck knots of men were disputing the merits of possible stances, jostling to demonstrate foolproof techniques, each of which resulted in splashed toe-caps; derision for the urinator when the moistened shoes were his own, aggrieved accusations otherwise.

Meyer lay on his side on his table, narrowed his eyes and watched our bucket square-dancing on the boards as if he were planning to net it. The sea was not yet ferocious but it was gusty. The bucket hopped, and slopped, between Schönbach's planted feet, dodging Finkl's thoughtful stream.

'Pfui!' said Meyer as the glistening rivulet scurried about the deck. 'The thing is to catch it when it's not looking. Excuse me, gentlemen, I'll have to be ready for it.' He unbuttoned, took himself in his hand and settled on his other elbow to wait.

I was hungry but I slept, swinging slowly in my hammock, wondering without conviction whether I should cede it to Rosenthal or Engel. One night. It could not take much more to reach the Isle of Man.

By morning, the deck was sodden. Schönbach's eyes were streaming. Meyer had stiffened on his table-top and we had to prise his limbs away from his body to get him upright. He swore and sobbed but Schönbach said to take no notice.

Someone shouted, 'Food!' They were lugging two-handed metal vats, dumping them on to the tables, dealing out metal plates and cutlery. It was food, good food. An Englishman's breakfast.

The soldiers came clattering down again with brooms, more buckets, shouting orders.

Schönbach was in charge of us, unelected, unopposed, grimly buoyant. 'We're going to clean this place up. They're opening the latrines. Washrooms there too, they're saying. I'll be back.' But with a longer face. 'Ten places to shit, and how many are there of us? How many hundreds? You want to wash? You wash there. You want to wash your clothes? Same place. Salt water only. You want to smoke? . . . Get the picture?'

'Take me there,' said Meyer. 'Quickly.'

Schönbach lugged him across the deck, mincing a path between pools of the previous night's excrement. I followed Schönbach's big-footed spoor, the press of other men's bodies growing more dense as we neared the latrines. Schönbach was shouting, 'This one's urgent. Make way for the sick.' Lugging Meyer, stiff as a tailor's dummy under his arm, he lowered his huge head into the crowd and bull-headed a passage into which he and Meyer disappeared as it closed again behind them. Suddenly I thought:

But I can't see him, I can't see Schönbach, I'll never make it.

Elbows in my eyes, in my back, all the bodies were pressing and leaning towards a narrow doorway, dishevelled, sweating men, wild-eyed and fiercely alone as they crowded together. I seemed to be further from that doorway, not nearer, as men who were stronger, more determined, with a greater urgency, pushed past me and ahead. And then, there it was.

Ten lavatories, without doors, each topped with a straining whey-faced internee, his trousers round his ankles, one hand over his eyes to shield himself from acknowledging that absent door. A row of basins but no soap, no towels, and, beyond, another struggle of men. In the way that people do I was drawn to join them, for they couldn't be pressing towards nothing. And they were not. At the head of the rough queue, when eventually I arrived, was a single open porthole.

We sat round our table, the six of us and eighteen others, motionless, silent, chewing our lips, rehearsing what we would say to the relevant authorities, should we ever locate them. The soldiers had been down again, singled out a table and ordered the men to empty their pockets. One of them had pulled at the wedding ring on someone's finger, and when he had struggled his hand back, shouting that the British army was recruiting barbarians, the soldier had jabbed him in the back with his bayonet and then, embarrassed by the blood, carried him off to the ship's hospital.

'Where there's a hospital there has to be a doctor,' said Schönbach, his unshaven face glowering like a gangster's. 'That's the place to start. Doctors have to behave differently.'

'Don't count on it,' said Meyer. 'We're dealing with the British here, fine old Albion with her love of freedom. How has she managed to kid the rest of the world for so long?'

'That's not fair.' For a moment I had been thinking the same until I heard him say it. 'You can't judge the whole country by these people.'

'No? These people are official. Someone decided to put them here with us. With what instructions? You've seen the officers. Don't tell me it's some sort of accident, English Leo from Oxford. What we've got here is the British army representing His Majesty the King to whose welcoming country we all came running for help because we were too stupid to know better.'

I shook my head. 'I know someone in the army. He's not like this lot.' I wanted to see Major Laing with his dog and his binoculars, but all I retrieved was his shotgun pointing at me from the kitchen corner.

Meyer scoffed. 'Good for you. You know someone in the army. Aren't we lucky to know you. Perhaps you should scribble him a friendly note and we'll all be released in a matter of hours. Go on, why don't you?'

'Still going west.' Rosenthal, twirling a tiny compass and looking at his watch, stepped between us with his observation. 'If it was the Isle of Man we should have been there by now.'

'If.' A unison of voices. People had been saying Canada. People had been saying America. Schönbach had met a man called Hoffmann who couldn't stop smiling. The Americans had refused him a visa, and now it looked as though that was where he was going anyway.

'He shouldn't smile so much,' said Schönbach. 'There's more people saying it's the Isle of Man.'

'Excuse me.' From the far end of the table, Manny Finkl. 'Excuse me, but I heard there are some people here who came *from* the Isle of Man.'

'I heard there are Nazis on board.' Fat Engel, green round the mouth, had only opted for the sailing in order not to be left behind with people he didn't know, waiting for German bombs. A pond was enough to make him seasick – even thinking about a pond.

'Where?' Manny Finkl looked round the deck.

'Up there.' Schönbach jabbed a thumb at the ceiling. 'Behind barbed-wire, just like us, but different wire.' Schönbach who always knew. Up there? Giusè Tolini's anguished face. He must be wrong.

'They're not Nazis.'

'You know something we don't?'

'They can't be. I know someone there.'

'He knows someone everywhere. Such a well-connected boy. People on both sides. Perhaps you'd like to write to your friends up there too. Ask them to stop the war, give in, surrender, go back home and milk their cows.'

'Shut up, Meyer, or you take yourself for your next shit by yourself. Who is it you know?'

'An Italian, a chef at a restaurant I used to go to. He's my age practically, a Londoner, been here . . . there . . . all his life. But he had a granny in Tuscany. I thought he'd gone to visit her with his dad. But now they're here with us. They're not Nazis.'

'They wouldn't be. They'd be Fascists.'

'They're not that either. You should have seen his face. I didn't see his dad upstairs.'

'Maybe he's not here.' Schönbach was very quiet.

I wasn't with my father either, it was true, but there was something about Schönbach's expression that made me think he had more to say. 'What do you mean?'

'Those people, the ones up there, they came from the *Arandora Star*.'

Rosenthal covered his mouth. '*Ach*, poor things.'

'What's the *Arandora Star*?'

'It was a ship, Leo, like this one. They said with prisoners of war. Going to Canada, a week ago. It got hit by a torpedo and went down. So they put the survivors on here.'

'You mean to say', said Meyer, forgetting Nazis, 'that they put people on one boat, and when it sinks they immediately put them on another?' He turned to me and laid his gnarled claws palm up on the table. 'I rest my case.'

I thought of Mr Tolini, soft and portly, flailing among the splintered boards and floating oil of a shattered ship in deep water, and remembered the scrabbling toes of the man the two soldiers had dragged across the deck.

There was a silence. Out there, in the swell, in the depths, there were U-boats. Having other things on our minds, we had forgotten about that.

'North,' said Rosenthal in tones of surprise. Then drowsily, hours later, 'South-west. What's going on?'

Twenty-four plates, twenty-four knives and forks exactly, dealt across the table by the two Schönbach had said could be on kitchen duty for the day. Other tables had elected their leaders. Schönbach had arisen, unchallenged, for no one could imagine organising us better than he could. No one could imagine wishing to. The bucket had some meat in it, potatoes and cabbage.

Engel poked his diminishing jowls over the edge of the bucket. 'Not much meat,' he said gloomily.

'Not a problem,' said Schönbach. 'Give us the bucket.' And he swung away with it, off between the tables to the corner of the deck.

'What's he up to?' Engel, fearful that Schönbach might dip a paw into our lunch under cover of the crowd, stood on the bench and craned after the butcher. 'I can't see him.' He sounded plaintive now. 'Why doesn't he come back?'

He came back, exaggerating the weight of the bucket with a lop-sided shoulder. He heaved it on to the table. 'Meat,' he said, and pointed. 'But not so many vegetables. You win some, you lose some.'

Engel was a carnivore. 'You're a marvel. However did you manage that?'

Schönbach nodded towards the corner of the deck. 'Them over there, the koshers, the Hasids. They won't touch the meat, so we did a little trade.'

Engel raised his fork, pronged through a lump of meat, in comradely greeting to the orthodox corner who couldn't see him.

Engel was the only one to get a taste of that meal. *Dunera* lurched, seemed to slide backwards, hesitated and plunged downhill. Three hundred and eighty-four lunches slid off the tables in synchrony, as if they had been laid on an invisible tablecloth pulled by an invisible hand. On one side of our table, men with lunches in their laps grabbed at the table as *Dunera* tipped them back. On the other side, we were thrown on our faces where our plates should have been. Then we were lunging for the table as they were tumbled on to it. Up and down she went, on and on and on.

There was no one on that deck who wasn't sick, where he was, on himself, on his neighbours, the orthodox into their beards, Schönbach into the food bucket. The vomit flowed as *Dunera* ploughed on, each man producing more than he could have had in him. It mixed with the spilt food and the sight of it made us throw up more.

168

I want to die, I thought, we all thought, and we very nearly did, for just beneath us there was a booming and a wrenching, and *Dunera* flinched throughout her bulk.

'We've been hit!' someone's voice spluttered. We began screaming, all of us, although perhaps not out loud, crawling towards the hatch steps even as the pitch of the sea bundled us together in a heap. I looked up and saw Meyer, unmoving, with his arms round a pillar to keep his balance. He shook his head at me and shrugged. He wouldn't make it, he seemed to be saying, so he wasn't going to get excited either.

Beyond the barbed-wire of the hatch door the soldier on guard, his face pea-green, his knees blustering in the wind, raised his gun to his shoulder and pointed it down at us. 'Stay down there, Nazis,' he hissed between his teeth, 'and drown like rats.' But *Dunera* swivelled on the summit of another great wave and the soldier doubled over with retching.

We did not sink. We did not drown. We had not been hit. We had been missed – just, or so we later came to believe. For a moment we were frozen in a tableau of panic, hands stretching out for the barbed-wire door, men standing on one another on the hatch stairway, more pushing forwards to reach the lowest step, the deck emptier behind them. But alone in the centre stood Meyer, embracing his pillar, and from the further corner the dark, rocking coats of the orthodox, praying through their noses and trusting to God.

Next morning *Dunera* calmed herself and waded disingenuously through the water as if she had quite forgotten the scene she had made a few hours earlier. Schönbach returned from a table-leaders' meeting. 'It's not the Isle of Man,' he announced. 'It can't be. We should have arrived there yesterday if we were going to arrive at all.'

Rosenthal pulled out his pocket compass. 'Going west again,' he said.

'So then it's Canada or America, like they've been saying. We're not getting off tomorrow, so we're going to have to get ourselves sorted out. I looked out of the latrine porthole. The sea is flat. There's sunshine out there still. And fresh air. But there's shit all over the floor, sea-water and God knows what else. And there's this.' He squelched a foot in our collective vomit. 'We can't sleep in this stink. So we've decided on a clean-up team. Who can face it gets something to cover his nose and maybe extra rations tonight, 'cos, looking at what's on the floor, nobody's eaten since yesterday breakfast. We thought one from each table. Who wants?'

We all looked at Engel, who looked at the floor, shuddered and weighed his priorities.

Finkl put a stringy arm on his shoulder, encouraging. 'Think. Roast beef, maybe. Irish stew, because Rosenthal says the bad weather was the Irish Sea. It has meat in it, the way my landlady Mrs Mitchell used to make it. Come on, Engel, where's your determination, your ambition? You're wasting away.'

Engel gazed at us unhappily, and hungrily.

'I'll do it,' I said inadvertently.

'You?' said Schönbach, amazed. 'You don't eat enough for one, never mind extra. D'you know what you're letting yourself in for, shovelling this gunk? You think it smells now, but when you're in it up to the ankles, moving it about' – Engel's face paled – 'it'll be so bad you won't want to eat at all.'

'I don't mind,' I said, gallantly. 'I can take it.'

'Good on you.' Schönbach handed me a bucket and a shovel.

As I marched off, head held a little too high perhaps, towards the latrines, with their porthole, I felt Meyer's pupils pricking my spine. The arch of his eyebrows lodged between my shoulder-blades.

We ate well that evening. Having earned my extra rations it was understood that their allocation was also in my gift, so I divided them between Engel, whose bulk we all, for some reason, felt an urge to maintain, and Manny Finkl, because his ferret's face suggested malnutrition. This was misleading. Finkl just looked like that. No one complained since food was not, yet, that scarce.

Later, lying on the table and feeling *Dunera* swaying rhythmically beneath me, I watched the rows of hammocks swing and pause, swing and pause, their motion lagging fractionally behind the ship's, but in unison. In the strange semi-darkness of the blue lights that burned day and night there was something beautiful about those hammocks and their silent, sated burdens.

Next to me Meyer's stiff skeleton stirred. 'So you're a friend of the noble gesture?' he whispered.

'I have always aspired to heroism,' I fibbed, and laughed, pre-empting an acerbic riposte.

But Meyer was taking me seriously. 'Don't do that. You only get the applause when it's too late, and it's no fun at the time, believe you me. And look where it lands people.' I had not thought we were on board ship bound for Canada in recompense for under-rated heroism. Meyer, however, hadn't finished. 'The worst thing is when your friends and your enemies become confused. In a German prison one knew where one was. But this . . .'

'Give over,' Schönbach growled from his berth under the table. 'We need to get some sleep while the damned ship lets us.'

'Don't blame the ship,' said Rosenthal. 'She only goes up and down with the sea. Incidentally, we're not going west any more. We're heading south.'

'South?' In a chorus.

'I don't know. Dodging torpedoes, maybe. What they call taking evasive action. Good night.' And, having reminded us of our earlier terror, Rosenthal went to sleep.

In the morning it was still south. South in the evening.

'Show me that.' Schönbach grabbed Rosenthal's pocket compass, twisted it about, tapping it viciously as if the little needle were responsible for the ship's perplexing course. 'Maybe there's something wrong with it?'

'No. It's fine.'

'How do you know? Things go wrong all the time.'

'I can prove it to you, but we'll have to wait for dark.'

'Why dark?' Out of his depth Schönbach was uneasy.

'Because I can show you the stars.'

'I don't know a damn thing about stars. I keep my feet on the ground and my eyes in front of me. I haven't the time to be staring at the sky.'

'Well, let's say,' said Rosenthal, placating, because Schönbach was a restless bunching of irritable muscle, 'let's say that staring at the sky is part of my job. It's what some geographers do. Sailors too, you know. And birds.'

'Birds, for Chrissake?'

'Migratory birds. They navigate by the stars, we think.'

'Well, butchers don't.'

'No,' said Rosenthal and turned away with his hand over his mouth. 'Butchers don't.'

'I need some exercise. We all need some exercise. We'll go crazy cooped up like this.' Schönbach stamped his feet and swung his arms. I looked at our unchallenged leader and wondered if we'd made a mistake.

Meyer caught my eye. 'You know, if Rosenthal is right, if we are going south, that means forget Canada, forget America. I think you should tell people. I think you should call a deck meeting.'

'Yeah, yeah, maybe. Is it dark enough yet, for your stars?'

Rosenthal held up a finger that said, wait, I'll have to go and check, and he walked weightily towards the latrines, gratified as a man whose true value has finally been recognised. We lined up to follow him, Schönbach pressed up behind the geographer, tapping him on the shoulder, asking questions. The door to the latrines was, as ever, jammed with waiting men. Rosenthal faltered politely and, delighted, Schönbach elbowed him aside. 'Let us by. We have urgent business.'

'Believe me,' said the queue, holding its trousers bunched in its hand, 'we all have urgent business.' But Schönbach barged past, drawing us in his wake.

Rosenthal manoeuvred his narrow head out of the precious port-hole, twisted his neck and looked skywards. His arms flapped like fins, then reclaimed his head. 'No question. We're going south.'

Thirteen

Someone had miscounted. Twenty-four men to a table but when the people on kitchen duty brought in our dinner and we opened the pot there were only twenty-three tinned plums. There was a second of complete silence, then the shouting began, my voice wailing with the rest, Schönbach bellowing, forgetful of his role. 'Our table' splintered.

'Please! Please!' Like the tenor who outsoars the chorus, Lieutenant Andrew Mayhew's naval larynx gathered up our babbling and stilled it. We stared at him, towering because he stood and we sat, because he was pristine and clean-shaven in his uniform and buttons, because, below apologetic but streaming eyes, he held a handkerchief to his nose. We touched our faces, held our grimy fingers up to our eyes.

Lieutenant Mayhew stepped back, picked a path between the benches to the side and edged round the deck to the latrines where he disappeared for a full minute. Then he was in the doorway, his shoulders filling its space, looking out at us, our eyes, all of them, fixed on his. His lips were thin, twisting with anger, and he raised his arms once and let them fall.

Then he was back at our table, bending over Meyer. 'I'm the medical officer. Do you speak English?' Meyer held up a crippled hand, finger and thumb almost touching. 'But you understand?' Meyer rotated the hand, wincing. 'I think you'd better come with me. Who speaks for you?'

His mouth distorted by the plum he had hurriedly placed in it, Schönbach got to his feet. Lieutenant Mayhew nodded appreciatively at the butcher's square build. 'Would you please give me a hand with him?'

Schönbach grinned his willingness, plum juice glistening on his beard, his tongue working away at the plum, teeth scraping at the stone, which he kept in his mouth like a sweet. 'My pardons,' he said finally, wiping his chin on his sleeve. Together they levered Meyer, clenching his teeth, from his place and carried him to the hatch stairway, crabwise up the narrow opening and away into another world.

When Schönbach came back he had an orange which he peeled and divided. We had half a segment each.

That night they unbattened the hatch and we took turns to stand underneath and look up at the handkerchief of sky, breathing in the stars.

In the morning they brought us a cake of soap for each table and tiny ripped squares of towelling. My piece was white. In the corner were the letters B.M. 'Look.' I held it up.

Professor Mandelbaum reached over and stroked it with his fingertips. 'This is mine. But when I packed it it had the rest of the towel attached.'

'*Ach*, who's counting?' said Schönbach. 'At least we know they didn't leave our cases in Liverpool. Go easy on the soap. You wash yourself or your clothes.' In salt water.

'I owe you an apology.' Meyer, enthroned on the table-top, had walked uncertainly down the hatch stairs. We sat at his feet, the man who had spent three nights 'up there'. 'Medical Officer Lieutenant Mayhew. It has a ring to it, wouldn't you say, Leo? An excellent man. An excellent Englishman. Let's assume those others are aberrations. An excellent doctor,' he repeated. 'Admirable.'

'What did he do? What did he give you?'

'Two aspirins a day, a bed, an apple and a bath.' Meyer had shaved and his nails were clean. 'And I lay for a few minutes in the sun. There's a lot of sun out there, and there's going to be more.' So he knew something.

'Did Lieutenant Mayhew say where we're going?'

Meyer wrapped his arms together, savouring the moment. 'Mmm,' he said, breathed in, then out. 'As a matter of fact. Australia.'

*　　*　　*

174

Without doubt an excellent doctor but Lieutenant Mayhew could do only so much. The hatch was opened and remained so, though not the portholes through which we might be tempted to throw ourselves into the boiling sea. 'Who would want to do a thing like that?' asked Finkl, apparently minutes before someone on another deck propelled himself over the side. They said it was the day his visa to America expired, leaving him no choice but to expire with it. We were able to dab at ourselves with flakes of soap scraped off with the fingernails, retrieved from under the fingernails; some of us washed our clothes but the salt water which dried on the skin, leaving crusts of crystals and matting our beards, rusted the fabric of our suits in the armpits and on the knees so that our joints poked out of the shredded material and the lining hung free, streaked sticky with salt.

Lieutenant Mayhew ordered a daily ration of fresh air up on the top deck, recommending the exercise that Schönbach had been itching for, but the ship's medical officer could not supervise the activity. I dare say we must have looked as entertaining as the soldiers found us, scampering about the deck while they bounded after us, prodding our buttocks, drawing blood with their bayonets. 'Gooworn!' they bawled, as one does to recalcitrant cattle; they took away our shoes and we ran, the portly and flat-footed, the dark-hatted Hasidim, Schönbach foul-mouthed but helpless, hobbling Meyer. And what fun too for the little lascars, finally, to watch one group of white men humiliate another.

For ten minutes every day in the sunshine I learned that to have power is to hold someone else's dignity at the point of a whim, and that properly armed anyone can do that; and I learned too that the humiliated come to believe that they must, in some measure, deserve their humiliation because they have been chosen for it, because they have not prevented it. They were young, those soldiers, some of them as young as me, but mildly mutilated. Pitted skins, an eye-tugging scar, a twisted shoulder, a limp. It seems now that every one of them was flawed, which cannot be true, so that I look askance at my memory and accuse it of superimposing blemishes to add colour to the villainy.

In a corner we could not reach, behind a railing, we would pass our suitcases piled haphazardly, bayoneted open. Somebody's dressing-gown had been tied on to a wire where it swung jauntily in the wind. Somebody's novel, work in progress, still only a manuscript, had been tossed overboard. They said that the floating papers had been gathered by a passing U-boat whose captain, seeing the German script, concluded that *Dunera* was carrying German prisoners of war, and thereafter escorted her at a distance to keep her cargo from harm. Who knows? We needed a little irony and it would have served nobody's interest to discover that a story like that was not true. It was Meyer who told us and Lieutenant Mayhew who had told him.

'I'm grateful to you,' Meyer had said, sucking an aspirin. 'Why only you do this thing for us?'

Lieutenant Mayhew had handed him a glass of water. 'There are regulations governing the treatment of prisoners of war, and it's not the British way to flout those, no matter who the prisoners are.'

'But we're not prisoners of war.'

'You are Germans.'

'But not prisoners of war. We fight for Britain. We want.'

'And where do you come from?'

'I? From Berlin.'

'And you would fight against Berlin?'

'Natural.'

Lieutenant Mayhew had eyed Meyer for a moment without expression. 'That', he observed, 'is treachery. When it comes to war every man should fight for his country. But perhaps that's a concept you people don't understand. I will do what I can, because it goes against everything I stand for not to. Those young troops have had a hard time. They shouldn't be doing what they are but I'm not surprised they despise you. Be grateful. You're being shipped, at our expense, far from the dangers of battle.'

'How far?'

'As far as it's possible to be. To the other side of the world.'

That knowledge had turned *Dunera* from a ferry into a prison ship. 'Australia?' we had chorused, wondering, tasting the word which for a moment was no more than a sound, faintly ridiculous, connoting nothing. But then, after tears of impotence, there was a sense of relief. To know, for the first time to have information, meant that we could, together, decide how we should try to live out what would be, said Rosenthal, another six weeks.

We weighed our slivers of soap in our hands and knew when there would again be none left; we took pieces of lavatory paper and wrote on them in minute writing, diaries, polemics of complaint, poems. Some people drew. Finkl taught me how to make paper boats, paper hats, paper aeroplanes, his small fingers flicking the paper into shape like a magician. His artefacts were somewhat limp and destined to be unfolded again immediately. Professor Mandelbaum gathered a class of would-be physicists about him; a renowned mathematician of whom I had never heard patiently explained theorems to those who could understand, and to those who could not but were improved by the trying. A choir rehearsed in four-part harmony, at half voice, Walter Michel the conductor cupping his ear and waving the other hand frantically. 'No, no, no. What's the matter with you all? Listen!' He sang, then whistled each of the interweaving melodies, and kept his singers at it, relentlessly, as if they were preparing for a concert at some international venue. When finally they performed, some of the ship's crew crouched over the hatch to listen, and to applaud.

It grew hotter and the air round the unwashed bodies of men who had not changed their clothing in a month muffled our breathing. Among us Meyer was the most distressed. 'I never thought it was possible to be revolted by one's own smell. My only comfort is that everyone else is as disgusting. But you wouldn't know that, would you?'

'How d'you mean?'

'You can't smell a thing, can you? Well, can you? . . . How do I know? Simple. You've been on latrine duty every night long after there were extra rations, and for what? Just to be thanked? I don't think so. Some of us here wouldn't be able to bear it, so I asked myself first, why is the boy putting himself through this? Then I thought, he doesn't look happy but he doesn't look the way I would feel. Why not? So I started watching you. The rest of us inhale our bits of soap sometimes when it gets too bad down here. The rest of us gag when we have to come back down from the top deck. The rest of us drag out our meals by smelling the food slowly before we eat because that way it seems to last a little longer. But not you. And there was only one reason I could think of why that might be.'

Dunera docked at Freetown to take on supplies and all the time she was in port they kept us locked below decks. Finkl perched under the hatch door and slid a hand through the meshed barbed-wire. Between his fingers was a cigarette. Within minutes a young lascar was on hands and knees. 'Where?' whispered Finkl. 'Freetown.' The cigarette disappeared. The ship stopped again at Cape Town; in harbour the portholes were unshuttered and we saw the lights of a great city. At Fremantle we thought, this is Australia, surely they'll let us leave, but the ship set off again. Then they sent down razors and instructions to shave.

Although Schönbach barbered Meyer, who shook with eagerness but whose hands were unreliable, he tugged his own beard belliger-ently. 'So they want us to look better all of a sudden. No thank you. This was a present from Britain and I'm keeping it.' I looked from him to Meyer and reached for a razor. Schönbach's suit hung tattered from his gaunt shoulders, his face was greasy and his hair, darkened by dirt, was of no known colour. Any country harbouring a man who looked like Schönbach could be forgiven for transport-ing him to oblivion.

At Melbourne we heard shouting, running feet, orders bounced along a line. People were leaving. Finkl had grown so small he was almost invisible. He sidled up the stairway, peered through the barbed-wire of the hatch door and scuttled back. 'They're off-loading.'

'Who?'

'The ones from up there. The prisoners from the boat that went down. The Nazis.'

'They're not all prisoners and they're not all Nazis,' I protested. Lieutenant Mayhew thought we were Nazis; Finkl, Engel, Schönbach, even maybe Meyer thought Giuseppe Tolini was a Fascist.

'Yes, yes.' Who was a prisoner and who was not had become a matter of suspended interest.

On 6 September, fifty-eight days out of Liverpool, we slipped into Sydney harbour. It was early morning and we stood, as many as could fit, out on deck in a tangible mist. Police boats puttered alongside nosing *Dunera*, like seals fussing at a beached whale, towards her dock. On the shoreline a bank of trees shook off the overnight dew and watched us pass. Overhead, the droning of the traffic on the Harbour Bridge brought our hands to our unaccustomed ears. The people of Sydney had assembled on the quay behind a line of soldiers.

I think, unless I forget, that most of the citizens simply stood in silence; a few offered restrained hisses, and somebody threw something glutinous.

Our guards behind us, we disembarked at the trot, the only pace we knew. 'Hey, steady there. No hurry.' A voice as warm as the brown of his boots. All along the quay the Australian troops standing in position were smiling, trying to hide their smiles. We were not what they had been led to expect.

A train had brought us to the quayside at Liverpool. Another was waiting to remove us from Sydney. There was a seat on it for every man, for every man a paper bag. Inside the bags were ham sandwiches and a banana sweet as candy floss.

Meyer sank back in his seat and pressed his bones into the upholstery. He bit alternately into a sandwich and the banana, his cheeks filled like a hamster's. The train pulled slowly away from the berthed ship, passing the letters of *Dunera*'s name in reverse order. In the portholes and over the railings the faces of the British troops looked down on us. Schönbach, looking back up, jerked up a half-eaten banana in the crudest gesture he knew.

'*Bon giorno*.' Under his slouch hat, in his green uniform, the Australian soldier's face contorted round the words. We gaped at him and he tried again. 'I said *bon giorno*.' Silence. His face fell. 'I was trying to be friendly, dammit,' he said grumpily.

Schönbach nudged me. 'Say something.'

'Good morning to you too.'

'Hey!' The soldier rubbed his face. 'You a Pom?'

'In a manner of speaking,' I said, my voice plummy with sandwich and education.

'You're not Italians?'

'Not one.'

'But they said . . . Oh, Jesus! So who the hell are you all?'

'Internees. We're Jews from Germany, from Austria . . .'

'Refugees from Hitler,' said Meyer, blowing the crumbs from his knuckles and sucking his teeth where a shred of ham had lodged. Then his eyes widened. 'Thank you for the food, but we are not all eating.'

'Why not? What's wrong with it?'

'Nothing is wrong. Excellent but for some not good.' He pointed to the far end of the carriage where a small group of orthodox sat disconsolately holding their untouched paper bags. 'For some is . . .' Running out of English he wagged a forbidding finger. The soldier rubbed his face again. Meyer shook his head. 'The ham. For them – not good.'

'You don't say.' The soldier whistled at the ineffable ways of the world and edged warily towards the silent group in their salt-stained coats and high hats. They had combed out their beards with their fingers. 'Excuse me.' He took the bags from them, filling his arms like a visitor to a children's hospital, turned to leave and turned back. 'You lot want seconds?' We held out our hands. He addressed the koshers again. 'I'll see what else I can get, but you might have to wait.'

'We have waited a long time already. We can wait longer. We are grateful. Please, no meat. No meat at all. Thank you for your trouble.'

'No trouble, mate. No trouble.' Pausing in the doorway to the next carriage he surveyed us briefly. 'Jesus wept,' he muttered, and was gone.

They fed the rabbi's people on plain bread, fruit and lettuce. They gave us all cigarettes. When the train stopped for water they would not let us get out, apologising, sorry, orders.

We had left the cities and towns behind, the light wooden houses bordering wide streets. We passed through grey-green forests of eucalyptus and out into a pastureland waiting for colour, so flat that as the train curved through it we could see the great engine labouring ahead of us.

Meyer tapped my arm. 'Look.' A pair of kangaroos dangling effete arms bounded by the track, racing the train, then slackened their pace and veered off into a desiccated grassland.

Later, when outside the night was total, the soldier came

again and crouched down between the seats. 'Getta hold of this a minute.' He held out his rifle. 'Don't drop it or I'm in shit.' I held the thing upright, gingerly between my knees. He took a bottle out of his jacket and pulled the cap off with his teeth. 'Just the one. Pass it round.' A single brief swig of his beer and our heads were swimming. He took the bottle back, rubbed a hand over the top and shook the remaining drops into his own gullet. 'Yeah.'

'Where are we going?'

'Hay.'

'What's Hay?'

'Don't ask me, mate. Hay is Hell.'

Hell is red. On all sides the desert had been thrown like a bolt of terracotta corduroy, rucked and wrinkled over the horizon. But there was a petrol station and small airy houses, low-built, along the railway. Some people, only a few, had come to watch us, curious but silent. The platform was too short to accommodate the train and they shunted us off in shifts to walk us out over the desert along ridges of churned sand to an encampment of barrack huts with speckled asbestos roofs behind double barbed-wire fences measured by watchtowers.

Meyer squinted up. Machine-guns nosed from the watchtowers. 'Generally speaking, the arrangements are pretty much the same wherever you go,' he said, sounding less chirpy than he intended. 'No doubt in their place we would do the same.'

Beyond the barbed-wire the reach of the desert mocked the fencing. On a distant rise grew a single stunted tree. The opposite horizon shimmered with the trees fringing the Murrumbidgee river. Grey and red parrots flocked in daily forays from somewhere to somewhere else. Beneath them our huts stood shoulder to shoulder raised from the dust, erected in haste to enclose the prisoners the British authorities had sent. The troops on *Dunera* had overstepped their duties, there was no denying that. But people are not shipped across the globe for no reason. We must have done something, we must have had the intention of doing something or we should not have been earmarked for Hay. But you could take a cold shower in the sun. You could walk, or sit. Food was provided, and our cooks, every one of them Viennese, were going courteously to take over the kitchens from the Australians.

In the unfamiliar you cling to what you know, so we clung to each other: the koshers congregated in one hut around which they threw an invisible cordon; the few non-Jews, whom we dubbed 'the Vons' or 'the Barons', shared another; the people who had huddled round a mess table on *Dunera* kept together and Schönbach was redesignated hut captain, doing press-ups at dawn to reconstruct his shoulders. Meyer and I stood outside each morning, the sleep dry as sand still in our eyes, and marvelled that the drama of a desert sunrise should lose nothing in repetition.

Someone brought a newspaper. The very day we had arrived in Hay the Blitz on London had begun. Lieutenant Mayhew had been right. We were as far from the centre of battle as it was possible to be, saved, privileged, plucked from danger. Schönbach roared over a photograph of a London street whose houses had spilt their guts on to the tarmac. 'My wife is under that. Without me my wife is under that.' So that I saw him demeaned, stripped, by his unbidden safety, of his masculine duty to look after her.

We were issued, each of us, with a single beige POW's postcard, instructed to fill in only the name and address. Our address was printed. So was the message. 'I am quite well. Letter follows at first opportunity.'

A delegation of hut captains went, ritually, to make representations: we are not POWs, we wish our status to be recognised, how is it that we, anti-Nazis to a man, can still be considered the enemies of Britain when we want only her success in this war? And were answered: these are the only cards that have been provided, kindly make use of them if you intend to communicate with your families, there will be no others, consider yourselves fortunate that there are regulations governing the treatment of POWs, no such regulations exist for internees, and true POWs, some of them admirable men in their way, could, not unjustly, question the privileges accorded to you even though you have never seen battle. Cease complaining.

It is not in anyone's power to make another cease complaining altogether, but it is possible to ensure that the grumbling is kept under the breath. We sat down to write our postcards, in rotation, with the pencil provided. On completion the pencil was to be returned. Schönbach was first and wrote to his wife. Meyer, next, insisted that, however laboriously, he would do his own filling-in, the pencil bolt upright in his inflexible fist. His sister, he said, would only be convinced by the misshapen letters that illness had made of his handwriting. The rest of us left the hut to make a couple of rounds of the perimeter fencing to give Meyer time to finish.

Walking slowly, it took ten minutes to circuit the fence and I made the journey twice, then called, 'I'll be last', the hut's youngest politely ceding to seniority. 'I'll stay out here a little longer.' Such a small beige card to turn over in the hands. I am quite well. I am *quite* well. Someone had composed a message adequate for all prisoners, whoever they might turn out to be, printed in advance of their arrival, maybe even before their arrest. Boxes of cards had been waiting for us in the Commandant's office. More than the fence, more than the huts and watchtowers, those cards suggested permanence. For the first time since the constable had accompanied me to Willesden Green police station I entertained the past. I had one card. Now I must decide to whom to send it.

My mother. But, if my mother, then only she – and my father, if she had located him – would know where I was. In England the mornings would be misted with autumn, the evenings more leisurely than the abrupt nightfall of the desert. EL's boots would glisten in the damp grass as she called out to the growing foals, dodging Mirabelle's malevolent teeth. Mrs Laing would be struggling with her book-keeping, the major limping over the fields with his old Bounder, heavy-hearted with apprehension because his daughter must soon return to the university. Where she would be reunited with Jeremy, uniformed and on leave, a man who gave orders with the expectation that they would be obeyed, a man with his dignity intact and his hands on the tender places of my girl, in her maroon hair. My mother knew nothing of EL. EL could not know, if she received my card, that I had had no others to send, even if, sharing her narrow college bed with visiting Jeremy, she were to care. There was only one person who would understand the import of the small beige oblong, who might remark on it so that my message might be passed on.

They had waited for me in our hut, their completed cards stacked in front of Schönbach, the pencil beside it, and stalled the guard who had come to collect. 'What's with you?' growled Schönbach. I sat down and addressed my card to Mr McKechnie.

'Meanwhile,' said Meyer, the man with experience, 'we have to live.' Light-fingered Finkl had filled his pockets with nails from the huts still under construction and we hammered them into the edges of our bunks with our shoes to make clothes hooks. We made shelves from the planks Finkl transferred from the other side of the camp. The hut captains met to form a vociferous parliament; we set up a camp school, as I suppose all such camps do, each man teaching what he knew, sometimes even what he didn't. Professors of this and doctors of that drew on the hut walls with pieces of limestone and on the backs of the upturned tables. Their pupils huddled into the blue shade of the huts until the guards came to watch, and waggle their fingers in incomprehension.

Meyer's voice had weakened, but he drew me aside. 'It's a shame about the books.'

'What books?'

'The ones in your case. I had hoped you would read me your poets, your English poets.'

'I can recite them for you, some of them.'

'Then fetch me a chair and we'll find some quiet shade.' Between two huts, where the afternoon sun didn't reach, the sand was black. Meyer sat, stiff as wire, his claws in his lap, his feet planted. 'So?'

'I feel a fool. Like a performing animal.'

'You are a performing animal. That's what we all are, performing animals. Turn your back if you want, then you won't see me. And I'll close my eyes.'

'A cold coming we had of it . . .' A useful memory Mr McKechnie had called it, a memory to suck in other people's words, ingest them, hold them somewhere in readiness.

> 'Just the worst time of year
> For a journey, and such a long journey:
> The ways deep and the weather sharp,
> The very dead of winter.'

We both listened, Meyer and I, but heard differently. Until I began I had forgotten what I remembered now so easily, and was surprised again by those careful words, 'And the camels galled, sore-footed, refractory'. But Meyer's head wagged to the music, the sense escaping him.

> '. . . I had seen birth and death,
> But had thought they were different; this Birth was
> Hard and bitter agony for us, like Death, our death.
> We returned to our places, these Kingdoms,
> But no longer at ease here, in the old dispensation,
> With an alien people clutching their gods.
> I should be glad of another death.'

Meyer opened his eyes. 'You have a voice, did you know that? And what a language, whatever the poem was. No, don't tell me. I don't need to know what it meant.' I sat on the sand, then stretched out at his feet and drew patterns in the grains. 'I may ask you for another concert another day. No objections?'

'Of course not.'

'It's a strange business.'

'What is?'

'Poetry, music, pictures,' Meyer said, waving a hand that implied 'etc.'.

'What's strange about it?'

'All that unnecessary effort.'

'Unnecessary? Poetry doesn't just arrive, one, two, three, you know.'

Meyer laughed at me. 'Look at your face. Of course I know, but that's not what I meant. Perhaps I should have said "wasteful", wasteful of energy. It's not needed. We don't need it.'

'What do you mean, we don't need it? Of course we need it.'

'No, we don't. Not to survive. We can survive without it in the way we can't survive without food or water. That's what I've asked myself. Why does a group of creatures engage in an activity that has nothing to do with survival when it takes so much effort? It's uneconomical.'

'And what did you answer?'

Meyer leaned forward to get to his feet. 'Well, it's a problem as yet unresolved. But for the moment I'm saying to myself, there's only one answer. They're freaks. All of them, freaks of nature. Good to have around but life goes on without them – which is true for most of us anyway – and they help to pass the time.'

'And that's all?'

'I think so.'

'That's too bleak.'

'Why bleak? What else do you expect? Purpose? There isn't any. There doesn't have to be any. Look, you listen to a piece of music that you like, and you enjoy it. You recite a poem that you like, and *I* enjoy it – even though I can't follow a word of what you've said. You're thirsty and someone gives you some . . . whatever it is that you like . . . and while you're drinking it the combination of your thirst and the taste of the drink gives you pleasure. Let's say you're in love – and with your girl . . . Do you see what I mean? That's what the point is, and it doesn't have to be more. And meanwhile, all around you, there's life. All of it interesting, so much of it, so many different forms of it, so many different ways that things live. All as good as one another, all striving to be better, to be stronger, to leave their mark – even if they don't know that's what they're doing.'

'Writing poetry is leaving a mark.'

'Yes, but not one that nature recognises.'

'You don't know that.'

Meyer, standing, knocked the top of my head with a crooked knuckle. 'No. I only believe it. Don't ask too much of it.'

At midday, the summer raging, the Murrumbidgee ambled over its banks in a mirage that ebbed and flowed, the promised water receding only when the temperature dropped. Nightfall crashed and those who could stand the cold gazed, puzzled as children, at the unfamiliar stars, the phases of the moon back to front in a wild wide sky. Some of us thought about God and eternity. Some thought only of eternity. I knew better and saw EL and Jeremy, arm in arm.

Months had passed and not one of us had had a reply to our cards. The newspapers they let us have, three days old from Sydney, told us about the night bombing of London, so that sleep

186

was forbidden to its citizens. But when the horizon got to its feet and hurtled over us, whipping up the red dust and stones in the sandstorms they called 'the bricklayer', we lay face down on the boards of our hut, clutching our heads and choking. Only when the wind had veered away, overnight rain had settled the swirling ground and the sky reappeared, vaulted and cloudless, did we remember the bombers, and vowed never again to forget, did not forget – until next time. Who can think of others when he is in pain himself? 'Only the koshers,' said little Finkl, pulling the sand from his eyelashes, scraping it from his anus, admiring the closed and uncommunicative orthodox hut, but also uneasy.

Meyer wept because he could not sleep, so that we feared for him. His eyes were crusted and rheumy from lack of rest and the ever-moving dust.

Schönbach assembled us in a hut meeting. 'We're responsible for him. We've got to get the man to sleep or we'll lose him. You, young Leo with your head in the clouds, think of something. The old fellow's been good to you.'

My head in the clouds? 'How does one get people to sleep?'

'I dunno. How did your mother get you to sleep?'

'But I was a child.' She had sung. She had told me often enough how she had sung, she had a fine high voice, liked to say so, liked to sing. I remembered none of it. 'Can you sing?'

'At the right time,' said Schönbach, 'when I'm in the right mood, with a bit inside me. Not in front of you lot to a sick man.'

Maybe a sick man was like a child at night, afraid to leave wakefulness, longing for sleep but needing to be lulled, unawares, into it. Meyer lay twisted in his bunk, no position comfortable. 'Meyer,' I began hesitantly and crouched on the floor beside him. 'Meyer, once upon a time . . .'

Squatting on the boards of our hut I retold the fairy tales of my childhood reading, for those too had waited in my memory. As I was talking I sensed Schönbach, Rosenthal, Finkl and the others grouped in silence around the table, and I heard the fishermen, the giants, the canny peasants clamber out of the confines of their roles. I saw the lines on their faces, heard their bickering and wondered what they would do next, so that it seemed I was also sitting at the table listening to this bedtime story.

187

When I finished I heard myself say, 'And that's all for to-night.'

In the dark Meyer hissed with laughter. 'Thank you,' he said. 'Now I think I will go to sleep. Will you tell me another one tomorrow night?'

I went every afternoon to the camp mail distribution, for weeks without reward. Then on a single day there were three letters for me. My mother had located my father, on the Isle of Man, where apparently it rained without cease. She said nothing about the Blitz and I recalled that there was no cellar in Melrose Avenue. A tall young English girl had come to the house and given her the address. She didn't know I knew girls like that but did not say what sort of girl that was. She asked me to write everything I could think of to her and promised to send only the most cheerful episodes to my father.

The other two letters, disconcertingly similar, were from Jeremy and EL. Oh, how they had been outraged to learn where I was, shocked was not too strong a word, there was a rumpus about the whole business in Parliament. They were stilted with embarrass-ment and EL, making it better I suppose, added that at least I was lucky to have had the chance of such a voyage through the tropics. They were hiding their truth from me, they imagined out of some sort of delicacy.

I folded the letters, each into its envelope with the censor's stamp-mark, the censor's knife-mark. Wasn't this what happened when soldiers went away to war, and others moved into their vacated beds? But then the soldiers returned, bearing wounds and decorations, and there would be tears, recriminations, separations. Usually, I supposed, the soldiers prevailed because they returned changed men, damaged perhaps, but also augmented. I was not a soldier but supplanted by one. I was E 76431, rounded up, in charge of neither my own destiny nor anyone else's, diminished. I wondered whether in EL's cool mind lurked the thought that those who allow themselves to be pushed about deserve it. I wondered whether, conceivably, I thought the same. An internee is no hero; only, if he's lucky, the object of somebody's compassion. I could not in future take EL in my arms because she pitied me. If ever she were to ask me to make love to her again it might be out of charity. There would be no way of knowing.

At the height of summer they would take us to swim in the curve of the Murrumbidgee and the guards leaned their rifles against the trees because we were not the sort of people who make trouble or run off. Nor was there anywhere to run. Meyer stayed behind, discouraged by the walk, but each time asked me to find him some living creature from the water. I would bring back a wriggling thing in a mugful of river, and that afternoon Meyer would propose, staring into the mug, how, over millions of years, spread across as many individuals in each generation, that thing had come to be the way it was. But after nightfall it was my turn and I would weave him a tale about the monstrous ancestor of that wriggling thing, how it had set out into the wilderness seeking a place it could call its own, where it might found a colony. Behind the breathing of the tired men I heard my voice, again not my own, speak without pause, sonorously plucking adventures from a decade of daydreams.

Come the morning and I would set Meyer's chair in the gorge of deep shade between the huts, towels folded as padding, and stretch out at his feet, lying propped on one elbow in the dust.

Beyond the huts they were all at school, learning about photography and travel, simultaneous equations and iambic pentameter, drawing the lines of erosion streaming from the delta of the Nile. The distant Murrumbidgee undulated above the horizon and the guards dozed under the canopies of their watchtowers. Beneath them Uwe Schumacher, square as a filing cabinet, with forearms wide as my thighs, chopped wood for the boilers. Holding a lump of rock-hard redwood in one hand, he wielded a small axe in the other and with the rhythm of a turning wheel sliced identical wedges into a heap at his feet. By dark the wood was stacked to the eaves of the kitchen hut; by the following evening it had been consumed and Uwe Schumacher chopped on . . . thwack, thwack . . .

Meyer wouldn't let me take notes. 'I'm not teaching, only thinking out loud.' He scraped a toe in the sand and a small chestnut beetle scurried out, stopped abruptly, motionless, scurried on and disappeared under the red grains. 'Not bad, is it? What else would manage to make a home here – except a couple of thousand bedraggled foreigners, for whom they have to build houses, dig drains, erect fences, import food . . . ? It knows to stay under the sand in the day, it doesn't need water, it's wellnigh invisible, and best of all it's found a place where there's almost no one to compete with. I wish to God I knew what it eats. So you see, it's almost perfect, only as perfect as it needs to be, and no more, until something comes along to challenge it, and then it will have to become more perfect.' I loved Meyer. 'But the thing is, it doesn't know any of this. That's the beauty of it. It doesn't know what a history it has, and of course it can't imagine what a history it may yet have. And nor can anyone else because no one, no one, Leo, knows. It's like the rest of us, perpetually on the way to becoming something else – maybe, maybe not – and then something else again. We're just part of an unfinished painting which will never be completed and which has no plan and no artist. Everything on the canvas is on the move, and nothing any one thing does is of any significance itself, although we may like to think otherwise. When my bones hurt, I can think only of my hurting bones. When they don't I fret about being here and what I might have been doing, what I should be doing in that struggle out there that we aren't considered fit to join. But then, I say to myself, that evil man and his extraordinary doings, perhaps they're just a manifestation of nature too, a speck in the passage of time. And then I shake my head because, thank God, I'm not yet capable of thinking like that for more than a moment. So we have to set all that aside and concentrate on making sure good wins over evil, even though, who knows, good and evil don't mean a thing. What do you think, hmm?' He prodded me. 'And look at you! You can't look me in the face. Some doctor you'd have made.'

It was true. His eyes were so inflamed and crusted by the frisking sand they made me feel queasy but I imagined laying a hand on them, removing the inflammation, leaving them clear.

'Mind you, I like the bedside manner, you with your fairy tales. I tell you about a membrane accidentally sensitive to light in one individual something-or-other which benefits that something-or-other just enough for its offspring, and then the progeny of that offspring, to hang on to that membrane until bit by bit its sensitivity to light increases and all the something-or-others without the membrane die out because they're out of date. And what do you do? You come up with the tale of a fully fledged eye wandering about looking for a head to inhabit so that the two of them can go out and conquer the world together. So I despair of you, my son who is not my son, because I am trying to work out a truth for you, and you invent sweet nonsense to send me to sleep.'

'So poetry and music are unnecessary, and stories are nonsense too?'

'All right. Not nonsense. But don't confuse them with the truth.'

I wrote to EL. She replied. A letter every two months. I wrote as she wrote. Informing. The Society of Friends – what good, generous people – had come to hear about us, come to visit, and were supplying paper, textbooks, pens; they were arranging for people to sit recognised examinations. They were trying to find a piano. In a hut two down from ours Walter Michel, *Dunera*'s musician, was fretting, his fingers drumming, pining for the keys; he had plans, he had ambitions, and the Quakers were going to help him realise them. We had started a newspaper for which I wrote dry commentaries and the odd piece of ironic doggerel. I said nothing of Schönbach or Meyer, nor of the nights when he slept but I lay awake, heckled by his myriad generations, his never-ending painting which could not be finished – like our imprisonment, because no one had set a date for its completion. On the other side of the wire they were too busy waging war, on our behalf, to remember that they had sent us here lest we hinder them in their efforts.

There were more pregnancies, more births, on the Laings' farm. One insignificant generation out of Meyer's millions but a year of my life. EL was going to visit my mother, befriend her, doing the right thing. My mother, of course, would become excited and misunderstand. Dear EL, do not befriend my mother, she will become excited and misunderstand with cleverly devised biscuits and coffee that she'll make you believe is real. My small waddling mother alone in her house looking up at the tall girl who won't wear a hat, who will smile too brightly, sip the hot liquid, nodding, pretending she understands the garbled language pouring from the short-legged woman on the sofa. My mother sits back in her cushions and her feet dangle. She has grown used to the bay window and the tiled garden path outside. But the tall girl who doesn't wear gloves and holds her hair up with a single pin is unaware that there is any other way to live a city life, doesn't realise that she is my mother's first English visitor: that, crossing the threshold and noticing the foreign furniture arranged in a foreign way, she is reclaiming the house. When she has eaten her biscuit she offers to visit again; and my mother, saying yes, please do, fears she may.

'What people don't want to understand is that the perfection of every living thing is temporary. It's a perfection, while it lasts, because that living thing is alive – its existence testifies to the perfection. If it were not perfect it would have been replaced by something that was. But change the place, or change the climate, above all change the competitors, and that famous perfection is suddenly tenuous. Let newcomers arrive and you have to start struggling all over again. Maybe they've got something you don't have and you go down. Maybe you're the lucky one, and you've got that little extra something, you're better at laying more eggs in clever places, or you've got a bigger tail than that fellow who looks so much like you in every other respect, and the ladies prefer you for your tail, or your fur blends better with the trees where that fellow has been living so long without any worries until you came along, and it's your progeny who will take over from his and wipe out all memory of him. Meanwhile, you don't even know that you're inevitably on the way to becoming extinct, along with all those millions of others that have become extinct before you, more than there are creatures living at any one time, because nothing stays still, nothing stays the same. And I'll tell you something else, Leo. I'm hungry. Go in and struggle for something for me to eat. Get Manny Finkl to filch me something good, something sweet.'

Finkl produced a slice of cake from a box under his bunk. 'You should eat a piece of it yourself, kid,' he advised. 'When we get out of here you'll need to be fatter than you are. You need to live. Nothing's going to keep your teacher going much longer.'

'I'm going to, if it kills me.'

Meyer took the cake and split it in two, holding out half to me.

'I heard that. Very kind. Altruism. Good for the species. Bad for the individual, and this individual' – pointing his cake at me – 'needs to keep his strength up. Finkl's right, the little bastard.'

'It's not altruism. It's –'

'I know. But go on anyway, you like cake, I've seen you.'

The hut leaders had elected a camp spokesman, a man called Boskowitz, distinguished by his extraordinary height and the fortune of a great-grandfather, still his for the having, perhaps, some time in the future, depending on how things went. Boskowitz had been in the diplomatic service which, he said, did not qualify him for the task of being our representative. 'You expect me to put direct questions and get direct answers,' he cavilled, pleased as punch at his electoral success, 'but diplomats are taught to do the opposite. Nevertheless . . .' And he bowed, a burdened but obedient public servant.

One day Boskowitz was asked, most courteously, if he would attend the Commandant in his office. Off he went, and off went half the camp after him, at a closing distance, suspecting the arrival of some information. Within a few minutes he emerged from the Commandant's room with the Commandant behind him. His face was crumpled by tumbling expressions – anger, incredulity, hilarity, jostling over his cheeks. By his side the Commandant was so expressionless it was clear the man was suffering.

Boskowitz stepped forward and held up a hand to still the noise from a crowd that was already silent. 'The Commandant has an announcement he would like to make.'

The Commandant looked at Boskowitz like a man betrayed, but he knew his duty. 'Yes,' he said so quietly that we all swayed a pace forward. He swallowed, prevaricating, thinking of escape. 'I have been asked to inform you that you have been sent here in error. His Majesty's Government regrets the mistake.'

Boskowitz's eyes gleamed with malice. 'And when may we expect our release?'

'Unfortunately', mumbled the Commandant, 'you are the prisoners of the British authorities but the guests of Australia. Now of course you will understand that Australia's original willingness to be your host does not imply her readiness to accept a flood of immigrants, so you can only be released in Britain. But you are here. And in the present, um, situation, the war and so on, it is not possible to envisage a return to Britain. A representative of the Home Office is on his way to meet you. I would be grateful if you could address any comments you may have to him.'

Then the Commandant hurried back to his office and sat heavily on his folding chair which he tried to pull out of sight of the window. As the size of his room was paltry for a man of his responsibilities we were able to make out the jutting tips of his despondent nose and chin.

Fourteen

Seven months had passed and Major Layton from the Home Office had installed himself in the Commandant's office without protest from the Commandant. Layton was benign, utterly correct, hampered by his position. He was not the Australian government, not the British Home Office – only its representative carrying in his briefcase no more than the powers someone more senior had placed there. He repeated the Commandant's apology, confirmed that there could be no automatic release, promised that there would be compensation for stolen articles up to a specified amount, pointed out that we should not in any way expect unusual consideration, others were less fortunate still. Who could disagree? We could not, did not, but were not comforted. He was distressed to see some instances of ill-health but gratified that, in the main, most internees were fit and keeping themselves occupied.

He made one announcement and one offer. Internment Camps 7 and 8 at Hay were unsuitable for Europeans. The climate was too extreme. We should, therefore, expect to be transferred to another, more temperate location which was being prepared according to instructions he had sent by cable. In the meantime release would be considered for those who were prepared to sign up with the Pioneer Corps in units on the Home Front. It would, naturally, not be a question of bearing arms, which was not yet thought advisable, although we could rest assured that our status would in due course revert to that of 'friendly aliens'. Anyone who wished to sign up should notify him within the shortest possible time but must be prepared also to sign a document indicating his willingness to travel on transports as they become available, recognising that these would be unescorted vessels. Safe arrival could not be guaranteed under the circumstances.

'Shit that!' yelled Schönbach, still aggressively bearded despite the heat and looking like one of the rabbi's people. 'Give me a gun, for Chrissake. I don't want to sweep the streets. I want to go out and kill somebody.' Sagely, he kept his yelling for that evening's hut meeting.

'Perhaps that's just his point. You might kill the wrong person.'

'Look, Klaus. I beg your pardon and all that, but you're not going to join the Pioneer Corps with or without a gun, are you? I mean, can you, if you get my meaning?'

'Never clearer.' Meyer, tired and ironic.

'So, if you don't mind, this is for people who could sign up to decide.'

'Ah. Disenfranchised. Do I not have an opinion?'

'Yeah, sure you have an opinion. But you don't have a choice. And Major Layton said everyone should choose for himself.'

'So far we have tried to do things together.'

'But there won't be spaces for everyone.'

'Why are you so upset? You don't want to sign up. You just said so.'

'But I might want to.'

'I'm going to lie down and revel in the luxury of not having to choose.' Meyer was bitter but accurate. 'Leo, have you chosen or do you want to leave it for today and sit with me?'

Don't be disappointed, my father had written, restored to Cricklewood from the Isle of Man where it rained. A pearl of a girl had been visiting, but accompanied once by a young British officer, who professed concern about me. Clearly her friend. Did you hope she might be your fiancée? Was she special to you? Leo, these things happen. I could only find out what was happening, forestall, prevent, if I were there among them. It might all of it, whatever it was, be too late by the time I got home, I might not know what to do, I might not know what I wanted to do. But if I went home I would have to leave Meyer.

'I haven't decided.'

'Good. Then let me tell you about ducks' feet.'

'Ducks' feet! Meyer, we're trying to have a meeting here.'

'Count me out, Schönbach. As you pointed out, I have no contribution to make. I'll talk quietly.'

The feet of ducks are irresistibly attractive to newly hatched molluscs which attach themselves to the damp surfaces and will not, thereafter, be removed until the ducks have flown to the next whiff of water, whereupon the molluscs loosen their hold and allow themselves to be deposited in puddle or pond along with feetful of seeds lodged on the wide webbing. That's why groups of the same species can be found simultaneously in various and remote parts of the world. Live fish, it has been said, might be swept up in an ocean whirlwind and hurled to alien locations, where they will encounter new conditions to which they must adapt themselves or perish.

'I get the point,' observed Schönbach sourly. 'Call it war. But which is more alien? Here or there?'

The camp splintered. Meyer was right, we had done everything together before, but now, depending on what you were prepared to accept, some people – young enough, fit enough, desperate enough – might go back. I don't think we had been behind the wire for so long that freedom itself was daunting, but we were being asked for the first time since each of us had been arrested to make a decision that would affect us separately – and completely. No one could ask the advice of anyone else. Each one of us, alone, had to ask himself, how much do I fear that return journey, unprotected? Now that it's a possibility, do I want to walk the streets of London at any price, conceding – by failing to hold out – that the British authorities are justified in withholding their trust, justified in refusing my unconditional release? Am I not unduly self-regarding to be so absorbed by a matter of principle when the war, essentially my war, is being fought out there, above all by the British who have borne the brunt of it alone for so long, whose cities are targeted night after night while I pace the circumference of the safety of my prison trying to decide if I want to go free? The reasoning was hypothetical. Transports home were not promised.

It was July and raining. Meyer lay on his back in his bunk, his arms by his sides, his head turned towards me. Outside, a few huts down, they were rehearsing an oratorio to the accompaniment of the piano the Quakers had procured, and the energetic bowing of a five-man string orchestra. The performance of *Israel in Egypt* –

how everyone smiled – was scheduled for the following day, programmes had been circulated, pinned up, dignitaries invited: Major Layton, the Commandant, even some representative of the musical press who would drive bumpily over the desert with his notebook and pencil, expecting little, impelled by curiosity. 'They sound good, don't they?'

Walter Michel, who had rehearsed his singers on *Dunera* and drummed his fingers on his hut table, gave no quarter. Lack of instruments, lack of sheet music and the desert's excesses were no excuse. You want sheet music? Here, I've one copy. Make your own. You want to sing with me? Then you sing like I say and you don't stop till I say. You don't want to sing with me? But you have the voice I need. You will sing with me. So they sang, faltered, and we could hear Michel's impatience, and they sang again. Then a furious 'No, no, first violin! You may be all alone but I don't want to hear you so loud. Keep it down. Listen to what the music's telling you. This part they're going to hear in their heads, not just with their ears. Understood? All right. Take it from D.'

Meyer, alone, could advise me. 'But it's not my business to advise you.'

'"And the children of Israel sigh'd by reason of the bondage: and their cry came up unto God. They oppress'd them with burdens; and made them serve with rigour . . ."'

'Again! Again!' shouted Walter Michel. 'The words matter as much as the notes. If they don't, why do we bother with them, why did Handel set them? Think what you're singing, what it means and then let me hear it!'

'"And the children of Israel sigh'd by reason . . ."'

'Well, it's not quite like that, is it?' Meyer laughed. 'Major Layton come like a latterday Moses to lead the children of Israel from the desert.' Major Layton wore a navy suit so dark it was almost black. When he shaved with precision in the early morning, he stroked his chin up and down, always with the back of his hand, grimacing.

'"They loathed to drink of the river: He turned their waters into blood . . . Their land brought forth frogs, yea even in the king's chambers. He gave their cattle over to the pestilence. Blotches and blains broke forth on man and beast."' The phrases repeated, turned back on themselves, gathered voices, swelled and faded. ' "He spake the word: and there came all manner of flies and lice in all their quarters. He spake: and the locusts came without number and devour'd the fruits of the land." '

'I think you should go,' Meyer said.

'Why?'

'Because you have reason to be back there . . . sooner rather than later . . .'

' "Then said the Lord, then said the Lord, then said the Lord . . ." ' The singers passed the words like a baton between them, laying down layers of notes, but as the music grew richer its melodies stretched the syllables like elastic over criss-crossing stairways of sound and the story quietly got to its feet and slipped away.

'What's the matter?' asked Meyer.

'This is too beautiful.'

'How can it be too beautiful?' Meyer was straining his head over the edge of his bunk as if he wanted to bring his perfect hearing closer to the rehearsal outside. My grandfather's version had been harsh, narrated in the grating tones of bad temper by an aggrieved old man with a rough tale to tell. My grandfather's version had been real, steeped in panic and sticky with congealed blood.

' "They loathed to drink of the river: He turned their waters into blood, He turned their waters into blood, turned their waters into blood, into blood . . ." ' The boy soprano Walter Michel had unearthed held a slow arching line and the basses, all staccato, reiterated their message.

This isn't a story, my grandfather had yelled, it's the truth. Now, I thought, it was neither; it had become the skeleton for a composer's art, an excuse for a man for whom the words were only words.

I said, 'But it's not like this at Pesach. I mean, when you were a child . . . who told you the story? Your father? Your grandfather? Your uncle?'

Meyer shifted on his bunk. 'Nobody, Leo. I'm sorry but I'm not a Jew.'

* * *

Schönbach's roar of rage pursued me. 'Of course I knew. Everyone damn well knew except you, and that's because you walk about inside your own stupid head like there was no world outside. Then all of a sudden you find out and ask me did I know Meyer's not a Jew? And what did you think I was going to say? "Oh no. What a shock. Let's throw him out of our hut and banish him to the Barons." What sort of creep are you, after all this time, when the guy's been with us since the first day in that police station, remember? And he didn't have to be. He could have stayed at home in Frankfurt, done as he was told, kept his head down like everybody else. But did he? Did he hell! You and me, it wasn't choice, was it? And who knows what we'd have done if it had been. Have you asked yourself that one? I reckon you'd best get back to England where you belong and ask your damfool questions there. And after all the care the old boy gave you. You make me ashamed. You make me sick.'

'You don't understand.'

'I don't fucking want to understand. Just clear out of here. You're polluting the air.'

Kicked out of Germany for being a Jew though I thought I was German, kicked out of England for being a German though I thought I was English, and now a pariah in the camp for wanting, at last, to be a Jew because of Meyer – who wasn't. It should have been funny. I had been at home here with these men, where I had thought the one thing we did not need to do was explain ourselves to one another. Now, suddenly, there was too much explaining to be done and I could not begin. I could not make them understand that I didn't hold it against Meyer that he was a Gentile, nor could I tell them that only Meyer had made me glad to be a Jew. I was out of place again and must find myself another, although it was beyond me to imagine living at ease with anyone who had not shared the past year.

Sulking, Schönbach was, and so were the others. Even Finkl and Engel diverted their noses as I packed my bag. From all over the camp that July morning only twenty other men had opted to sign up and take their chances on the ocean. I could see them gathering at the gate, scuffing their toes in the sand, fit, well fed, a little shamefaced to be the first but all with better reasons for leaving than mine. They had wives, they had children. The story was that I was running from bad conscience.

Meyer sat stiffly on his chair at the back of our hut. 'Leo. No hard feelings?'

'You're asking me?'

'Mmm. I knew what you meant. They don't.'

'Then why don't you tell them?'

'Because I think Schönbach is right. You should go back to England. You fit in there well enough, which is as much as anyone should hope for. Well enough. Don't ask for more than that. And better than he ever will, which is why he was so rough about it. He's jealous. We're all a bit jealous of that – you and your accent and so on. But also you've got to sort out that girl of yours.'

Hot face again. 'How do you know about her?'

'You talk in your sleep. You sleep on your stomach. Your bunk is above mine and sometimes, believe me, it seems your mouth is right in my ear. I haven't been eavesdropping. I couldn't get away from it.'

'Sorry.'

'Don't be. It's been very entertaining, but you must sort it out, as I said. There's a few other things you could sort out too.'

'Like?'

'Like, for example, worrying about the wrong things. For a start, you're entranced by what we've got here, what we've made of it. It's a perfect socialist society, isn't it? Almost no crime, all very democratic, all the little ministries working, people studying and playing music. Don't mistake it for what it isn't, Leo. You think it's special to us. But we're given food and shelter and no one is threatening us. No one. On the contrary. But we've got the memory of threat, and that binds us. So what could be easier than playing at democracy? Don't imagine that in other circumstances, in other places, we would all be as community-spirited as we are here. We wouldn't. We'd behave just as everybody else does. There is nothing special about us. How do I put this? Supposing I said, there's no such thing as a Master Race. There's no such thing as sub-humans. But there's no such thing as a Chosen People either. All there is is people, a type of mammal, which sometimes behaves in a way no other mammal ever has – so far as we know. This business

201

about nations, about belonging, about *Volksgeist*, for God's sake – it's all so much rubbish. Just at the moment the group I'm supposed to belong to is doing appalling things to just about everybody, most specifically to the group you're supposed to belong to, in the name of living space, as if it was a matter of survival. Now you may say I have a reason for special pleading here, and I'm in no position to contradict you, but, if you can, try and see that it's people being foul to people. Mankind doing to mankind what only mankind knows how to do. It could have been any group of people and any other group, it just happens not to be. So that doesn't make all Germans evil – nor all Jews good. We're all just people, as much as that, or perhaps I should be saying as little as that. Do you see what I mean? And if I'm ashamed – and I am ashamed – then I'm ashamed of the whole damned species. I will not hang my head as a German – but as a man.'

He stopped and waited for me to say something but I didn't know what to say.

Then Meyer blushed a colour of the deepest sadness. 'I'm sorry. It's not my place to say things like that, not even to you, although I thought I might have a chance of explaining myself to you. Sorry. Sorry. Mistake. Ill timed. Clumsy. Crass . . .'

But at that moment I cared more for Meyer and his opinion of me than for anything else. I felt so sorry for him but almost laughed because he was comical in his anguish, his limbs angular as a marionette's.

He said, 'May I accompany you to the gate?'

I held out my hands and gripped him by the forearms, taking his weight on my thighs to lever him out of his chair. Practice had taught us how to bring him to his feet in a single, almost painless movement. Upright, more stooped in the last year, he was still taller than me. He looked slightly down into my eyes and left in them a glance which said he did not expect to rise so smoothly from his chair again. 'Give me your arm.' He walked from the hips as if both legs were wooden, sliding his feet through the sand leaving a dual unbroken track. It took us ten minutes to reach the wire, where Meyer stood panting. I edged him into the shade of a watch-tower and the guard, bored in his eyrie, leaned over and said, 'You all right, mate?' I ran back to the hut where they were all sitting in silence round the table and said, directing my words to the opposite wall, 'Meyer's come to the gate with me. Someone's going to have to bring him back.'

As I left, Schönbach shouted after me, 'Here, kid! Leo!' I stopped and he came to the doorway. 'We made this up. Expect you'll be needing it.' He handed me a package wrapped in the *Sydney Morning Herald*. 'Tell him I'll come out for him when you've gone. Wouldn't want to get in the way. Take care of yourself.' He slapped my arms and turned back into the hut, the back of his neck burning red as the sand outside.

They opened the gate. We walked through. They closed it. We turned as one and waved to the wavers on the other side of the wire only a few feet away, turned again and marched in a tight column down the dust road towards Hay. On the first ridge I looked back but the camp had gone about its business and there was no one watching our departure. Leaving, we no longer belonged.

Free to disperse we hung together on the station, a lean group of young men in assorted suits carrying cases strapped with rope, not soldiers, not prisoners, not yet free. At the far end of the short platform there was a kiosk selling cigarettes and newspapers. Somebody asked for a newspaper from a woman perched on a stool. When she opened her mouth to answer, a faint twittering emerged, the sound of a bird, not of a human being.

My head trilled with the alien cheeping of a woman's voice. EL's voice had not been like that. I could not remember EL's voice, the girl I was returning to, instructed by Meyer who must be obeyed, I could not remember her face. On the train eating the bread and cake Schönbach and the others had packed for me, on the surging deck of our transport, I drew and re-drew her in my mind, clustered floating maroon hair around a pale heart, arranged slim shoulders beneath, thin arms, long legs, coloured in the violet eyes, retrieved features but no face. If I could only sketch her mouth – not the lips I had invented to fill the space – I might then catch the tones of the elusive voice. What did she do with her hands? Her hands had been important. She had used them, I knew, to accompany her words, lending emphasis. Wild hands spined with fingers proliferated along the railing, fingers uppermost; long fingers with nails whose growth I couldn't impede prodded the sky like frenzied cacti until I was forced to hack away at the wrists and the hands dropped into the churning surf peeling back from the ship's bows. Swathes of hair spinning from magenta to vermilion spread over my face at night and I woke tugging at the fronds covering my mouth, wrapped in skeins round my tongue. Mrs McKechnie was knitting something from a basket of red hair, her husband's arms manacled by red hair. Behind them Lucy was bent over a jigsaw puzzle, saying, 'I can't find the green piece to go in here', but a hand over her shoulder pressed the missing piece in place and Lucy clapped her hands as Jeremy, unmistakably Jeremy, leaned on the table and said, 'Let's do that bit up in the corner next.' Smiling, and getting for his smiles smiles from the McKechnies to whom I had not written so that Jeremy had slipped into my place there too, eating a wedge of Mrs McKechnie's cake, iced by Lucy, crumbs at the corners of his mouth and between his teeth, sucking at the crumbs with his tongue, a hand on Lucy's shoulder, the other pressing piece after piece into the puzzle. Then Jeremy departed, Lucy hanging on his neck, the McKechnies standing together at the basement door, and he rode away on a brown and white pony, an old black dog panting frantically to keep up, waddling at the pony's side.

Six months after Major Layton's arrival, having sailed from an Australian winter, we sailed into an English autumn, and the sky faded, the colour bleached from it until it disappeared entirely behind banked clouds that sat over the sea, and the sea turned to liquid lead. I was cold. When we docked I could not believe that England had been so grey and wondered whether the war was sucking up colour with each life lost and spewing it out again somewhere else, where it would be safer so that as England dulled by degrees the desert by degrees grew brighter. Brick-red sand. The bricks of London were not red. Even the red bricks were not red.

It was raining outside my parents' house. At the bottom of the road the rain lay in wide flat puddles where houses had been, between toppled walls. I raised my hand to knock at the door, lowered it, raised it and knocked. The door opened and my parents stood in the hall, side by side, small and anxious. For the moment that no one spoke I looked beyond their shoulders thinking there might be someone else in the house with them. Then my mother was weeping shrilly, crying my name, lifting her arms to my neck while I stood, and my father was weeping too, saying, 'Let me look at you, only let me look at you.'

Part III

Fifteen

'Why won't you understand? It was a condition of my release that I join the Pioneer Corps and that means I can't go back to the university. It's what they said.'

'Look, Leo. Look. Times are changing. The mood's changing. Believe me, I've seen it on the streets. They made a mistake, and they're sorry about it. You'd be surprised what you might be able to do. There are people about with influence. We have only to find them.'

'No!'

'What's the matter. What's got into you? It was only a suggestion.'

'I don't want anyone intervening in my affairs. I feel . . . I feel that, as things are, I should be doing my bit for this country. That's what it's about.' (Was I blushing? I was not.) 'I mean, I'd rather join up, but there we are.'

My father furrowed his forehead, proud that his son understood duty and loyalty but distressed to see the latent doctor displaced by the navvy.

Some of the furniture had been moved. A chair that I was certain had stood under the window now faced another, almost identical, by the fireplace. There was a new table in the centre, smaller, more modern. I grasped the chair by its back, preparing to shift it.

'What are you doing?' asked my father, mildly interested. I replaced the chair. This was not my house to decide upon the positioning of chairs but I wished they had asked, or warned me before adjusting the landscape.

There were new curtains. My mother's hair was a haze of incredible yellow and she had spent the morning baking, using – I had seen – real eggs. 'Did you get all this just for me, for the lost son?'

She had led me to the kitchen, flung wide the larder door. '*Kleiner,* we live.' Inside was a tray of eggs, a slab of butter.

'But how . . . ?'

'I pay. Like anybody else.' But my father had written that the business had gone awry with 'the boss' away.

'Well, well,' said my father. 'And tomorrow you can tell us all about it.'

But in the night, as I lay in bed in the room next to theirs, my mother's penetrating sibilants seeped under the crack in the door. 'We'll ask Eleanor to help. He'll do as she says. Believe me, I know.'

I propped myself bolt upright on my two fat pillows with their frilly pillowcases, ground my teeth and inadvertently slept. Dreaming again I teetered on an immense swaying deck which stretched to the horizon. There was no one about but two figures far away in the bows, leaning together, one pointing out something distant to the other. I could not recognise who they were but as I drew closer they turned abruptly and I stopped. One of them seemed to hoist the other on to his shoulders. In a moment Jeremy sauntered by carrying on his back an idiotically grinning Meyer. 'No!' I shouted, bringing my parents to my door, my mother, inexplicably, carrying a mug of Ovaltine.

'Go away.' I waved them out. 'Go away. Go away.'

My mother placed the mug by my bedside. 'He's talking to his dreams,' she confided, and they tiptoed out.

'Well, and we've got a surprise for you.' My father smacked his hands together as if he had finally drawn up a tricky but favourable agreement. 'A friend of yours is going to visit.' He presented the announcement as a gift.

My mother took over the story. 'And I'm going to make dumpling soup because I know that's what she likes best. She's even asked for the recipe because her mother doesn't know how to cook it.'

'I'm going for a walk.'

'Yes, you go. You need to get out and see what's changed.'

There were no longer any leaves on the trees. An early autumn or high winds or dejection had caused them to drop prematurely.

It was a fine day but the blue of the sky was muted and the grass was grey. I walked the circumference of Gladstone Park, following the perimeter path, following the fence. When I saw what I had done I passed out of the gates and walked, as I had once walked with my suitcase, watching the stretch and bend of my feet, watching the paving stones slip past. Some of those small suburban streets were as quiet and unaltered as if I had last been along them the previous week. Then, as I rounded a corner, there was nothing but debris, cavities between houses whose walls bulged. Weeds clambered among the tumbled brickwork, wound among the spokes of a pram wheel. Past the next corner and all was silence and normality again. There seemed something so arbitrary yet so precise in the destruction. You've got to sort that girl out, said Meyer. On the contrary. She was being brought in like a reserve battalion to see to me. What if I didn't go home but left them to eat their dumpling soup in a trio? 'And you'd like dumpling soup too, wouldn't you?' my mother had said. 'It's a long time since you had any.' Far from it. Those chefs of ours had turned out vats of the stuff. But I lacked the courage to disappear, even to be deliberately late.

By the station a woman was selling flowers parcelled in newspaper, mostly chrysanthemums. 'A present,' I would say, or 'These are for you', as if they might be for anyone else. Her hand taking them. But I saw instead the fluttering fingers growing along the railing of the ship and only slightly slowed my pace by the flower stall.

In our three chairs we sat in the front room and waited for my visitor. My father took out his watch, as he had always done when he was expecting someone, urging them to be punctual by the ferocity with which he examined the little hands, the impatience with which he dropped the watch back in its pocket, shaking his head as if the appointment was threatened. My mother verged on silence but was restless, running to arrange and rearrange the table. She was nervous. My father was nervous. Outside it was already dark, the blinds were down, the streetlights were shrouded and I wondered how she would find her way.

My father spoke up, to himself, it sounded. 'Good thing she's been here so often. She'd get lost otherwise.' Of course. Was there any need for me to remain? Let them have one of their evenings together, without me. They had not needed me before.

'Does she know I'm back?'

'It'll be a great surprise, won't it?' My father looked up from his watch, beaming in expectation.

'You mean she doesn't?'

'She doesn't. No, she doesn't. How could she know? There hasn't been the time to tell her.'

'Then how come she's coming to dinner?'

'She always comes on a Saturday.'

'Always?'

'Nearly always.'

'Since when?'

'What's the matter with you? You don't think she should visit us? She's a good, kind girl who's been trying to keep our spirits up, I know that. I know she wouldn't spend her free time with two people like us for the fun of it. She's a young girl. A lovely young girl. She could go anywhere but she comes here. So of course your mother makes a fuss of her. We've been very grateful. She's kept us in touch.'

'In touch? Who with?'

'With everybody. All the people who were worrying. That teacher, Mr McKechnie. Mrs Chapman, the old one . . .'

'Marrrm!'

'What? Yes, and of course your friend Jeremy. You remember I wrote you . . . about Eleanor and Jeremy?'

'What about it?' Every time I spoke my tone sounded more rude, more offhand.

'Well, I think –' A knocking at the door and I suddenly couldn't swallow. 'Will you go and open it?'

I got up – oh, all right – and slouched through into the hall, and there leaned against the wall, one hand already reaching to open the door. I had planned to plan what I would say.

She was waiting, a dark figure in the dark whom I could not fully see, with a bag over her shoulder. 'Leo. Oh, gosh.' I held out my hand politely, she took it, stepped over the threshold and bent forward. 'Oh, your beard's gone.' She brushed her fingertips over my chin and I shivered. Then, 'Look behind you.' She put her arms about my neck as if it didn't matter, as if I had no reason to be angry, and spun me round until I was facing into the house. Poked round the front-room door, eyebrows high on their foreheads, my parents' twinned heads vanished.

Shifting rubble suited me. I carried sandwiches in a tin box and rolled up my sleeves. On the site we were clearing, a library had been sliced away from its white portico, which now straddled an inconsequential threshold leading nowhere. I would eat my lunch sitting framed on the top step of the entrance stairway, like a passing workman who has stepped into someone else's portrait. 'You wanna watch yourself.' The others were not so foolish. Deep cracks meandered about the supporting columns and when the wind blew the pediment grated irritably. The occasional air-raid warning would send us burrowing briefly underground; otherwise I passed bricks, hand to hand, as part of a chain whose beginning was the residue of a rear wall, the end a wheelbarrow. We had come to the scene late. Others had already removed the books, although I found a portion of a page.

My companions were garrulous with boredom. I was silent, but in the evenings wandered home content, realising that whatever had passed through my mind had not lodged there but trickled helplessly away leaving only the standing images of EL and Meyer.

Purple buddleia grew from the tumbled bricks in the cavities of wasteland, Hitler's weed they called it, suckling butterflies. They seemed to be painted on to a landscape of grey, because fallen walls are greyer than those still standing. The numbers of our company remained the same but people departed and were replaced. In a matter of months I had become a senior figure, by virtue of long attendance, second only to the Royal Engineers, who carefully destroyed the teetering and threatening shells, leaving the debris for us. I grew wiry, and felt well.

'But we have to get him back to his studies,' my father wailed. His promised ally was letting him down.

'I think he should do what he wants. I do what I want. So should he,' said EL.

It was more than my parents could bear. 'Eleanor. It was medicine!'

'My father approves' – to silence them, Major Laing, after all. 'He says it's only a pity he can't join up. He says it's a disgrace. He says Leo's sacrifice is noble, and he can study later.' Noble? Not a word of the major's, I didn't think.

'Is that what he says?'

'Something like that.'

It was our complicity. 'What was it like? What happened?' But there were some things I would not tell her, some I could not, some I wanted to keep, jealously, for myself. It had been long ago in a brighter light, framed by the sea before and after, a closed time. 'All right.' She crossed her legs, in nylon stockings, a present, she said, from my mother. Patience was written on the curved lips I had, for some reason, not been able to bring to mind. If she waited long enough, the crossed legs declared, I would be bound to tell. 'It's Caroline's birthday. There's going to be a party. Will you come?'

'Caroline?'

'Jeremy's sister, don't you remember? And he's going to be on leave. He's dying to see you.' My sister, Caroline. Blonde as you, Leo.

'Where's the party to be?'

'At their house outside Oxford. A lovely big place. You should see it.'

'A big posh party?'

'Yes. A big posh party.'

'I haven't the clothes. It'll need "clothes", won't it?'

'Oh, it will, it will. They're going to make a big splash.'

'Jollity and gaiety and pretend nothing's happening.'

'Don't be so sour. Jeremy's going to be on leave. Afterwards he'll be going back. Can't people celebrate occasionally?'

'Sorry. Of course. But anyway I haven't got the clothes.'

'Jeremy will lend them to you. He's got two. He wants to.'

'You mean, he knows? You've already asked him?'

'Of course. You're not a state secret. He's been asking all the time.'

'What's all the time?'

'All the time. Just all the time. He's very concerned. You should know that.' Concerned that I had returned, most likely.

'His clothes won't fit.'

'They'll fit well enough. There'll be so many people anyway, no one's going to worry what you look like.'

'If there's so many people I won't be missed.'

'You will be missed. I'd miss you. I want to see you there.'

'You see me here.'

'I want to see you there. With other people. I want other people to see us there. And Jeremy . . .'

'How does my mother manage to give you stockings? My father said the business wasn't the same with the boss away.'

EL grabbed my hands in something approaching fury. 'What on earth is the matter with you? You're so incurious. Why don't you ask her. It's so simple. If you want to know something, just ask.'

'I am asking. I'm asking you.'

'Well, ask her. She wants to tell you. Or ask your father. He doesn't.'

She knows them better than I do, I thought, my parents sitting tactfully in the kitchen leaving us alone, although once EL had left they would examine me, all question marks. Late-night whisperings told me my father had forbidden my mother to enquire but she was bursting.

I raised my hands with EL's clamped to them and counted the slender fingertips. 'When is this party?'

'In a fortnight. Will you come?'

'Maybe.'

She wore dark green and had her hair scooped up. Her neck was white. 'All right?' She wore high heels raising her to my height, and gloves to the elbow.

'It suits you,' I said clumsily.

On the mantelpiece of the room in the Oxford digs she shared with Caroline there was a photograph of the two girls, arms about each other's waists, their lips stretched with beaming. I did not ask who had been the photographer. Blonde Caroline had left early to prepare herself in her parents' house, to receive her guests.

'And this is yours.' EL opened the wardrobe. A black dinner

suit hung over a stiff white shirt. 'I'll do the tie if you want.' She turned her back while I undressed. 'Actually, come to think of it, I've seen you in your underpants, and less, remember?' Which bolted me into Jeremy's trousers just as she spun round, laughing, to face me.

I buttoned the crackling shirt, pushed the ends into the trousers. 'They're too big, look.'

EL slipped a fist into the waistband and we were both immobilised. Casually she withdrew her hand. 'It could be a disaster. You're going to need a belt.' She rummaged in a drawer. 'Of course, Jeremy is stockier than you. Aha!' Triumphant. 'And it's black.' She threaded the belt, a man's belt, through the loops, and the trousers bunched as she fastened it. 'It won't show with the jacket over it. Put your head up.' She tied the tie, used to tying ties. 'And now, if Sir would kindly try the jacket, would Sir?' The shoes were my father's, barely tight, which he had polished again and wrapped in paper. EL stood away, examining me. 'Golly gee! Well, I do declare. The gentleman is transformed. How does it feel?'

I put my hands in deep pockets. 'They're very baggy.'

'That's the fashion. Or it was. You'll be able to keep your hands in your pockets and no one will notice.'

'It's not one of my habits,' I said sourly. 'Shall we be going?'

You could already hear them, through the honey-stone walls, the acquaintances and friends of Mr and Mrs Benson, and of their son and daughter. A young man with a glass in his hand opened the door. 'Coats to the left. Drinks to the right. Caroline and everyone through there' – pointing. 'Make yourselves at home.'

'Who's that. Do you know him?'

'Never set eyes on him.'

'D'you want a drink?'

'Do you?'

'Not yet. It's too early.'

'Later may be too late.'

'What do you mean? Are they going to run out?'

'Not them. But I never leave things till later.'

So each with a glass of punch in our outer hands, EL wary on my arm, we made our entrance into a room of bared shoulders and glossy hair. The walls were panelled, the vast table set to one side, piled with cold cuts and bowls of steaming vegetables. There was a cake in the centre and, incongruously, a large red round jelly.

'I knew it would be like this – they're rolling in it. Shortage isn't a word they know. Yum.'

She was right. I sipped my drink, downed it.

'Shall we eat?'

'I'm not hungry.'

'Yet. Is that the idea? Well, I will. Hold my glass.'

I watched her circle the table filling her plate, missing nothing.

'Eleanor! At last. We'd almost given up on you.' She disappeared as they closed in from all sides, my popular girl. I put my glass on the table and downed hers too, sticky-palmed. There were uniforms, unknown people inside them, and pillars of dark suits. Girlish voices were screaming, male ones grumbled. As they swarmed towards me, so I retreated, backing towards the door.

Hands on my shoulders from behind. 'Leo. It is Leo? You look excellent.' Jeremy's smile was still wide in his wide face but over it his eyes were apprehensive. 'Sorry about the suit. This one's even bigger. Have you had a drink? Let me get you a drink. I've had too many, we all have, but one might as well. What'll you have? You're as thin as ever. Shall we go out, where it's quieter, and we can talk? What'll you have? I kept wondering when you'd make it back. I can't tell you what I've been thinking.' He was talking too much for one who couldn't find words to apologise. It was too late for apology, too late for a Benson apology, too late for Jeremy who had wasted no time once I had been dispatched.

'How do you do, Jeremy.' My voice chilled me too. 'Are you well?' He ladled out two glasses, handed me one, nibbled at the other. I watched him. 'Why aren't you drinking beer?' I asked.

'Why should I drink beer? I don't like it.'

'You always drank beer. You never drank anything else.'

Jeremy held his glass out and twirled it, pretending to be interested in the playing on it of the last slant of sun. 'I do what people do, don't you know.' He seemed to be offering a confession I did not wish to hear, asking for forgiveness I had no intention of providing, implying that I, particularly, should understand what he was trying to say. So I too twirled my glass in the sun and swallowed its contents, and all my neck and the lines beside my nose prickled with sweat.

The cluster of EL's friends was advancing, buzzing, but parted to release her. 'Boys,' she said brightly – placing herself between us, linking us to her through her elbows, one each – and faced her friends. Faced out her friends, I thought suddenly. The scrubbed faces, the bare shoulders and square shoulders, the wide and round mouths appraised us. 'And this is Leo.' As if they couldn't tell, having been told all about Leo, who was well worth scrutinising. I was EL's trophy, her pet project perhaps, along with my parents whom she had visited so regularly and so graciously.

I disengaged my arm. 'I think I need something to eat. Excuse me. How nice to meet everyone.' And I plunged back into the main room where the unnamed guests warbled around the loaded table. Beyond it I had seen french doors opening into the garden. Halfway across the room I turned instinctively and there was Jeremy behind me, closing the gap, and there where we had left her stood EL, her curving lips ajar and disconcerted, her two arms empty.

I ducked behind an ancient uniformed waiter shouldering a tray of champagne glasses which were plucked away from all sides, but another waiter with another tray followed on and yet another stood waiting. The guests swayed together, swayed apart, the time to drink the birthday girl's health approaching, impatient to taste the fizzy stuff, too well mannered to pre-empt the starting pistol. The hands reaching for the trays behind me meshed into a barrier that left Jeremy struggling and I fled through the garden doors alone.

There was a broad terrace leading down to the lawns in wide steps on each of which was the body of a limbless stone girl barnacled with moss. I crept around the lowest and squatted gingerly at her feet, chilly, in safety and in a temper. She had paraded us, the man she made love to, the smiling man, magnanimous in his riches, and the boy she felt sorry for. Did she think I wouldn't notice? Did she imagine I did not mind? But then I remembered her laughter when I stood, untrousered, in that welcoming kitchen, the major's shotgun trained on me. I remembered her mother's advice, 'Never take riding lessons from Eleanor, she's much too intolerant.' Briskly competent on the river bank pummelling the life back into me. EL did not feel sorry for people. Whatever it was that drew her to me, it was not charity. Then my temper rose further, directed now at myself for snivelling in my soul for a heartless girl. In the distance the line of a river and a regiment of dark cypresses suggested a boundary. In between the lawns rolled and twisted, cushioning specimen trees. On the lawn looking down over the gardens stood a man and a woman, arm in arm, owning what they surveyed. They turned together to officiate at their daughter's celebration, and Mr Benson was facing me, walking with his wife up the generous garden stairway, passing me without a glance, as one passes people who are of no interest, people one does not know. But I knew him.

I let him pass me without a word, my mouth suddenly filled with ice in which all words hung petrified; Mr Benson, until then known to me only as the Magistrate, with whom I had been closeted for a month while he stamped letters of the alphabet on the flotsam of Vienna and Berlin; Mr Benson, who had as good as sent two thousand men across the world without giving us a second thought; Mr Benson, whose son had tampered with my girl while I was behind barbed-wire and then lent me his second-best suit for a family champagne party. Mr Benson walked up to me, past me and away into his mansion without a flicker of recognition because for the Magistrate his interpreter had been merely a voice, not a face.

I watched him go in and thought, I will make you pay. For all of us. But I meant: for me.

'Ca-ro-line! Ca-ro-line!' They were braying in the house. EL was among them. I must find her, remove her and run from this place and the people who belonged to it.

'Ca-ro-line! Ca-ro-line!' Hands that were not holding glasses thumped the table: get the girl and we can drink.

'Where's Daddy? We can't begin without Daddy.'

'Mr Benson, we want to sing Happy Birthday. Mr Benson, Mrs Benson! Ho, Mr Benson! We want to wish your daughter a very happy birthday.'

'Want to drink my bubbly, more like, wouldn't surprise me.'

I pressed myself against the wall, camouflaged entirely by the massed bodies.

The Magistrate's bust rose above the heads which turned to him like sunflowers. He tinkled a long sliver of spoon against his glass, bringing instant hush. 'Ladies and gentlemen! Pray silence!' His public retreated a co-ordinated pace and I was flattened against the fireplace. 'You all know why we are gathered here today. My daughter, Caroline . . .' ('Hooray!') '. . . and a very lovely girl she is too . . .' ('Hear! Hear!') '. . . is twenty-one today!' ('Yaaar! Hooray for Caroline. Well done, Carrie!') 'You don't need me to tell you how much we've all been looking forward to this day when we can forget the outside world for an afternoon. So I suggest we raise our glasses and say, here's to you, very many happy returns and . . .' I tipped some of the gassy drink into my mouth but nausea rose to my gullet and I put my glass down, rather roughly, on the mantelpiece. '. . . and thank you, Caroline! So everybody. To Caroline!'

'To Caroline!' Welcome, Mr Benson's champagne – wherever did he get it? The glasses were raised again and I reached out for mine to do as the others were doing, all the while trying to pick out the girl in whose honour my stomach was heaving. Unguided, my fingers missed the glass and closed on a slim hard object standing on the mantelpiece. I looked down into my palm. In it lay a small antique candlestick, its tarnish suggesting silver. Briefly I bounced its weight and made to replace it, changed my mind and slipped the Magistrate's heirloom into the cavernous pocket of the fashionably wide trousers I had borrowed from his son. Now I saw her, a peck from mother, a peck from father, blonde as me, rounded and appetising, her brother's sister, no doubt about it. Mr Benson, his duty done, removed himself to his estate once more and I edged away from the fireplace. I must retrieve EL and make myself scarce. Banging low on my thigh, hidden beneath Jeremy's jacket, I had something belonging to the Bensons – and I was taking it away with me.

EL stood in the doorway, her mouth set in a tight line.

'Quite a place they've got here,' I observed, noticing her hair flame in fury.

'Managed a tour, have you?'

'Not a comprehensive one. A bit here and there. Have you had enough?'

'Of what?'

'Oh, festivities . . . you know. The excellent company.' Excellent, the company's improving, Meyer had said, on the first day.

'I didn't think much of yours, going off and leaving me like that.'

'All alone? Among your friends? Hardly.'

'It was appalling. You made me look a fool.'

'And what did you think you made me look? Your foreign victim brought along to embarrass the upper classes.'

'Leo! How could you even think that?' But for the first time since I had known her she coloured. Bull's-eye.

I took her by the elbow and pushed her out of the house, off the elegant porch and on to the gravelled drive. Footsteps ran behind us.

Jeremy caught up with us at the gate. Disappointed. 'Going so soon?'

'I've got a long journey.'

'So have I. My leave's over tomorrow. I'll have to be back.'

'Where?' It did not hurt to be polite now.

'Northampton. We fly out of Northampton.'

'Ah.'

'Do keep the suit. It's miles better on you.'

'I wouldn't dream of it.'

'Please. I'd like you to. Keep it. All of it.' His eyes flickered to my right leg and I swivelled a few degrees on the gravel. Did he know what I was hiding in the trouser pocket? 'I shan't be needing it.'

'Very probably, neither shall I. I can't imagine another occasion like this one.'

'Then keep it as a memento. Best of luck.'

'You too.'

'Bye, Eleanor.'

'Bye, Jeremy. Take care.'

For a moment they looked into one another's faces as if I wasn't there, then Jeremy nodded, touched his forelock in a gesture of irony unknown to me, and said, 'Yes, Ma'am.'

In the dark, behind blackout blinds, the lights out none the less, EL prodded my thigh, outer and inner. 'What have you got in there?'

'That's not for you to ask,' I said, jocular with nerves.

But she only laughed. 'I didn't mean that. I meant the other one.'

'A souvenir.'

'He said memento.'

'So he did.'

On the floor, on our clothes all crumpled and strewn, I met with such a soft slipperiness I was clumsy. I was not nearly as clumsy as we had expected. Then we found her bed, crawling and groping for it, climbed aboard and lay, bone against bone, our thin legs interlaced, our noses in each other's necks.

Then EL said, twisting a sudden knife in me, 'What have you got against Jeremy?' I sat up and leaned across her, hand flailing in the space by her bed. 'What are you doing? What are you looking for?'

'I'm looking for the damned light.'

'Oh.' She stretched out an arm – it was her bed, her light after all – and pressed the switch. 'Why?'

'I want to look at you.' I looked at her, lying stock still, even her breathing barely detectable, her curved lips set in an uncertain smile. She had not expected this. She was not quite mistress of the situation, used, so she had claimed, to love-making, unused to such an intent post-coital scrutiny. She was uncomfortable, above all because she mustn't show it. Her skin was astonishingly white, from her cheekbones, over her small breasts to her ankles. She blenched under my gaze but her hair, all her hair, smouldered.

'Now,' I said, still raised on my elbow, 'what was it you asked?'

She seemed truly puzzled. 'I said, what have you got against Jeremy?'

'You ask me that? You seriously ask me that? After the two of you . . . ?'

'After the two of us what?'

'Even while I was still in Oxford, and then later, when I was out of the way. You've been seeing a lot of him while I was away, I know. My father told me. And do you remember when I nearly drowned, how the two of you looked at each other over my sickbed? Because I remember. And I didn't care for it. I'll tell you how it seems to me.'

222

'Tell me how it seems to you.' Disconcerting triumph already lurked in her eyes.

'It seems to me that you've been playing us both along, enjoying the competition. Maybe you didn't really want either of us, I don't know, but you didn't want anybody else to have us either. But events beyond your control altered the plot. I was removed, so you only had one of us left . . . so . . .'

But again EL was laughing, incredulously, also angrily, also – and this was most confusing – because she was finding what I was saying funny. 'Yes, you stupid, self-centred boy. You're quite right. There was competition, between Jeremy and me – for you. Today he finally acknowledged I won. All right?'

I lay back, flattened and foolish, thinking of the lonely men behind the wire who, passing, had offered their affection and their bodies, then pleaded to give them, but never once insisted. Jeremy, and the women who'd surrounded him, Jeremy and his friends. Jeremy and his smiling. Since how long? And I knew: always.

But EL's tongue was tracing the corrugations of my ribcage, circling my navel, her face was buried in my pubic hair, she took me in her mouth, her fingertips drawing fine lines around my testicles. She raised her head and climbed astride me, the tops of her inner thighs glistening. 'Besides,' she said, easing herself on to me, 'you should have known something else, anyway. I couldn't possibly have gone to bed with Jeremy.'

'Why not?'

'He's too . . . English.'

Sixteen.

My mother stood in my bedroom doorway watching me hang Jeremy's suit in my wardrobe. Then she could bear it no longer, pushed me brusquely aside and rearranged the jacket on the pink satin hanger.

'You bought this suit?'

'No. A friend lent it to me.'

'What friend?'

'Jeremy. You know, EL's friend.'

My mother frowned. 'Too good a friend, if you ask me.'

'It's okay, Mutti, and yes, he is a good friend. You used to like him.'

'I used to like him? I never met him before.'

'Yes, you did. When you came to my school finishing day. He showed you to your seats.'

'That boy? That's the boy?' She fingered the suit. 'This isn't quality.' She peered into the back of the trousers. 'Not even lined. How could you wear something like that to a ball?'

'It wasn't a ball. It was a birthday party. And I needed a suit.'

'You should have told me in time: I could have had one made for you. I know a man . . .'

'This one was fine.'

'Are you going to wear it again?'

'I shouldn't think so.'

'Then you should give it back, maybe.'

'He's given it to me.'

My mother sucked in her top lip and blew it out again. 'Some gift. The trousers are all out of shape. It's the pockets. What have you got in the pockets? You shouldn't put heavy things in pockets, it pulls the fabric out of shape and you can never get it back again.'

She put her hand in one of the pockets. 'Some heavy thing –'

'Leave it. What does it matter if it pulls out of shape? You just said it's not quality.' I closed the wardrobe door so roughly she barely had time to whip her hands to safety. She clasped her hands together, then clasped mine. '*Ach,* look at them. The nails.'

'That's what happens when you hump bricks about.' No longer doctor's hands.

'You tell those people, it's been long enough. They'll understand.'

'But I don't want to, Mutti. I'm enjoying myself.'

'Enjoying yourself! You have a future and you're enjoying yourself. Never mind. You sit down there' – she plumped up the cushion on my armchair – 'and read your poetry books. Enjoy those.' She rearranged her disappointment about her plump shoulders like a shawl and trotted out.

Closing my eyes I was again deep in EL's moist body and a wave of desire made me shiver. *That's more or less what I meant by sorting out,* said Meyer. *And now what? Are you going to get that girl, or are you going, perhaps, to listen to your mother?* I'm going out, I said.

We were sitting in a row on a low garden wall which remained, solid, in spite of the bomb that had removed the houses opposite. We were eating our sandwiches. I had in my pocket Meyer's latest letter, saved to read in the peace of a crowd. I pulled it out.

The second camp, draconian in its discipline and awful in its drainage, had nevertheless improved his health. On his release, promised soon, he was going to stay in Australia. His sister Frieda was already on her way to Melbourne, a reunion he both dreaded and anticipated with joy. 'I'll fling my arms round her – insofar as I can – and then pray she'll shut up. My prayers, of course, will remain unanswered, there being no one there to comply and this particular demand being beyond the powers of any deity. Schönbach has swallowed his pride and gone off to pick fruit for the Australians in their Labour Force. Rosenthal has left for England – someone found him a position to go straight into, teaching probably. Finkl got himself arrested some weeks ago for pickpocketing on a night out in Melbourne, even though he returned his booty. He says he only did it to keep his hand in, which I take to be self-evident. He talked his way out of trouble, as one would have expected, and left for Britain. No one knows how he got his release. He said he intended to make his living as he always has. He also said he was going to look you up, he feels affection for you. I would keep a sharp eye out for his affection, if I were you. As for you, what are we to say? I have restored you to your father, which was not easy for me. Now you must outgrow us both – in whatever manner you choose. Make sure, though, that the choice really is yours.'

Tears stood in my eyes. Not easy for him, he said. Not easy! But easy words, written so far away that I could not shake him to his senses or make him come back. He was deserting me, and wrote that it was not easy.

Someone suddenly punched me in the shoulder so that I all but dropped my tin box and my letter. 'Fuckin' Leo. So they let you out too!'

'Giusè!'

He was older than the two years should have given him. 'How you been doing?' His face – thinner, bonier – had hardened.

Yet his father, soft from sitting at the back of the restaurant, had not survived the oily waters and splintering wood of the *Arandora Star*. He had seeped beneath the surface and not come up again, not even once. 'And what was I supposed to tell my mum? It took 'em long enough to find out. You know, they didn't even bleedin' know who was on that boat an' who wasn't.' He kicked the wall, kicking them, whoever they were. But they remained serene, unknown and unknowable. Giusè pulled his face back to mine, his tears for his father finding mine for his father, for Meyer and, in retrospect, for us all. 'So whatcha been doing? Not a doctor yet?'

'I'm not going to be a doctor.'

Giusè enquired no further. 'Gotta girl?'

'Yes.'

'Marryin'?'

'Good grief. I haven't thought that far ahead.'

'Well, you oughter.'

'Why?'

'Nah, nah. You just oughter.'

226

'Are you getting married?'

'You bet.' He rubbed his hands. 'Soon as I can get goin' again.'

'The restaurant, you mean?'

'Yeah. Bit of the readies an' I'm away.'

'So where's that going to come from?'

'Problem, that is. You got any spare cash?' I turned my pockets inside out, pulling a clown's doleful smile. He put an arm round me. 'I was only kiddin'. I wouldn't take money off of you. My old man would've had me for that.' He got off the wall and stretched, muscled under his shirt. 'Know what I reckon? I reckon this is fate, us meeting like this after all that.'

'Coincidence,' I said. 'There's no such thing as fate.'

'Ru-bbish! Him up there' – he pointed skywards – ''e's got it all worked out. It's just you don't always know at the time what the big plan is, so you 'ave to be a bit patient.'

' ''Know then thyself, presume not God to scan, The proper study for mankind is man''?'

'Whatever.'

'You believe that?'

' 'Course I do. I'm Italian, aren't I? Good Catholic. It's a job lot. You got one, you got the other all thrown in. Never been anything else and don't wanter be. Same as me dad, me mum, me nan, me Uncle Toni. Remember Uncle Toni?' In shirtsleeves over coffee and cards. 'I'm staying up at their place. Ours got took over.'

'Someone else moved in?'

'Rented property. Never safe in rented property. So when I get the restaurant goin' again I'll buy me somewhere small, then sell it and buy me somewhere bigger. But I'll buy an' it'll be mine, no nonsense.'

'How are you going to run a restaurant and cook without ingredients?'

Giusè struck a pose, reminding me suddenly of old Mr Tolini. 'Do me a favour! I don't cook. I'm a bleedin' chef. You give me a tin of spam and I'll give you a carbonara.'

'You can't.'

'I can. Magic. That's what it is. Nah. The cooking's not the problem. It's the organisation.'

'What about Uncle Toni?'

'That one? He's a good geezer, but 'e ain't got it up 'ere. Lazy bugger too. Best man in the world, though.' We each have one of those, I thought. 'Anyways . . .' Giusè yanked Meyer's letter out of my hand and scrawled on the back of it with a pencil he pulled from behind his ear. ''Ere's where you find me. Evenin's. Make sure you do, or I'll be out after you.'

I laughed and he took my hand, shaking it in both of his. 'But you don't know where to find me.'

'No problem, mate, no problem.'

We hadn't mentioned *Dunera*, either of us, I thought, walking home. Nor Australia. I shared this thing with Giusè and with no one else I knew here in London. Perhaps having been a part of it together precluded talking about it. Perhaps, though, his *Dunera* and mine had been different. They had kept us separate, his people behind their wire on a deck above ours, his people off-loaded before us. Perhaps, just as I could not speak to EL or my parents in anything but general terms, so he could not speak to me lest we discover that our experience had not, after all, been the same. Nevertheless, we knew something others did not. It marked us out, and it bound us.

My mother was waiting at the door and said, 'That candlestick. It's worth a lot of money.'

'Mutti!'

She was not contrite. 'Somebody has to tidy your room. You're out working for those people all day. You can't do it.'

'Thank you for tidying my room but my wardrobe didn't need tidying.'

'It was those trousers. I couldn't bear the thought of those trousers. If you don't want people in your wardrobe you should lock it.' And she patted her bundle of keys. 'Anyway, it needs polishing. It's black. Silver goes black if you don't polish it.'

'I like it the way it is.'

'You can't have it standing and looking like that.'

'I'm not sure I'm going to have it standing.'

'So why have you got it if you're not going to show it off? Why are you keeping it in that pocket?' I said nothing. 'No! Leo!' I still said nothing. 'Where does it come from?' I looked at her, my silence an effective prosecutor. 'The ball. You brought it back from the ball.'

'It wasn't a ball, it was a birthday party.'

'The birthday party. At that boy's house. It comes from that boy's house.' She stepped forward and hugged me. 'That'll teach him.'

'What?'

'Trying to get your girl behind your back. That'll teach him. You show him.'

'But Mutti. He wasn't trying to get my girl. He was trying to get me.'

My mother's eyes grew perfectly round. 'Pfui!' she said. 'Pfui! Pfui! Pfui! Don't tell Pappi. And sell that candlestick.'

'No. I want to keep it.'

'Why? From a boy like that.'

'He's a friend of mine.'

'He's no friend of yours. What do you mean, a friend of yours? What are you suggesting?'

'I'm not suggesting anything. I'm just saying. He's a friend of mine.'

My mother resorted to experience. 'You don't know what you're talking about . . .' I fancy my face was not cordial. She dropped her eyes and tried another route. 'It might be a lot of money.'

'I don't need money.'

'And when you marry Eleanor you won't need money? How are you going to keep her if you don't have a proper job and you don't have money? I can give you money, but not enough. She's a lovely girl, and she has style. Pappi says.'

EL had said I was incurious. 'Mutti, how come you can give me money?'

She was delighted. 'Pianos.'

'Pianos?'

'*Ja*, pianos. When there's a war people play the piano more.'

'How do you know?'

'If they didn't play the piano more why would they keep buying pianos?'

'Are they?'

'Of course they are. I told you. From me.'

'And where do you get them from?'

'I bought them from someone else. While you were away, while Pappi was away, I bought pianos and sold them again.'

I thought of the front room packed with pianos. There were no footprints in the carpet. 'But where did you keep them?'

'I didn't keep them. I sold them before I bought them. It's simple.'

'And what does Pappi think of that?'

My mother put her hands to my mouth. 'Ssh. Pappi doesn't know. He mustn't ever know.'

'Why not? Aren't you buying and selling pianos any more?'

'Certainly not. Not once your father was home. I have my work to do when he's home, and he has his business' – which was not, I suspected, prospering. 'So now, this candlestick. Get rid of it because when that boy finds out he'll come after you.'

'He won't. I didn't steal the candlestick.'

'He gave it to you? With the trousers?'

'Not exactly.'

'You stole the candlestick.'

But I didn't want to sell it. I owned something of Mr Benson's. I had taken it away. Mr Benson was now without it. Every time I looked at it I would be reminded of that fact. On the other hand, if it really *was* worth something, then I knew what I would do with the money. *Make sure the choice is really yours.* Okay, Meyer, I muttered, and turned back to my mother, who was about to become my ally.

'I've decided to sell.'

'I knew you would,' she said. 'I already asked around.'

'Before I –?'

'Leave it to me.'

'But –'

'Leo. I've been in this business longer than you.'

'This isn't pianos.'

'It doesn't matter what it is. Sugar is sugar. Pianos are pianos. Candlesticks . . . What difference does it make? Besides. I'd like.'

She had lost her husband, and her son for a year. Now she had them back, but something was missing. I studied my mother with new eyes. She looked exactly the same. Yet I was uneasy. An innocent in these matters; but who leaves such a project to the discretion of his mother, with her keys and her lavatory brush? Nevertheless, these things were bound to take time; time enough for me to thicken my wrists on rubble and think of other things. Until, too quickly, my mother announced triumph. 'There are always the right people if you look carefully. I'm told, fifty pounds.'

I was unpeeling my overalls in my room. 'It's not enough!' An unpremeditated, ignorant retort.

'Isn't it?' My mother had enjoyed her telephoning. My curt response made her doubt her success. 'Are you sure? Perhaps you're right.'

'Who's your contact?' The words came to me from books, from films. 'I need a name. An address.'

'Erwin Blum. He gets me a lot of things. He's a good man.'

'What sort of things?'

'The eggs, the sugar.'

'What does Pappi say about that?'

'He doesn't say anything. He pretends he doesn't know.'

'Why?'

'Because we're here – what does he say? – "by the kindness of the King's government", so we ought to behave better than other people. We'd never have done something like this at home, so we shouldn't do it where we're strangers.'

'And what do you say?'

'I say he's quite right. Pappi is always right. But at home we didn't need to do it. Here we do. He likes his eggs and his sugar, so he has to pretend everyone else has them too.'

'But everyone else doesn't.'

'*Kleiner*, that's not my fault. Somebody sells eggs and Mr Blum helps me buy them. If I didn't buy them it doesn't mean you'd find them in the market. So what should I do? Not buy eggs so that other people can not buy eggs too?'

'It would be fairer.'

'What's fair? It's not fair that we're here. Wouldn't you rather be at home in Berlin? That's not fair. Ten young men go out in aeroplanes and one doesn't come back. Is that fair?'

'All ten are going out for our sakes.'

'Nonsense. Nobody ever fought a war because they were sorry

231

for someone else.' It was the one pronouncement of that sort I was to hear my mother make. I wanted to hear no more and changed the subject.

'So, Erwin Blum's address.'

She gave me a piece of paper. 'He has a partner. He's branching out. This partner's been travelling, he says, knows what's what.'

'And the partner said fifty pounds? Has he got a name you know?'

'Mr Blum said . . . I've forgotten. Wait a minute . . . he said . . . Finkl. Manny Finkl.'

'Who? . . . Ha!' I couldn't hold the laughter in.

Excluded from my hilarity my mother was wounded. 'What's the matter?'

'Nothing, Mutti. Nothing.' *If I were you I'd keep a sharp eye out for his affection.* 'Does he know you're my mother?'

'How should he know that? Do you know him?'

'Let's just say I've been travelling too.' All of a sudden I was apprehensive. 'Who has the candlestick?'

My mother paled. She had blundered and therefore grew defiant. 'How can they value something if they don't have it?'

'You could have shown it to them here.'

'Leo! I can't have people like that in this house.'

'So you went there?' I tapped the paper with the address.

'No.' My mother waggled her shoulders a little. 'We met for a cup of tea. At Lyons Corner House.'

'Tea!'

'That's what everybody else was drinking.' Then, 'You know, it's a good thing Pappi is away in Birmingham. He wouldn't like this.'

Catch him early, I thought, on a Saturday morning. Finkl was always last out of bed.

Walking the sleeping suburban street, the summer, mindless of destruction, rippling in the trees, I thought of EL in her room revising for her final exams. She was confident, methodical. She knew her subject. In three weeks' time I was to join her to celebrate her inevitable success and the end of a separation she had imposed.

232

She has her priorities right, that's a smart girl, said my father, his approval of EL's priorities laden with innuendo. My girl was bent over her books while I was counting the house numbers looking for a minor criminal who had taken possession of my candlestick.

Only the gardens distinguished the houses one from another. Tea-roses and geraniums, tiny ponds with paved shores, little lawns bisected by pink stone paths curving between house and gate, the last fronds of yellow laburnum. Blue hydrangeas and monkey puzzles. One could get lost here. One could disappear.

Finkl's landlady also had priorities, on her knees in a flowered pinafore applying red stuff to the front step. Her hair was grey, her menfolk away obliging her to take in lodgers.

'Good morning,' I said under my voice, hoping not to alert the neighbours. 'Is Mr Finkl at home?'

She looked up, embarrassed to be caught on all fours, balanced on her wide forearms, and abrupt. 'He is.'

'Might I speak to him?'

'It's very early.'

'I know. I do beg your pardon, but I've come a long way.'

The lady clambered up. 'They all say that. Who shall I say it is?'

'Would you say Leo? An old friend. I'd be most grateful.'

'He seems to have a lot of friends.'

'He was always popular. You're very kind.'

'I don't know about that.' But she liked my manners. 'You'd better wait in the back parlour. Mind my step.'

I skipped over her morning's work and followed her into a dim small room, the light hindered by the leaded lattice of the window. The linoleum of the floor was as red as the front step, the armchairs spotted with sleeping cats. She held the door open for me. 'You can throw them off. Think they own the place. Leo, was it?'

Bees bounced about raspberry canes and a wigwam of runner beans in the back garden. The earth was ridged for potatoes. At another time there would have been flowers and a stone sundial. Finkl had chosen his lodgings with acumen.

'I thought there could be only one Leo who was an old friend.' Finkl, a dressing-gown wrapped around his diminutive body, had

233

slipped into the room and stood now, almost invisible, beside a high-backed chair. 'I was thinking, maybe we should have a get-together, all of us who've come back. And you've pipped me to the post. How are you? You look well. Did you see to the business with the girl?' This was not how I had intended our meeting to proceed. 'Oh, come on. Everybody knew. Mostly old Meyer, but he was close, that one. The worst gossip I ever met. You couldn't get a thing out of him he didn't want to give. Has she offered you something?'

'Who?'

'My landlady. Mrs Mitchell. Mrs Mathilda Mitchell.'

'Should she?'

'I pay her good money. It's board and lodging and courtesy towards my visitors.' No wonder she had remarked on how many there were.

I plunged in. 'Does she know why they come?'

Finkl darted round the chair and squinted up at me. 'They come', he confided, 'to see an old friend, just as you have. Have you seen Rosenthal? No? Schönbach? Also no? Then I'm honoured. I really must get that woman to provide you with something. I remember old friends too, you know. Mrs Mitchell! Where is she? Mrs Mitchell!'

'She's doing something to her front step.'

'Then she should stop. I have to have my breakfast. Will you have some with me, or do you still live on air?'

'Still air.'

'Well, sit down at least.' He patted a chair. 'You came to say hallo and welcome back, and something else.'

Several possible opening gambits rehearsed themselves in my mind. Now, you're a fence, right? Chewing gum or sucking on a sagging cigarette. Finkl, I've got a friend who needs . . . Finkl, suppose someone had something they wanted to sell . . . 'Finkl, have you met my mother?'

'Your mother? Why should I meet your mother? Are you going to introduce me? I'm delighted.'

'I think you have met her. Or perhaps it wasn't you. Perhaps it was Erwin Blum.'

'Ah!' He put his hands together as if he were about to pray, and rested the tip of his nose on the fingers. 'And what were we negotiating about?'

'A small candlestick? Probably silver? Fifty pounds, you said.'

'That was your mother.' A statement, not a question. 'I didn't know she was so broke. She should have gone to a pawnshop if she was hard up and had to raise capital on the family heirlooms. Mind you, they'd have done her no better there. Mean, those people. They take advantage.'

'That candlestick is worth more than fifty pounds.'

'You know this?'

'I should. It's been in the family long enough. There are some things, you know, when you grow up with them, you get to know their value.'

'Funny thing,' mused Finkl. 'A family like yours, comes from Berlin, running away from Mr Hitler, and bring in their luggage a silver candlestick – yes, it is – made by a known English silversmith.' So fifty pounds was probably too little, and Mr Benson had lost an item of worth. 'So I ask myself, if the thing is so important to the family, how badly off must they be to part with it? Or are they trying to get rid of something they came by in . . . unusual circumstances? There is a difference, you know. Ethically speaking. Of course, the money you get boils down to the same.'

'Why?'

'Because you need me. You can't manage without. You don't know your way around. For me, it's a lifetime's work. If I'm not a professional I don't know what I am. But since it's you, Leo, and I'm in your debt, I think I can arrange with Erwin fifty-five pounds.'

'And how much do *you* get?'

'That's not a question you should ask. I have to make a living, so I charge a small commission.'

Was it worth the risk? 'I've changed my mind. I think I'd like to go elsewhere. So give me my candlestick and I'll leave you in peace.'

Finkl spread his child's hands. 'I don't have it.'

'What do you mean, you don't have it?'

'I don't have it here. This is where I live, Leo. Nothing more.'

'And what would Mrs Mitchell say if she knew what you're up to?'

Finkl wagged a finger. 'Not nice, Leo. But, since you ask, I think she'd keep her mouth shut. And for why? Because, like I said, I pay her good money, and, good honest lady that she is, no one is so honest, when they need the money, that they'll risk losing it by asking the wrong questions. So please, for old times' sake, don't spoil a friendship with that sort of talk.'

'But I want my candlestick.'

'Only it isn't yours, is it? You . . . removed . . . it from someone. Someone who's already missed it? You know, Leo, you have to learn not to blush if you want to succeed. Be sensible. Take the fifty-five pounds. It's a generous offer and it'll go a long way if you're careful. I don't have the candlestick here, but if you don't believe me I'll bring it to show you this evening. We can meet again, you and me and Erwin Blum. And if you like he'll explain the situation to you more thoroughly than I have. He's altogether more experienced.'

'Where this evening?'

'I'm very fond of the ducks in St James's Park. So is Erwin. He feeds them on bread crusts. They know him well so you won't miss us. Or you could bring your mother. She knows him too, I think.'

'You shouldn't try and cheat people's mothers.'

'I? Cheat? I'm cheating no one, believe you me. And some people's mothers can look after themselves well. Very well. Eight o'clock. Not too many people then, not too few. Are you sure you won't have something?'

'Not a thing.'

'Perhaps you're right. Mrs Mitchell cooks everything until it's dead.' Finkl held out his hand and I shook it, assuming Erwin Blum's was bigger.

I was not proud of myself. Five pounds extra. I had expected to achieve more. Certainly I had left my mother with the impression that I would achieve more. Instead, I had neither the money nor the candlestick – only a rendezvous by a duck pond with two men who could do very largely what they liked. And I would be alone. Or perhaps not.

*   *   *

236

'*Ciao! Ciao!*' Giusè's Uncle Toni locked his round forearms about my neck and squeezed as if he'd been waiting for me to visit ever since his nephew announced our reunion; the cigarette between his fingers singed my ear. Over his shoulder I saw Giusè grinning and waggling his fingers. And this was his Aunt Gianna, there his two young cousins Stefano and Luigi, there his mother, a woman in black of no determinate years but aged, rocking her grief, offering her hospitality.

Giusè waved her away, explaining, I supposed, that I was an unsatisfactory guest. He slapped my arm a few times. 'So, watcher got going?'

I dropped my voice. 'I need help.'

'Yeah?'

Someone was trying to cheat me, trying to cheat my mother, who had hoped to sell a candlestick for the right price, and been offered the wrong one. Giusè translated and the family gathered round. I had been to see this person but failed to persuade him to improve much on his original offer, failed too to retrieve the candlestick. I was to meet him again, in the evening. He would not be alone.

'And nor will you be, mate.' Giusè had asked no questions at all. 'We're right behind you, eh?' He nudged his uncle's paunch.

'Sure thing, sure thing. We together with you.'

'We gotta stick together, ain't we? Know a thing or two what others don't, you an' me.'

'The man we're going to meet. Manny Finkl. He was on the boat too.'

Giusè whistled. 'I dunno. It takes some.' Then he put an arm round me. 'So you know this geezer, eh? Never mind. Can't all be saints.' Hadn't Meyer said the same? 'Bit of a laugh. My lot against yours. And you in the middle. Piggy-in-the-middle.'

I spent the day with the Tolinis, teaching Stefano and Luigi to make paper boats and swans (Manny Finkl's deft fingers folding and pressing the creases down before my eyes), declining the family's food and then eating it. Erwin Blum was a source of fresh eggs, I told Giusè; my mother bought them. 'Some lady, your mum. Get her in with mine, give 'em a bit of fun, what d'you say?' Mutual incomprehension might make them friends. The widow Tolini, in her brother-in-law's flat, stayed on her feet, bending and sweeping, kneading dough, living somewhere behind her eyes where she nurtured a hollow filled with fury.

Suddenly the urge to give her something unleashed an incautious tongue. 'That candlestick. I stole it.' Giusè shook his head: don't want to know, mate. But I wanted to tell. 'Tell your mother. Tell her that the man I stole it from was the man or as good as the man who sent us all away.'

'No kidding.' He told his mother, who fixed her eyes on me while he was talking, smiled vaguely and shrugged. 'She says, if 'e's lost half as much as she 'as, you've done a great job. But 'e can always get another candlestick. Don't worry.' I must have seemed crestfallen. 'You can only do what there is to do. And we're going to have some fun tonight.'

The water of the duck lake was already dark with approaching dusk but the sky was clear, blue and violet. Silhouetted couples meandered arm in arm, braving the unpredictable skies, and under an overhanging willow ducks and geese churned the water, others skimming arrows of light over its surface, hurrying towards a tall, stooping man with a paper bag in his hands. Pigeons and sparrows bickered at his feet. Manny Finkl perched on a bench.

The Tolinis touched my arms, in concert, taking charge, and melted behind trees. I sat down next to Finkl, my bowels uneasy.

'Nice evening,' he said. 'I forgot what these English evenings could be like.' Side by side we remembered desert sunsets crisscrossed with parrots making the journey home. For a moment I was drawn to him. '*Na ja*. Business time, isn't it?'

'It wasn't like this before.'

'Before? Oh, you mean over there. Look, my friend. That was different. This is real life. Understand?' He was cordial. 'Erwin. Leave your damned ducks.' The tall man shook out his remaining crusts and the scavenging birds, overfed, tore the last fragments from one another's beaks. Carefully he folded the paper bag and put it in his left pocket. The right one bulged with candlestick.

Mr Blum seated himself on my other side. 'So you're Elsie's son?' He held out his hand. 'Erwin Blum.'

'I know.'

'And you're here to drive a hard bargain.'

238

'I wouldn't call it that.'

'Don't make mistakes, little Leo. You should leave these things to your mother.' Was he sneering? 'She knows what's the right price for what. We told her fifty pounds. You didn't like it. Manny offers you five more and you don't like that either. What are we going to do with you, such a greedy fellow? And what will Mutti say if you spoil our relations?' This I hadn't considered, her eggs and her sugar. Yet she had been the one who'd said the candlestick might fetch a lot of money. Fifty-five pounds was a lot of money. But not enough for my purposes.

'I told Finkl I'd changed my mind. I don't want to sell after all.'

'You told him you wanted to go elsewhere.'

'All right. I don't want to sell to you. I want the candlestick back.'

'What candlestick is that?'

'Do you mean you haven't got the candlestick?' I sang out in English.

The Tolinis, summoned, loomed behind us. 'You're not givin' my mate a 'ard time, are you?' Giusè had inflated his chest. His uncle's was anyway a barrel. One tall, one short, Manny Finkl and Erwin Blum were a pair of scarecrows and I thought, I don't want this.

Erwin Blum was on his feet. 'I was not expecting violence. I don't deal in violence.'

'Neither do we, mate. We just deal fair and we like to see the same all round. Which one of you's Mr Finkl?' Manny Finkl vanished into the bench. 'Shipmates ought to stick by one another.' Finkl's eyeballs goggled, disembodied in the gloom. 'Don't get me wrong. You can diddle who you want, not my business. But lay off *Dunera* people. The world's big enough without doing the dirty on us.'

'Us?' Finkl's anguished squeak sounded from under the bench.

'That's right. Him. And me.' Giusè thumped his pectorals. Erwin Blum had retreated towards the water but Uncle Tolini was marking him. 'So let's all stay pals, shall we? You give us what we want, an' we'll go home nice and easy.'

I closed my eyes. Out in this darkening park for my sake, Giusè

239

sounded no longer like my friend but like the raw troops who had taken such pleasure in our humiliation. 'Giusè.'

'Easy, mate. Easy. Won't be a moment, now. Will it, Mr Finkl?'

Finkl re-emerged, pulling money from his pocket. Uncle Tolini was steering Erwin Blum, unresisting, back towards us by the shoulders. The candlestick was in Blum's outstretched hands. Which was it to be? The money, naturally; if not, to whom would I go? 'I have seventy. That's all I have.'

'What's your cut?'

'If I give seventy, I get nothing.'

'Good. You've just done our Leo a favour. It's what old friends are for.' Giusè had come prepared. He took a torch from his pocket and counted out the notes aloud. 'Lovely. Nice doing business with you. *Andiamo*.' And he pulled me away as if afraid I might linger and spoil things.

As we departed Erwin Blum hissed after me, 'You should think who you're with.'

I could not, at first, share the Tolinis' elation, even in the warm lamplight of their kitchen as Giusè recounted and, perhaps, embroidered, our adventure. With a flourish he put the wad of notes in my hand. 'Your earnings, my friend. Spend 'em well. You won't see another sum like that, not in a long while. And cheer up, won't you? Your Mr Finkl's the one what started it. And you don't 'ave to worry. There's no way 'e give us all the money 'e 'ad. 'E ain't such a fool.'

My lot against yours, was Giusè's explanation. Wrong, I thought. Some people settling a difference with some others, no more. But when he turned from his card game, still jubilant at the evening's success, his finger and thumb making a circle of approval, I could have hugged him.

'Eh, fellow,' said widow Tolini, finally seating herself next to me. She took my hand and we sat in silence watching the others play. It seemed to me that Italian was not an impenetrable language.

Seventeen

Every generation's youthful celebrations seem old-fashioned to the next. Looking back now I can see how dull people will consider us, how odd we looked, and dowdy, in our square wide trousers and tailored hair. Photographs in black and white of young people in black and white, running from the notice-boards, some dejected, some exultant, exuberant in that fleeting moment before anti-climax, still students, not quite yet compelled to be adult – it was all there in the eyes crinkled against the sun, the shining teeth.

We were many, the onlookers. There was Major Laing, trudge swing, trudge swing, stumping the pavements as if they were his fields and old Bounder were behind his knee with a wet nose and milky eyes. *But*, and he shook my hand repeatedly, looking me warmly in the eye through his bifocals, *the old fellow's been under the turf six months now, haven't the heart to replace him, though Marjorie says I should*. And Mrs Laing, *you must learn to call me Marjorie*, brandishing the silver plate of her hair in its net container as a reprimand to her wayward daughter: your hair will turn colour and be tamed one of these days, sooner than you suppose. My parents – invited by EL, confidently certain of something to celebrate, in a letter I couldn't countermand – cowered together as uneasy as the Laings. These mothers and fathers, suspecting that there must be an appropriate conduct but finding no one to explain what it was, shared a distress. EL had recognised, as I had not, that their unease in the face of the jubilant young might overcome their unease faced with one another. There was no better place for them, finally, to meet. In a ceaseless swirl of black skirt and dark stockings she placed her father's hand in my mother's, Mrs Laing's in my father's, as if triumphant in reuniting people whom circumstances had separated, good friends wrenched apart whom she was bringing together again. So they joined, the four of them, shyly, to admire her, without words, which was just as well.

Among the guests EL had gathered on the summer pavement was Jeremy, in uniform, an interrupted student, wistful and responsible. His time would come if he lived that long. His face was marked with the lines of reminiscence for those who hadn't. We stood, a little apart, also onlookers who no longer belonged to this place but watched its antics with affection. We exchanged glances, smiles. Then Jeremy pointed to EL and gestured, go get her.

Things being as they were, there were more young women than young men, but the young men swarmed around EL not like bees around a flower, or butterflies on the Hitler's weed, or moths on a night-light, but like blow-flies. I was sickened by the image but Meyer said, *They're creatures like any other. Just because blow-flies don't produce honey, which you happen to like, which I happen* . . . You misunderstand, I countered. If they are blow-flies, then EL is carrion. *Which some day she will be.* I switched him off.

They were oozing eligibility in their black and white, these raw graduates, but I had capital. Batting aside the buzzing things I reached EL and took her by the arm. 'Say goodbye to your friends, we're leaving.'

Her eyes narrowed. For an instant she was motionless. Then, 'Okay.' A silence hovered over us, then broke away. The buzzing recommenced but swarmed off. Delivering EL to the custody of the quartet of parents, I looked back. Jeremy held up both hands, thumbs up.

'Take your time,' wrote Meyer from a rented bungalow in Melbourne by the sea. 'People always rush into things in wartime because tomorrow may be too late. But by the time you find out tomorrow is still there, it *is* too late.' He was planting out a small garden with his sister Frieda. She wanted vegetables. He wanted undergrowth.

I rushed. Giusè rushed. One marriage, then another. Giusè first, too impatient to wait for the readies, to his Barbara, imported from Bologna, bearing his grandmother's imprimatur.

'And you're bleedin' comin' to the church, and you're goin' ter keep your big mouth shut. *Capisci?*'

'I wasn't going to say a word.'

'No smilin' or sneerin', neither.'

'Expressionless, I promise.'

We sat close together, EL and I, theatre-goers at an alien tradition, understanding nothing. EL inhaled the incense and relaxed against me. I regretted my nose and watched Giusè and his family, multiplied for the occasion, process without stumbling through the ritual they had all grown up with, and envied them. Giusè's mother wept silently, not entirely with sorrow. She looked across the dividing aisle and smiled for me. Afterwards we ate, all of us, at long tables in a bare boarded room over a club in Soho, tiny paper Italian flags pinned to the blackout blinds and a picture of Mussolini wisely, and prophetically, upside-down.

Giusè had cooked and vindicated his boast. His new wife, slim as EL, was not likely to remain so. She spoke English like a Mafia hood in a voice culled from films she had watched, secretly, in a dusty back room with a younger brother who had projected them on to a whitewashed wall. She put her arm through her husband's, removed it, returned it, sampling the gesture and finding it pleased them both. She ladled out food; Stefano and Luigi carried plates which they placed carefully in front of everyone except me.

'Hey!' EL, charmed until now, was slighted on my behalf.

But Giusè was bearing down on us holding a tray with a huge domed dishcover. He went down on one knee next to me and removed the dishcover with a flourish. 'Signore!' Three soft-boiled eggs in a glass. 'Right, me old chum?'

I wrapped my hands round the glass. 'Where the hell did you get these from?'

Giusè posted his lips into my ear and whispered, 'Your old friend and mine, Mr Blum. By arrangement. Present from the family to you.' The Tolinis applauded as if it had been my wedding. They watched me in solemn silence while I ate my eggs, Giusè and his uncle and I remembering.

'Perfect,' I said. 'Good as ever. You can cook after all – a bit.'

'Givover.'

By my side EL was brittle. 'What's going on? What's all this about?'

'We go back a long way, my love.' Giusè was soothing. 'Leo an'' his thing about eggs. You gotta get used to that, 'cos 'e won't eat nothing else, or not that I've seen. You should've seen my mum's face, trying to feed him on gnocchi, and 'e's trying to eat it but picking away, an' I says, leave it alone, Mum, it's a waste of time, 'e can't smell nothing, so 'e can't taste nothing neither. All 'e eats is bloody eggs, in a glass.'

'Can't smell?'

''E 'asn't told yer?' EL, hurt, shook her head. 'Blimey!' And Giusè retreated.

'You can't smell?'

'No.'

'Nothing?'

'Not a thing.'

EL set her handbag on her knee and opened it. She took out a tiny bottle of perfume. 'I wondered why he never commented. Wasting my time.' Her head was down. I thought, I should have told her, I should have trusted her the easy way I had trusted the Tolinis. But when she looked up she was laughing. She handed the perfume across the table to Barbara who dabbed some instantly behind each ear and said, 'Gee whizz!'

If Giusè, why not me? Not a church, but Willesden Register Office, decorated like a police station.

It was my mother's day, and EL graciously donated it to her. 'I have found everybody,' said my mother, smug with success. 'Everybody. All your friends. The old one helped me.'

'What old one?'

'Old Mrs Chapman.'

'She's not that much older than you.' But my mother ran a hand over her yellow curls, as if to say it's how you look that matters.

I wore Jeremy's suit, wide and baggy. EL was contained in something dark green. She mostly wears green – as redheads will. Complementary colours, so they say. My mother wore blue, my father black, Mrs Laing grey, like armour. The major was also in black, and uncomfortable. Uncomfortable about so much: his daughter's marriage to a man without prospects; the manner of the betrothal, no permission sought or given; the location dreary, godless (the major was not devout but there comes a time); the rest of the company. On a second meeting the Laings found the Becks less congenial. My mother was, I believe I overheard the major say, 'fluffy'. Less than you suppose, I mumbled grimly to myself, forgetting that I sometimes thought so too. My father's shoes were too shiny, his watch-chain too bright, his nails too polished, his expression too dazed. One military man failed to recognise the other.

Giusè and Barbara – old hands – flaunted experience, Giusè in dog's-tooth brown and white like a bookie, Barbara in a scarlet that should not exist in the British Isles. Henry and Elisabeth, woebegone and sniffing, and Marrrm, sharp as a bird, her hair crisped and coloured like smoke on an autumn evening. She had brought Jason – who was bandy-legged and could no longer walk – in a little cart on wheels which she pulled behind her. EL told me afterwards he farted throughout the short ceremony. The McKechnies had dressed Lucy in a flowered frock she had yet to grow into although she was almost up to her father's shoulder, but the frock had been bought to last. Mr McKechnie, glowering, had been talked into coming by his wife, who must have spoken up for me, excusing the discourtesy of a boy who had neither written nor called round. *Discourteous? Damned rude, Jean. And it's you I'm thinking of. Not to mention Lucy. The lassie's been wondering, you know as well as I do.* His tawny eyes, warm for my parents, were otherwise glacial. Major Laing had spotted the *Daily Worker* deliberately sported in the McKechnie pocket, darned at the edges.

EL, noticing all this, grinned to herself and, on signing the registrar's book, unpinned her hair. Behind her, yellow as butter, Caroline giggled and held out her hands for EL's posy. Jeremy had sent a telegram of cordial good wishes on behalf, he lied, of the family. A hired man took photographs on the steps outside.

Because my mother had baked, the guests were given a wedding tea at eleven in the morning in the front room.

Said Elisabeth to my mother, her hankie in her sleeve for easy access, 'I never thought to see this. It's so wonderful.'

Mr McKechnie was in conversation, in German, with my father, who answered in English.

The major sat, his wooden leg thrust out, and caressed Jason mournfully while Marrrm explained that, much as she believed in euthanasia, the recipient of any terminal treatment must take that decision when of sound mind and in front of witnesses. Jason had expressed no such wish.

Barbara admired my mother's furniture, Giusè her skills as a pastry cook.

Mrs Laing, Henry and Caroline stood in a row and said nothing.

Lucy and Mrs McKechnie gazed at EL, who took my manners in hand. 'We must circulate, I'll go one way, you go the other. Back to back, three steps forward. When I say "fire!", we begin.'

'Free choice of weapons?'

'Always.'

About turn smartly. EL pressed her shoulder-blades into mine, her buttocks too, and we marched forwards. 'Fire!' she hissed. I glanced back to see whom she would choose first and met her eyes on a similar purpose. 'Cheat.'

'Cheat yourself.'

'Thank you so much for coming.' She was holding Mr McKechnie's hand and might charm him. I selected Henry and Elisabeth.

'Oh, Leo.' Elisabeth's hair was greying, her neck weighted by an incipient dowager's hump. Henry held an absent-minded palm under her elbow. 'The old place hasn't changed at all. We wish you'd visit.'

'I shall. I should love to.'

'You look so grown up.'

'He is, dear.'

'Yes, but.'

'I'll . . . we'll come to tea.'

'What a striking girl.'

'Isn't she. Look, I'll be right back. I must just . . .'

'Of course. We understand.'

EL was still with Mr McKechnie. Mrs McKechnie and Lucy, by the wall, smiled wanly like women waiting, with scant hope, to be asked to dance.

'Hallo, Mrs McKechnie. Hallo, Lucy. You're very tall.'

'Why haven't you been to see us?'

'Lucy. Leo's been busy.'

'I've been working, Lucy, on the other side of town.'

'What at?'

'Carrying bricks.'

'Where to?'

'From one place to another.'

'What for?'

'Tidying up after the bombs.'

'We had a bomb in our street. It killed everybody in the house. Mummy wanted to send me to the country but I didn't go.'

Mrs McKechnie directed my eyes to her husband. 'Bob felt we should stay together. I suppose he was right. It's the first time I've been glad to live in the basement, though. How have you been? Bob was following your case, all of you, in the papers. He went to parliament to hear them talking about it. He was writing letters, calling meetings. I've never seen him so angry.'

'Daddy said the government didn't know who it was fighting. It was sending away all the wrong people.' I could imagine Mr McKechnie, at night, rehearsing his indignation on his wife, Lucy in bed, screened by her curtain from light but not sound. 'This is a war of ideas, Jean. And they're more scared of the communists than they are of the Nazis.' Lucy's imitation was exact. How many times must she have heard him say so?

Mrs McKechnie raised her eyebrows at me. And what was I supposed to do, she seemed to be asking. 'He left the party, you know, with the Ribbentrop–Molotov pact. Things have changed now, of course, but he won't go back. Don't tell him I told you.'

'What about the newspaper, then?'

'He only carries it about to annoy people. It's an old one.'

'I'm ashamed.'

'Don't be ashamed. You're young. The young are like that.' Selfish. But she didn't say so. Bob McKechnie would be less understanding and not in the least inclined to observe the proprieties due to the groom on the day of his wedding. Mrs McKechnie scented my apprehension. 'Never mind, dear. And by the way, congratulations. You've done very well for yourself. She's very . . .'

'I know.'

'Get along now. There's others waiting. But for old times' sake.' She hugged me, an interceding aunt. 'It's good to see you again, after all this time.'

'Thanks. I don't deserve it.'

'And me.'

'Lucy. And you, of course.' Lucy's embrace was wiry under her flowered frock.

EL and I passed, elbow to elbow, like dancers in a reel. 'Bob,' she advised. 'Him next, while the smile's still on his face.' Diplomatic relations restored, she left the concluding negotiations to me. Bob to her. To me, always Mr McKechnie.

'That's a fine lass you've hooked there, Leo. Quite a toughie too, I shouldn't wonder.'

'You may be right.'

We stood face to face.

'So what have you to say for yourself?'

'Absolutely nothing. Nothing that will do.'

'Well. I can accept apology. That was an apology, I take it?'

'It was. Abject. Crawling.'

He held up a hand. 'Now, now. I won't have excess. That's just words, which don't count for much in my book. Words come too easily to some people. Have you learned to read the papers?' He tapped his pocket with its old edition. 'The Eastern Front. They'll see to him. They'll see him off, you mark my words. They know what the fight's about. People here, you know, they're obsessed with North Africa, but that's a sideshow. It's in Russia where it counts, and it's the Russians who know it.'

'I thought you'd . . .'

'Jean tell you that? Good. That means she believes it. Makes her feel easier, you know, and I don't want her worrying. No, laddie. Why would I leave?'

'The pact?'

'Under the circumstances, a detail, although I won't pretend I was happy. No. I won't say that. But I would say that the way things are we know who's really taking Herr Hitler seriously.'

'That's not fair. Just because Russia was forced to join in . . .'

'Hardly the way I'd put it . . .'

'And who was fighting alone before, for nearly two years?'

'The people of this country don't know what the word means, Beck. They've had a bit of a shock now, for the first time in centuries, because they thought wars were always fought somewhere else, in someone else's garden. And all of a sudden there are bombs falling all over London, and people, ordinary people, are killed. But make no mistake. There's no comparison between the brave British spirit and what the Russians are going through. And don't let anyone ever tell you otherwise.' His voice had risen and some of his last words had carried. He fixed me with hard eyes which instantly softened as if he had remembered why he was in my parents' house. He put a hand on my arm. 'Your mother and father are in fine fettle.'

'My mother is. I'm not so sure about my father.'

'What do you think about his idea of going to Palestine?'

'What?'

'You didn't know?'

'He hasn't said anything to me.'

'Did you ask? No, you didn't ask. And why should you, I suppose. He's not easy, here, lad. Your mother's found her feet, you're right there, but your old man's not easy. He'll not go, of course, but he'll not settle either. Jumpy, do you understand? Doesn't dare put a foot wrong, scared that you might, scared that any petty crime committed by a Jew will reflect on the lot of you, and I, for one, can see what he means.'

'How can you?'

'Because, laddie, and it costs me something to admit this, there are times when thoughts I don't care for flash through my head, in and out, but flash they do. Now if that happens to me, what is the rest of the population liable to think, given a little ammunition? No, I think your father will only be easy when everyone around him's a Jew, and they can all be as good or bad as the rest of us. But, as I say, he'll not go. He can see your mother's planted herself on English soil and she's flourishing.'

We both looked across the room at my mother, who was, indeed, flourishing, her halo of curls jaunty with dye as she fed our guests, apparently insouciant of my father standing in silence, rubbing his knuckles and staring into the middle distance. *I have returned you to your father*, said Meyer, *but you have to outgrow us both*. It was not something I would be able to explain to my father. I would have to show him how it could be done, make him secure, give him red-headed grandchildren. And there she was, my tall, elegant wife, his good-hearted visitor, taking his hands, kissing his cheek until his eyes cleared, tucking her arm into his elbow and gliding over the floor with him to her parents.

'Leave it to her,' advised Mr McKechnie, reading her accurately. 'She knows what she's doing, that one.' For the time being the Laings smiled at my father for her sake and because an old embarrassment demanded it. 'You've married into England with a vengeance there.' Mr McKechnie snorted with pleasure.

'I didn't plan it that way.'

'Did you not?' The Laings bent their heads to my father with painful courtesy and EL moved on. 'So medicine's taken a knock, is that right?'

'You always knew it would.'

'I'm not saying I'm sorry. But of course your mother and father . . .'

'Yes.'

'Well, you can't become a doctor for other people's satisfaction.'

'You're not the only person who's said that to me.'

'And you listened, finally . . . So what's it to be, if it's not medicine? Are you going to support your wife by writing bad poetry?'

'Not at all. I'm going to become a restaurateur.'

The word dropped into a hole of silence and ricocheted off the furniture. Mr McKechnie's mouth was a cavern. More distant faces, indistinct, paled and bobbed. They swayed a step closer like children playing grandmother's footsteps.

I stilled them. 'I have a chef.'

'Fuckin' hell, mate.' Giusè whistled.

'And I have the capital.' The price of a candlestick. My mother's body swam into focus, piling up plates. 'It only remains to find the premises.'

Did my wife blanch? She did not. She crossed the floor and placed herself erect and defiant by my side.

Eighteen

Who now does not know the name of Tolini's? Four stars in Egon Ronay, recommended even in the *Guide Bleue*, never an empty table and bookings taken a week in advance except Tuesday lunchtimes, closed on Mondays. Don't bother to come if you're not creditworthy. The menu, only *à la carte*, also offers any dish of a client's own description if he's prepared to wait. Among the desserts a declared favourite is a flambé in kirsch on a bed of crisp cinnamon biscuits topped with meringue and ice cream. It goes by the name of Bombe Benson, which, the waiters will tell you, has a story behind it, tapping their noses and saying no more. Tolini's ice cream is celebrated, and sold under franchise by Harrods, Fortnum's and one or two other select purveyors of quality foods in a dozen countries. Its handmade chocolates retail at rather too much a bite, but customers have yet to complain. Nobody ever made money by being cheap – a maxim of my father's and entirely untrue. We began by being cheap, the capital's first Italian sandwich bar, serving from a hatch cut in the side of a van catering to my colleagues in the Pioneer Corps, moving with them like a wagon-train from bombsite to bombsite, nourishing appetites, nurturing a future clientele (some of the early stomachs now have offices in Hatton Garden and mansions in Millionaires' Row), building a reputation on Giusè's invention, with choice items – at a price – courtesy of Erwin Blum and Manny Finkl.

'A restaurant?' exploded EL in private on our wedding night, deprived of her poet. 'You don't even eat.'

'Well, and I won't be doing the cooking either. Think of me as the *éminence grise*. I don't need to eat, or be seen to be eating, to be that.'

'And you're calling it Tolini's.'

'What Italian restaurant was ever called Beck's?'

'But why?'

Had I done it again, floundered for the nearest word to save me from those who drummed their fingers waiting for me to present them with my future? I hedged. 'It needn't be for ever. I'll see how it goes. Nothing need be for ever. Besides . . .' The Tolinis had opened their door to me without a motive, beckoned me in, sat me down, suggesting, join us. Reason enough, I thought, if only for a while.

EL frowned, unconvinced. 'That depends on where for ever begins and ends. And what am I supposed to do in the meantime?'

'Whatever you want. Whatever wives do. Excuse my inexperience but I have only our two mothers to go by. Do you want to emulate either of them?'

'No fear.'

'Do you want to have children?'

'No. Well, one, possibly.'

'Only?'

'Judging by me, judging by you, one's enough. I shall teach it to ride.'

'You wouldn't teach me.'

'You're scared of horses. My child won't be. And what will you teach it?'

'I shall teach "it" nothing at all. I shall tell stories at bedtime.'

'In what sense of the word? Fables? Tall tales? Out-and-out fibs? It's bedtime now. Tell me one.'

'No. You're a lousy listener.'

'I'll make an effort.'

'Then you might fall asleep on me. Can't have that. Not tonight.'

'Of all nights.'

But later, when we lay sweating in our bed under the cracked paintwork of the small Bloomsbury honeymoon hotel, EL probed me with her nose and piped up again. 'But you can't smell anything. How will you know if what you're serving hasn't gone off?'

'I shall trust to Giusè's nose.'

'He's got a nose, all right.'

It was, without doubt, a snag. Still the child determined to outrage, EL was prepared to defend my project in public, but she did not actually like Giusè and Barbara, whose affection had made me love them. They were too loud, they were uneducated, their taste in clothes betrayed them.

'You're a snob.'

'I am not.' She was. She is, and fights it.

Giusè was my partner, but then so was my wife. So work and home were to be each in quarantine. EL didn't want us to be for ever with the Tolinis, nor they with us. Had she known more, anything, about the running of a restaurant she would have understood that there are few hours free of ordering, of shopping, dicing, chopping, slicing, mixing, cleaning, planning – quarrelling, though never with me; the Tolinis fought amongst themselves in stereo and in Technicolor. There were too many of them in Uncle Toni's rented accommodation. But when Giusè took out a loan and bought his first house, which was no cottage, he installed his Barbara, then sent a pantechnicon and a gang of men to remove his mother, his aunt and uncle, Stefano and Luigi and disperse them about his property; posted a one-way ticket to Bologna which extricated his grandmother moments before she opted for the grave; clapped his hands and bawled at his assembled family louder than ever, his voice now having a greater distance to travel.

Giusè was not a bully but the boss, in his father's image, which required him to maintain a modicum of volume. It also required him to reproduce. One, two, three children, so it went, not quite year by year: solid Catholic though he was, he was more careful of his wife's health than of his soul. By agreement, being anyway beyond salvation, I purchased condoms every Thursday, by the packet. How they subsequently found their way on to his energetic penis was a secret which even regular confession never revealed. Since I paid for them I felt I had an interest not only in the thwarted generations Giusè spilled into them but also in the few he allowed to escape, and was, consequently, a godfather to them all. I say 'a' godfather because Barbara was as principled as EL.

'You ain't gonna get woiked up, Leo honey, are you?' Godfathers who may be called upon to fulfil their obligations are expected to have some relationship with the Almighty, however tenuous. Mine was in doubt. Real godfathers, therefore, were imported for the baptisms and ushered out again, reserving their duty for the future. I was allocated a different role because I was Giusè's partner – an equal partnership incidentally, for the candlestick had been procured by me but secured by him – and the man who enabled Barbara to retain the ghost of her maiden figure, and their old friend. Being godfather to Andrea, Sandro, Paulo, Domenica and, finally, Leonora was to give me almost unlimited access to the ears of children.

'Rabbits,' exaggerated EL, without spite, unaware of the restraints being exercised. Every year that a Tolini child was born was one that EL failed to conceive, which distressed her less than my mother thought it should, who nevertheless dared not harry her directly.

'Leave him alone,' said my father with some impatience. 'God sends children when He wants to.'

'God?' My mother was doubly incredulous. 'That's not the way people get children.' And she nudged him lewdly in the ribs so that he blushed. What had come over her in this country? All the same he did venture to ask me if I got on well with my lovely wife. I got on well. Pumping furiously but getting no issue, forgetting sometimes to will my seed to take firm root because behind our flimsy front door we laughed and read aloud to one another and picked the splinters from our thighs when we got up from the chairs I had made out of orange-boxes.

Even at the time, we knew we were only playing at marriage, still living like undergraduates with a mattress on the floor. EL saw me to the door in the morning, closed it behind me and tied a scarf over her hair. She piled the orange-boxes together on the table, pulled our books from the shelves we had made from bricks and planks, and stacked them beneath the table. She filled a wide brush with dark paint and coloured our ceiling midnight, against the express wishes of the landlord. By the evening the furniture was restored and I was invited to notice that something was altered in our room – coquettishly, almost, arms round my neck, 'men never notice anything', in another woman's voice. But the moment would pass, and in the later lamplight she reverted to herself so that sometimes I was scalded by her sceptical appraisal when she hoped I was reading but saw I was totting up figures instead. Yet we would walk together, after dark, arm in arm, easy in our silence.

She ironed my shirts, inexpertly, on the table, and without conviction. We were only dabbling so I didn't much mind. I didn't much notice.

She swept the floor in the morning, was sweeping as I left, but hustled her energy through museums and galleries, fidgeted while lunchtime concerts played, then with white paint and a fine brush picked out the curlicues of the plaster rose in the centre of the ceiling. When I came home in the evenings I would find my volumes of poetry lying as if someone had just been reading them or was just about to. I noted how she noted that I did not pick them up. But I am a restaurateur now, I pointed out, without a word – just for the time being. I was doing well enough to buy a four-poster for my wife, had she wanted it. Yet we didn't even move from the flat I had rented in West Hampstead, two rooms and a kitchen corner, the bathroom shared with the tenants over the hallway. The ghost of EL's poet lingered in it, and I didn't mind. Giusè, his eyes already on a suburban villa with a conservatory and garage, was saddened. If he had the money, or could persuade the bank he shortly would have, why did I not do the same?

'Because they ain't got kids, sweetheart.' To Barbara it was obvious. Giusè winced at her lack of tact, her apron rucked over Paulo. Her skin had begun to coarsen, her ankles to thicken, and she no longer had time to put the hot irons in her luscious hair.

'Get a nanny, get a cleaner,' I counselled in return when Giusè related his wife's exhaustion.

'You think I 'aven't tried? She won't hear of it. "It's my kids an' it's my house an' I in't havin' no one messin' it about." That's what she says.'

He was proud, although EL was still the girl with the alabaster skin, unblemished by lack of sleep and undismayed by the reticence of motherhood. Her hip-bones grated on mine and clothes hung on her with unpremeditated perfection. As the war came to an end she sat on the lavatory, the door bolted, eating Erwin Blum's Del Monte tinned peaches (sliced and in halves) from the tin, and emerged, her lips sweet from the syrup and salty from the blood where the jagged edge had nicked them as she drank off the last drops of juice. Fresh blood and syrup, I thought, licking the mixture away, odourless but with the taste of sex.

Meyer wrote. 'I take it all back.' The newsreels in the cinemas

255

had followed the victorious into the camps to linger on the heaped and contorted corpses and on the stiffened living whose buttocks had withered away. 'I had no right to lecture you about humanity. My people have done this to your people, and I don't know why. What frightens me most is that we may never know why, in which case I may have to accept that there is something peculiarly evil innate in us.'

'You're an Australian now,' I responded lamely, preferring the old lectures to the new breast-beating. 'Besides, someone once told me that it was not a question of peoples, but the iniquities of mankind, the failings of the species.'

He retorted by return of post. 'Don't give me excuses. I don't want them.'

But I didn't want to hear Meyer's proxy confession.

He was disconsolate. 'Your trouble is that you have an inadequately developed sense of vengeance.' Which startled me. How had I financed Tolini's – no longer a sandwich bar but a neat eatery of medium size – if not out of a sense of vengeance? But Meyer was on the other side of the world in a white-painted weatherboarded bungalow where the light was bright. London, no longer fighting, had resigned itself to boiled food and chipped plates. The Pioneer Corps, demobbed, were living in prefabs, the cavities where bombs had been were destined to become car parks, the Hitler's weed was fading and the sky was suspended low. Now the only points of colour were Tolini's tablecloths and EL's hair.

And EL chafed. The passing years were resembling for ever. She was nearing thirty. One can wait only so long. 'I don't have enough to do.'

'I don't have much.'

'You're running a restaurant.' Still, after all this time, after six years. You should be doing something else.

'Actually, I'm not.' Tolinis ran the restaurant, a family concern as it proclaimed itself to be, leaving to me only the mathematics which I did in my head, my mouth clamped shut, then with a slide-rule, later still a calculator. Now, of course, a young woman and an accountant – on whom I check more often than he knows – have made even that effort unnecessary. 'What's the matter? What do you want?'

'I'm going to start a business. Can you lend me something to get me going?'

'EL! Lend? Why lend? How much do you need?' Then, 'What business?'

'Cosmetics.'

'Gee whizz! – as someone would say. Why that?'

'Ah. Now you're asking me. Because I'm tired of the tawdriness of everything and everyone. This country is overcome with allotment mentality, all of them growing sprouts. And have you noticed, if ever you ask people why they're so dull, so down in the mouth, they say, "There's been a war on, you know", as if that was the answer to the whole damned caboodle? I want people to be frivolous and gorgeous and kick austerity back where it belongs.'

'But you're so colourful already, you don't need cosmetics, you don't use cosmetics.'

'And you don't eat.' So there.

Tipsy with excitement, crowding over a small table on the upholstered chairs – a concession to a boss's dignity – we launched the House of Laing. It was a joke, and meant to be, and my idea. She laughed at the swagger of it. 'That's a bit much.'

'If I know you,' I said warily, 'I doubt it.' And I watched her stirring her first tentative inventions like an apprentice kitchen-hand, watched her grasp the label impatient with conviction, watched her grow into the skin that deserved the bumptious company name.

I take it for granted now but at first I was tickled by the notion that the clientele of Tolini's were decorated in my wife's colours. She kept her unadorned face with its violet eyes to herself. Eleanor Laing was to be as invisible in her company as the name of Beck in Tolini's. Shrewd. Avoiding publicity she attracted it. She has known what she was doing from the beginning when the nation yearned for a washing machine, and she poured her potions into jars of pure white, the colour of hygiene, set the white jars into white boxes, and let it be known that within them was the key to an alternative epoch. And who did not wish to believe her?

She learned to be an early riser and drank her coffee black, no lipstick mark on the cup, setting out crisp and clean, her skirt swinging like a girl's, to join the men and women who worked for

257

her. She knew about the wives and boyfriends, the awkward land-lord and the ailing cat. The men and women warmed to her, and were a little frightened too.

'And I want to make money. If you like, I'll race you to the top.' She meant it.

So we locked our feet into the starting blocks, buttocks high, knuckles down, nodded to one another and bounded off, following our tracks, keeping within the lines. Instantly EL was ahead, a more determined racer, a worker, gritting her teeth for the frivolity she had determined to espouse.

As for me, in three decades I have chosen and negotiated as many new premises, buying always when the market was down, selling when it was up, have decided on the furnishings and their source – another family concern – and arranged the exclusive marketing of our sidelines. I have played the stockmarkets by tele-phone and, taking my mother's lead, dealt in futures. The lunch-time diners, noticing the man at the rear table eating soft-boiled eggs, have been told with a wink when the chef made his rounds to assure himself everyone was content, 'That's the gaffer' – explaining away the eccentricity and implying that the statement was not to be taken entirely at face value. On Mondays I ate with the Tolinis at home, my cars growing in horsepower as their residences increased in splendour. Small Tolinis in high-chairs made to measure chattered in Italian, mouths ringed with tomato sauce, and fed me morsels from their plates with grubby fingers. It was understood that not one of them would consider the after-noon nap of Barbara's regime without Uncle Leo's bedtime story. Little Leonora's first English words commanded, 'You say one-a-pon-a-time', her head in the grip of her mother's fingers, her grim-acing face obliterated by a hot face-flannel. In houses big enough for them to have a room apiece they were dealt into beds and cots in the nursery they shared, variously sucking thumbs and fingers, while I lay on my back on the thick white rug, arms folded under my head, and began. None of us knew how the story would go; all were eager to find out.

The tales that fell from my unwitting mouth grew with the chil-dren. The teddy bear who had no nose – a handicap when it came to competing with others in the business of sniffing out honey –

258

yielded to adventure and mystery, ill-doers apprehended by nous alone, no blows exchanged so no muscle required. By the time the story-telling was transferred from siesta to dusk, Giusè at work, EL at work, only Barbara at home, I fabulated for the growing girls, whose ponies were at livery not far away, and serialised a saga about Janie and her immense black stallion, King Kong, with whom she could converse and who made Champion the Wonder Horse snort with envy. Distant but indulgent, EL schooled me in the necessary vocabulary of fetlocks and spavins, martingales and brow-bands, although Janie, naturally, rode her friend bareback, spurning reins and bit. We would all fall asleep, they in their beds, I on the floor, and in the early hours Giusè would tap me awake and send me on my way.

We were still almost young, not much past thirty. It was a Wednesday and the beginning of the season of funerals. I was called to help them bury Marrrm, who had died in her sleep, prescient, for the face they let me see was irritated that she should precede anyone into the grave.

EL held my arm as the daffodils jogged at our feet and men in black put Marrrm in her place. Elisabeth wept, for now she was released too late and would be lonely. Henry stared bleakly at the box in which his mother lay and said nothing. My parents, younger than Marrrm but older than Henry and Elisabeth, shook their heads warily. Then EL vomited.

My mother, relieved, hurried to her aid. 'She's young. She hasn't seen death before.' And she pulled a bottle of House of Laing cologne from her bag. Millions had died but one need not have seen death before.

A week later an envelope arrived, black-rimmed, containing a black-rimmed card on which Frieda Meyer, having found a German printer, announced the death of her brother in Gothic script.

'What's that?'

There was nothing I could say, having said nothing before. 'Someone's died.' If you have not spoken of the living, how can you begin to describe the dead? On the other side of the world, Meyer, in his clapboard house, had kept me in place. Must I start all over again without him?

EL picked up the envelope and looked at the postmark. 'Australia,' she remarked, frowning over the lettering on the card. 'Klaus Meyer? Who's that?' – and vomited again.

Giusè's grandmother was ninety-eight and glazing an apple tart. Usually she stood to do it. Suddenly, leaving half the tart unvarnished, she sat. Receiving the news EL vomited for the third time and went to find her black hat.

We closed Tolini's for the day with a notice in the door and followed the coffin in a cavalcade of black Austins provided by the undertaker, until Giusè erupted from his and we completed the journey on foot. Leonora, still a toddler, sat on my shoulders, Andrea and Paulo held my hands. Barbara had her hands over the shoulders of Domenica and Sandro, Giusè's hands were over his eyes. My parents were more cheerful: Giusè's grandmother had been older even than Marrrm, but timorous. There were so many Italians that the noise drowned the rhythm of EL's persistent retching.

'Oh, lumme. Never mind,' wept Giusè, comforting his wife to be comforted. 'Can't say she didn't live 'er life. Place is going to be empty, though. Feels like there won't be no one there any more, not hardly.' He plucked Leonora from my neck and slotted her on to his, holding the chubby ankles in one hand. 'Praps we oughter 'ave another. Whatcher reckon?'

But tear-stained Barbara, dutiful and sincere, wriggled away. 'It's not my turn this time. It's hers.'

Behind a rose bush EL straightened slowly but flustered, the focus of an Italian village. For some reason she glanced at her watch, then down at her flat stomach and said, 'Crikey.'

Sometimes I thought I could feel my child growing under my hands. Get ready, I said silently, because I am getting ready; in future, when I say 'we', I shall speak for the three of us; others, looking at us, will say 'they', and throw around us a cordon of connection. Sometimes I thought if I did not keep my hands on my child she would not grow. Blue veins embroidered EL's straining belly and we would look at them, at it, astonished. She remained thin but for this grotesque, beautiful excrescence and we made love tentatively, the child between us shifting and stretching. But when

EL stood, eating a piece of toast and looking out of the window, a hand supporting her back, her profile brought me nearly to tears for the inevitability of it. Her hair was impossible in a slant of early autumn; her slender fingers, distracted, traced curlicues on the table-top, her mind wandering, who could say where. Everything that made her who she was and therefore no one else was undermined by the obdurate growth inside her which we had begun and which now would not stop. *One individual is much like another*, said Meyer, *except for the details. But then it's the details that make it all so interesting. Of course the process is the same, you don't change it, you don't escape it. The best you can do is describe it.* How odd that the baby for whom I had been waiting should so sadden me by personifying the relentlessness of existence.

When EL sat down she couldn't get up without help; when she lay down she could only roll sideways out of bed. She laughed. 'Good God, and to think some people do this all the time.' She was well, and she was curious.

Giusè's mother would have waited on EL if she had been allowed. My mother was forbidden entrance and squeaked piteously at the door. Only Marjorie would have been welcome because she wouldn't fuss, because she pulled the foals from her mares, for which reason she kept away, largely unchanged except for the deepening of her voice. The major, I thought, was wringing his hands on the other end of the telephone, unable to disguise his illicit anxiety. 'Good healthy stock,' he said tremulously. 'Shouldn't have any trouble. Only she's a bit narrow in the beam, if you get my meaning.'

To this day the only birth I have seen has been that of a horse. I think I regret this. They telephoned me and I heard EL's voice, an ordinary voice that had already put behind it I could not imagine what alien sounds. 'It *is* a girl.'

They held my daughter, wrapped, up to a glass window for me to see, but I was paying for this room and for this nurse and walked through the door. Under her bedclothes EL had been deflated, the tight high belly gone as if it had never been, its contents expelled and parcelled. The nurse I was paying for held the child and glared at me, held out but held on to the baby lest her father infect her.

We had agreed. Joanna opened her eyes, deep violet, and stared from them with a sort of drunken myopia, turned them on me and halted them. We looked intently at one another. 'I am listening,' she seemed to say, 'so begin, why don't you?'

I reached out to take her but the paid nurse retreated and at that moment Joanna's arms struggled from their bindings, she flung them behind her head where they remained, she arched her back and it stiffened. The nurse, whose grip had tightened round her, stared down at what she held, shouted something and ran with my daughter away.

'Follow her! For Christ's sake, follow her!' EL was screaming and tussling out of the bed, running ahead of me in her bare feet, a patch of blood on the back of her nightdress and blood dropping on her ankles. Ahead of us the nurse galloped shouting along the corridor, swallowed by swing doors, and we followed. Joanna disappeared into a welter of white arms. Side by side and mute, EL and I stood outside those arms, our own involuntarily reaching out.

'She's fine. She's all right. I'm sure she'll be all right now. Lovely child.'

But when I looked again into my daughter's eyes they had turned grey.

They came that day, the grandparents and the well-wishers, bringing flowers, bringing chocolates, to adore the late-come child, who slept. On a bank of pillows EL received her visitors and pulled a social smile from an old repertoire. Then we were alone, gazing down from our two sides into the cot, strangers searching for a future in a wishing-well, and when our eyes met across the body of Joanna we saw mirrored the knowledge that our daughter had been but gone again.

At midnight they called me out. A young paediatrician forestalled me outside EL's room. 'We don't know what's causing it. I'm afraid I cannot predict the effect.' Convulsions were whipping through the soft limbs as if a distant hand were toying with an electric charge, on and off, curiously and dispassionately. Colours had flooded over the baby's features, blue, deadly white, then returning her to herself. The malign hand raised from the button, she lay in the white arms limp as towelling only to stiffen, fingers and toes become claws, her cheeks sapphire, the colour drained from her staring eyes. 'We shall want to see her regularly. It's too early to say yet, of course.'

We had known already it was too late.

Nineteen

We fought Joanna for a year. She was healthy. She fed with inexorable insistence and she grew. But we could not hold her. The touch of our fingers seemed to return her to her early torment and she writhed, repelled, away. A hinged arm of metal over her cot held the bottle to which she clamped her mouth, sucking with breathless fury, the life in her demanding sustenance. We changed her nappies in turn, struggling with a small body powerful in its anger. She did not cry but wailed tirelessly without tears in a monotonous mooing. We fled from the sound in opposite directions to distant rooms of the foolish house I had bought, and separately, our hands over our ears, we opened secret bottles and emptied them.

When she slept she was round-cheeked, her hair darkening from strawberry to flame, and her arms were plump. Then one could pretend that the eyes would open, violet, that she would raise her arms and smile. But when she woke, revived after only a few minutes, her irises were leaden.

Outside Giusè was lighting candles.

'Tell him not to bother.' EL's voice was cracked with nicotine, her fingers yellowed to the knuckles. 'Tell him not to goddam interfere.' She had barked the grandparents away.

Then one morning she too was gone, leaving the curt instruction, 'Remove her. Please.'

I strapped lowing Joanna into her carry-cot and drove to the hospital where they had been waiting, predicting our defeat. Abruptly our daughter fell silent.

St Matthew's is a pleasant institution. They encourage visitors. They know what they are doing. In those days it was a two-hour journey by car. Now there is a motorway and one can make it in half the time. They keep bees beyond the orchards and the honey is popular. EL would not see the place, for she had never had a daughter. 'Perhaps', said the matron as they wheeled the pram away, 'you'd better leave it for a little while. Come again in a week or so. Give her time to settle in.' Other people's children watched my departure with neither interest nor anxiety.

I drove away at speed, the silence behind me weighing on my chest, my throat tight with what I had done. Twin violet eyes set in flawless skin regarded me without blinking.

There was a light in the upstairs front room of my house. I switched off the engine and braced myself for entry. Switched on again and drove to the Tolinis'.

'You gotta go back.' Giusè offered me brandy. 'You can't leave 'er like that alone in the house. You don't know what she's doin'. You gotta go back.'

'I can't.'

Barbara sat with Leonora encircled in her lap, her eyes vast with compassion and unspoken opinion. The little girl's eyes were heavy with readiness for her bed, her thumb in her mouth, her arm squeezing her teddy, upside-down. She leaned against her mother, whose chin rested on her dark head, whose fingers absently twirled a curl of her daughter's hair. She would not have given away her child so easily, I thought. She would have managed.

'Go with him, Giusè.'

'Better not.'

The brandy burned my mouth but I swallowed it. The four older children stood in a group inside the door, staring at me. I had not seen them for almost a year.

Suddenly Leonora wriggled away from Barbara's embrace and stumped over to me, chubby-footed on the floor. She tugged my elbow and held up her teddy. 'You. You say one-a-pon-a-time?'

Giusè snatched her up. 'Sorry, mate. She doesn't understand.'

'It's all right,' I said. 'I'd like to.'

The children by the door parted to let us through, Leonora leading me by the hand, and swung round behind us. Looking back I saw Barbara shaking in her husband's arms.

Leonora clambered up over the raised side of her cot – she hadn't

265

been able to do that before – and settled down on her bedding, her round thumb in her mouth, the forefinger hooked on her nose, eyes waiting. Still in their clothes the others sat on the floor.

'Aren't you going to lie down, Uncle Leo?' Sandro pointed to the white rug. I'm listening. Begin, why don't you?

I lowered myself to the floor and stretched out. The violet eyes looked down at me. 'Once upon a time.' But there were no words in my mouth. 'Once upon a time.' Only salt and saliva, and the dregs of brandy. 'I'm sorry. I don't think . . .'

Then ten-year-old Andrea was lying next to me, his arms folded under his head. His voice was high. 'Once upon a time, there was a teddy bear who had no nose. And when all the other bears went out into the woods hunting for honey, this bear sat at home alone and rubbed his ears.' Domenica sat astride my legs, then lay face down on me, her breath on my chest, her toes on my knees. I wrapped my arms round her. '"It's not fair," said the bear, "I'm fed up with grubs and insects. I want some honey."'

Domenica moved in my arms and a lock of hair fell across my mouth. What was the fragrance of a child? Particles of silver dust came and went in a column of setting light. They would be feeding her, those kindly strangers who had undertaken what I had abandoned, bending over Joanna in her bed, speaking soothing words, their practised hands calming the spasms from her. Why could I not do that? Why had I not had the patience or the capacity? My ears filled with a moaning wail and she flailed from side to side. I held her with all my strength to contain her as I had never held her before.

'You're hurting.' Domenica was struggling and my arms fell away.

'*E! Bambini. Andiamo.*' Giusè lifted Domenica on to his shoulders and knelt beside me. 'I'm gonna run you 'ome.'

'I'll go by myself.'

'No you bleedin' won't.'

'But my car –'

'Fuck the car.'

Leonora was asleep on her face, her thumb slipping from her mouth.

*   *   *

266

EL stood on a ladder, her hair tied under a scarf. Three of the walls had been painted. She had nearly finished the last. Bright white, the colour of hygiene. The room was without furniture. Across the street Giusè stood on the pavement under a streetlight looking up at the window. I raised my hand and he disappeared.

EL's arm swept the paint back and forth, replenished the brush in the tin of emulsion, swept again.

'How does it look?' She pulled the scarf from her head with a hand speckled white.

'Very professional.'

'The light's uneven. I've probably missed bits. We'll be able to tell in the morning. But I had to get it done.'

'Yes.'

'I'll leave the ladder for tonight, in case.'

'All right.'

'I think I'll go to bed now.'

'Shall I come too?'

EL stretched her arms above her head and one of her elbows cracked slightly. 'If you don't mind, I'd rather not.'

'EL?' She waited. 'Shall we go away together for a while?'

'Away? I couldn't. I've got work to do. Good night.'

'Good night.'

Halfway out of the door, her back to me, she paused. 'Elisabeth was lucky.'

Uncle Toni was said to be crippled with gout. 'Someone's got to get the veg.' Giusè's late nights were telling on him and the dawn markets in the dark before sunrise made him shiver. It was by way of an order. 'Barbara can come with you, so's you don't get done.'

'I won't get done.'

'Oh yes, you will. You can't tell a good cabbage from a cowpat. You got to 'ave the nose for it.'

'I'll manage.'

I learned, and have loved the dawn streets ever since. 'Where's old man Tolini? Laid up, is he, poor sod? So who are you when you're at 'ome?' I daresay they made a fool of me to begin with but my fingers still recognise a melon's readiness at the first caress and I can spot a poor tomato in the dark. Word came down and they called me 'the gaffer', but laughed. I drove the Bedford van with 'Tolini's' inscribed along the sides. The crates of vegetables were a more tangible contribution than balancing the books.

Letters from St Matthew's assured me my daughter had made herself at home and suggested the time had come to visit; they asked if previous letters had, by any chance, failed to arrive.

'We'll all go,' said Giusè. 'Make a day of it. Sunday. Picnic in the country. Kids'll love it.' The offer goaded me to go alone. 'Take her a present. Somethin' she'll remember you by' – demonstrating how little he had understood. 'Thought this would do. Real cuddly.' The fluffy elephant was planted on the passenger seat. 'If you don't like it, tell 'er it come from 'er Uncle Giuseppe.' He banged the roof of my car and sent me on my way.

The gardens were bathed in autumn, the lawns dried by the summer and still warm. At the gate they pointed her out. A young woman was pulling a low wooden cart on wide rubber wheels. In it sat a child dressed in green, red ringlets on her neck, flapping her arms stiffly from the shoulders as if she were considering take-off.

I stood in their path. 'Hallo. Is that . . . ? Is she Joanna?'

'Are you her father?' I waited for the reproach, which was denied me. 'Look, Joanna. Your daddy's here.' My daughter flapped her arms more vigorously, disappointed that her carriage had come to a stop. I sat on the grass and put the elephant in her lap. 'Isn't that lovely? You are a lucky girl.'

The arms halted. Tentatively she picked up the elephant and sucked on the end of its trunk, held it up in the air, and bounced it in her lap. She turned to the young woman and smiled, pressed the tip of her tongue between her curving lips and blew a long farting raspberry.

'Joanna! . . . She does that all the time. It's how she communicates.'

'What is she saying?'

'Nothing. Everything. Whatever you want, really.'

'But she smiles. She smiled at you.'

'She smiles at everyone.'

'May I take her?'

Walking backwards I trundled the little cart over the rounded lawns away from the young woman, and the arms flapped, up and down, strong arms, full of energy. In a dip by a stone bench I sat beside her and took the elephant in my hand. Joanna grasped it with both of hers and turned eyes of slate on me. I released the elephant. 'Listen,' I said. 'This is Oswald. He's very greedy but he's also very shy.' Joanna smiled at Oswald and her lips farted. The curls on her neck carried the sun.

'Mr Beck. How do you do.' The matron wore tightly laced brogues. 'I should have liked to have a word with you before you saw her.'

'You've done wonders. She's so happy.'

'She seems content, yes.'

'She's so much better.'

'No. No, she's no better, only different.'

The matron had forgotten what I remembered, forgotten the bellowing, wracked body. 'But she's sitting up, she responds.'

'There was never any doubt that she would sit up. And she's not responding. I'm sorry. At least not in the way you want.'

'She smiles.'

'Yes, she smiles. But it's neither here nor there.'

'But before she only . . . made noises.'

'Well, yes. That much has changed. She is calmer.'

I stood up and began pulling Joanna back up towards the house. It was too soon to argue but perhaps St Matthew's was not the right place for my child. They were overworked, inclined to be defeatist, blind to their own miracles. I would visit her again. I would take her out, and she would learn to listen.

The matron took the handle of the cart from my hand. 'If you'd care to see the Director. He'd be only too happy . . .'

'No. Thank you. Another time. Next time maybe.'

'So you'll be coming again?'

'Certainly. Soon. Very soon.'

'Well, we'll be very glad to see you.' Speaking on behalf of my daughter and, with careful manners, for herself.

How had they done what they had done? How had they wrought the transformation? How much more might not be achieved if there were time to spend with Joanna every day, one person every day with patience and concern only for her? The road stretched in front of me and I nursed the steering wheel in my hands. I sat myself beside her on the grass and she turned her head, and smiled. I knelt by the side of her bed and she put out her arms. I gathered up my coat, preparing to leave and she said, 'Stay.'

'So? 'Ow did it go?'
  'You must come. You must all come. Not just yet, maybe, but you must all come. Or I'll bring her out to visit. Something.'
  'You told the wife?'
  'I will.'

Once a week, sometimes twice, then daily, I made my way through the countryside along roads whose every bend became familiar, and I charted the turning of the leaves, the whitening of the naked branches, the renascent buds. Joanna smiled without fail, sitting in the cart from which she would not be parted. Oswald accompanied her. He had once been part of a travelling circus, which he disliked because the many faces of the audience distressed him, so he had wandered away unobserved, tiring of the circus hay, searching for fresh leaves. He had found them, row upon row of trees in an orchard, placed so low that he barely had to raise his trunk to strip the branches. In one night he denuded that orchard and, slightly drunk with his good fortune, blundered into a shed and slept. The owner of the orchard, waking next morning, ran about wailing that a new pestilence had struck and they must all beware. Then he climbed into his cattle truck and set off for market where he hoped to buy a prize bull for his herd. When he opened his truck Oswald emerged, nauseous, blinking and convinced that the press of faces around him meant he had somehow returned to the circus. He stood on his hind legs and semaphored messages of love with the front ones; he coiled his trunk around a fencing stake, drew it out of the earth where someone had spent a day hammering it into place and twirled it about, skilled as a drum majorette, stamping his feet in time to the music he heard in his head. The public took to their heels, dogs barked and cowered, policemen blew whistles whose shrill notes pierced Oswald's large ears. The elephant was offended and lumbered away as fast as he could manage in a direct line south, over fields and outhouses, flattening an empty goods train as he went. After him went the representatives of law and order, and of the zoo, with nets and cages and big-game guns. All would have been over for Oswald had not a small girl with blazing red hair fixed him with her violet eyes which instantly shrank him to the size of a toy. The hunters went home disappointed and baffled. Everyone else assumed that the soft elephant was what he seemed. Oswald, therefore, with reasons for his singular loyalty, never left my daughter's lap.

I took her down to the beehives, cut out a piece of turf with my penknife and showed her the teeming industry underneath. I fed her on honey sandwiches, a bite for her and a bite for me. I saw the breeze in her hair when she slept, sitting in the cart, her chin dropped forward.

It was slow, much slower than I had anticipated, enthusiastic with ignorance, but she greeted me. If she was in her dormitory and I came to the foot of her bed, she smiled and flapped her arms. If she was deep in the gardens so that I had to hunt her out, I would call to her, spotting the beacon of hair, and the arms flew up. I did not know if she missed me.

Driving home again I would pull over into a lay-by and, closing my eyes, slip into Joanna's mind, behind those iron eyes, and was so frightened that I found myself gasping to escape. There could be no confinement more horrible to bear, to see, to understand, as I knew she did, but because of those few convulsive moments to be unable to respond. Language was locked within her, battering to be released, but the key had not only been lost, it had been destroyed. If she was cold or hot, if she was hungry, if she was tired or bored, she must wait for someone else to notice, to divine her wants, and then to act. Could this go on for a lifetime?

There was snow. The wheels of the cart rolled deep tracks. Joanna was heavy. I tried to lift her on to my knee but she used her weight to tell me: leave me where I am, I'm comfortable. So I wedged the wheels with stones and drew pictures in the snow – Oswald, who bowed with impeccable grace; I drew my car parked on the gravel behind us; I drew a giant blackbird at tug-of-war with a monstrous worm, and Joanna smiled up at me, up at the sky.

In the spring when the lawns glittered with golden crocuses the Tolinis followed me in convoy.

'Wait here. I'll go and fetch her.'

But it was as if I were about to display a prized horse, and on the way into the house I paused. I could not exhibit my daughter like this. How would she feel, led out in front of an invited audience? Through the window I saw the Tolinis waiting, a family together, come for my sake. Barbara's hair blew round her face and she was laughing and spitting it out. Giusè was calling the boys to heel from a chase over the lawns. Different behaviour was expected in places like these. Perhaps I could explain to Joanna so that she would forgive my insensitivity. 'Some friends of mine have come to see us. It's lovely outside today, shall we go now and meet them?' And why not? – smiling, arms like a windmill. And they were smiling too, in readiness, grouped for a photographer, all the lips wide. All the lips in rictus.

I pulled Joanna out on to the gravel, the rumble of her wheels mingling with her farting tongue, and I waved to attract the attention riveted on us. I stopped, braked by their eyes. Barbara's hands had flown to her mouth, Giusè had plucked Leonora from the grass just as she was running forward. Uncle Leo beamed stupidly. Next to him, at ground level in a wide wooden cart, a fat white red-headed girl with saliva round her mouth was blowing an endless raspberry and conducting the heavens.

'Go!' I shouted. 'Go away! Go away! Why did you come?'

The Tolinis fled to their car and I returned Joanna to her quarters.

The Director's office was empty. 'He'll be right back. He's been hoping to talk to you for a long time. He knows you're here, if you wouldn't mind waiting.'

From the Director's windows the view over the gardens took in the lawns and the orchard and the tips of the beehives. You could see beyond the boundaries of St Matthew's, beyond the barbed-wire, into cow-pocked fields, in one of which grew a single baggy oak. There was an unbroken greenness whose prisoners would never be released. I waited, feeling the beating of my heart, listening to the rasp of my breath.

Balding, stooping, yellow-fingered, the Director shook my hand. He sat down behind his desk. He gestured me to the chair for visitors. He lit a cigarette, then so did I. He said, 'She's not suffering, you know.'

'How can you tell?'

'You can tell suffering in any creature.' I flinched. 'Mr Beck, what makes a human being?' I didn't answer. 'A sense of the past, a sense of the future, a sense of oneself? Self-consciousness? Joanna has none of those. Look. Those convulsions. She lost oxygen to the brain. We don't know exactly how much damage there was, but you have to understand . . . There isn't much of what we might call "mind". She's not going to walk or talk or improve any further. She's got as far as she's going to get.'

'You can't know that.'

'I do know that.'

'Then what was the point of keeping her alive?' Shouting.

The Director's self-control was intact. 'Because she was alive already.'

'Like any other animal.'

'But we're not talking about animals, we're talking about people.'

'And what makes a human being?' I parroted.

'It's what she might have been. What she would have been but for an appalling accident.'

'But she isn't. You're telling me that. She's nothing but . . . lost potential.'

'She's your child. She carries you and her mother within her but things went wrong. She's still your child.'

'How can she be my child if there's nothing there? If there's no mind? She's got no more intelligence than . . . I don't know . . . than a chimpanzee, you're saying.'

He hesitated. 'Actually . . . less.'

'Locked up in being less.'

'I don't think she's locked up, Mr Beck. She's not aware of not being aware.'

'Then send her away and perform experiments on her. Why don't you, so she can be useful to someone else?'

'What are you saying?' Now he banged the table, outraged finally.

I couldn't meet his question. A fly crawled up the window and I took some papers from the desk, rolled them and swatted at it

273

again and again without success. This fully developed fly, as a fly, had more life than my daughter, although neither of them knew it. She isn't suffering. She isn't aware of not being aware. How could he be so certain? 'I've got to go.'

'Will you come again?'

'I can't see why I should. According to you, it makes no difference to her whether I do or not.'

'It might make a difference to you.'

'I doubt it.'

'Look, I can understand you're bitter –'

'I'm not bitter, but I would have liked to have children.'

'You have.'

'I haven't. You've just told me what I've got.'

I sat in my car and closed the door. If it mattered to Joanna only to be warm and fed, in the absence of pain, if she were to grow up and grow old and die without a history, what was the purpose in keeping her alive? I had startled the Director. I had, briefly, shocked myself. But now I wondered, why is human life more sacred than any other if the life is encased only in the human shape without its mind? I started the engine. Why is human life more sacred than any other even with the mind? Why is life sacred at all? If a sudden explosion brought the entire planet to a close, to whom need it matter? *Be a human being*, said Meyer. *Just a human being, a member of the species.* I remembered the chameleon waiting for a phantom fly on its make-believe rock in the zoo, its tongue flicking in and out obeying instructions it knew nothing of. I saw Mirabelle's newborn foal struggling to its feet because the safety of its stable could not countermand the instinct to be ready to flee. I remembered EL's tight belly with our child, still carrying her potential, waiting for the moment of birth. Someone had written that human infants are born retarded, completing their development outside the womb because the human pelvis could not produce a child of the size it would have to be if it were born with the capacities of a fledgling chimpanzee. But my child had proceeded no further. She was less than a chimpanzee. *It's not a question of more or less*, said Meyer, drawing shapes in the sand with his toe, *of higher or lower. All living things simply are. They will change, and if they fail to they will become extinct and others will replace them. People too.*

We're neither the summit of creation nor the ultimate aim of evolution. We are simply here, for the moment, and one day that moment will have passed. So why bother? I asked. *Oh, to make life more pleasant while the living is got through. We can't help ourselves from doing that either. It's what survival is all about.*

A convoy of racing cyclists blocked the road, humped over their handlebars, the muscles of their thighs etched by their aerodynamic tights. One of them was going to be first. All of them wanted to be. On this Sunday afternoon they would find out which one and he would celebrate. The road widened and I swung out past them. There would be people eating Tolini's ice cream, giving presents of Tolini's handmade chocolates, daubed in the colours of the House of Laing, fragrant with its scents, writing poems, composing music so that others might pass the time more pleasantly. But Giusè, surrounded by his family, preparing them to produce families of their own, lit candles every Sunday.

The traffic dawdled by a weekend market spilling into the road. On the pavement a striped stall was selling whelks and eels. The stallholder, matched in a striped straw boater, plunged his pint cup shovelling into his wares, his mouth expert banter, his eyes turned inward on future success, aiming for better things. A young couple with a toddler in a pushchair ate their whelks with their fingers, talking of the future. People fingered flowered dresses and plastic tablecloths on rails between buckets of bundled scrubbing-brushes, all implements for the passing of time. A girl with her long hair loose down her back crossed the road in front of me, eating an ice cream cone and talking to her crop-haired blonde friend. Her face was pinched, pale with a long thin nose, her expression intense. The blonde friend was round-cheeked and listening. Such different faces, I thought, instantly distinguishable one from another, although all of them shared the same scattering of features, and all of them supposed their individual lives ought to amount to something. They too were unaware of being unaware, more unaware even than my daughter, for they thought they understood. What would they do if I stopped my car, leaped on to its roof and shouted aloud, 'Don't bother! There is no point at all in doing what you're doing, wanting whatever it is you want, dreaming your foolish dreams. All life is an accident and you are

275

accidental, incidental too. There is no point in anything at all'? I knew what they would do. They would turn their heads, nudge one another and wander on, mildly entertained by an event they might remember sufficiently to recount over tea and egg and cress sandwiches.

Thinking of the sandwiches I was hungry, left my car in the middle of the road among the idling traffic, and bought a pint of whelks. I set the pot between my thighs and picked the fleshy bits out with my fingers as I drove, enjoying them. It was too easy, this body whose demands to be satisfied took precedence. Programmed for that to be so, trapped in that programme, but able, sometimes, to identify the trap – and recognise too late that the ability itself is also a part of the programme.

My bowels twitched and I needed a shit. Out of the market crowd I put my foot down, thinking: sod the police, if they flag me down it'll be too bad. Another twitch and there was sweat on my forehead and upper lip. Anything, I thought, anything to get home in time.

I left the front door swinging as I raced, crablike and clutching myself, up the stairs. But when I sat triumphant, in safety, swilling out, a voice sounding much like my own said, *Got you*.

Twenty

'Are you feeling better?' EL waited outside the lavatory door, a girl in the dim light. 'You look awful.'

'Others have said so.'

She nodded, a small suitcase at her feet. 'Daddy's ill.'

I had known. But the suitcase. 'More ill? May I come with you?'

She was already on her way downstairs and spoke to the air in front of her. 'It's up to you.'

Marjorie was sitting alone in her hacking jacket. Although she had discarded the hairnet, the silver plate remained in place. 'Ah, Eleanor, dear.' She put out one arm. 'And Leo.'

They had been to collect the body, being expert. It was all in hand.

EL swung on her heel, her shoulders high. 'You could have waited. You could have waited for me.'

'But he was already . . . he had already . . . you know, dear.'

'I wanted to see him.'

Marjorie was bewildered by her daughter's vehemence. 'I'm sorry, dear.' She sat back in the lumpy armchair opposite the major's empty one. I drew up another and sat next to her. 'Would you make some tea, Leo? I should like some tea.'

The kitchen was unchanged; only the paintwork was older, yellowed, greasy to the touch. Marjorie's paperwork covered the table. I looked back through the dates. She had been neglecting it. I picked up her pencil, for I would have time while the kettle came to the boil. The gas flame hissed quietly behind me and I turned sheet after sheet, briefly consoled by a job well done, sensing at my knee the moist nose of an aged black dog. The kettle began squealing and I pushed back my chair.

277

'It's okay. I'm doing it.' EL had been standing at the door, where her father had wielded his shotgun, watching me. 'Are you having some?' She laid a tray, held the biscuit tin against her to pull away the lid. 'Only crumbs, look.'

'Any biscuits, dear?'

'No. I looked. The tin's empty.'

'Oh dear. I must have forgotten. I'm so sorry.'

'It's all right, Mummy, we don't want biscuits.'

'We always liked biscuits with tea.' She stirred her tea. 'I'm glad you're here too, Leo. We didn't expect you. We knew you've been very busy.'

'I haven't been that busy. I do remarkably little for the business except for the markets and the maths.'

'Well, you've had things on your mind, haven't you? Away a lot. Eleanor's been telling us. Anyway, there's so much to do and I shall be grateful for your help. We've got the tea to organise and the invitations to send out, and after that I would like you to help me sell the ponies and wind everything up. I want everything in order. No mess left behind, no loose ends.'

'Mummy, what do you mean, wind everything up? You can manage. I'd help. I can always come down if you need help.'

Marjorie drained her teacup and patted EL's hand. 'I know, dear.'

They sang 'The Lord's My Shepherd'. As family we took the front pews although the major had said he didn't hold with church. Who knew what his neighbours held with, all in attendance in coats and hats, and shoes against spring rain. They sang with solemn gusto and I sang too. 'I like that, no waste,' the major had said as the vole cut through the river barely disturbing the water, built for its habitat, belonging there as the major had belonged in his. Sorely missed would not be enough, said the vicar, for not only we but our children have had much to thank Derek Laing for. I have known him personally for over twenty-five years, and I can honestly say . . .

'It's so deep.' EL stood on Marjorie's right, I on her left, tacit but superfluous support.

Marjorie bent over the grave, plumbing it with her eyes as they lowered the coffin in. 'Of course, dear. There has to be room for me as well.' She was stern in her black suit and shook hands with everyone.

It had taken all morning to make the sandwiches, ham and tongue, with the crusts cut off, and laid-on lettuce leaves and pieces of cucumber. Marjorie made pots of tea.

Old Bob Bold's daughter was making a name for herself in the show-ring; she had light hands and a good seat but the man would always be untrustworthy. If the smith's son was really moving into town they'd have to advertise for a successor, but give it time, the boy would be back. Town life wouldn't suit him. Mrs Ellis had done a fine job with the flowers but you could tell her nose was out of joint over that business about the hymn books. Thank you, I will have another cup. Are you down for the day or staying on?

'So good of you, Leo dear. I hope you don't mind being the waiter today, it must be strange.'

We left Marjorie washing up, keeping busy, and went, booted, to look at the mares and their new foals. EL sat on a five-barred gate, a soft muzzle between her hands. 'I don't know any of these. They're all new. But then they would be, I suppose. The fencing's in an awful state.' She tugged at a sagging strand of barbed-wire. 'That's not going to keep them in for long.' She jumped down into the field and a bay foal nibbled at her anorak. 'Does Mummy really want to sell up, d'you think?'

'Do you mind?'

'Do I mind? Not about these.' She pulled hard on a long, winter-furred ear. 'But the place.'

'She didn't say anything about the place.'

'No, but you know what she meant. She's decided to die. Leo, I don't want her to die. I don't want to be alone.'

'You're not alone.'

'Yes, I am. And so are you.'

'Then can we not be alone together?'

'Who can be alone together? Daddy was so sad and I never said.' Tears streamed down the back of her throat but her eyes were fiercely dry. I had thought to bring our daughter to this place and walk with her across the tussocks to the river, sharing her hands with her grandfather, watching her red hair grow. I had thought to root with her here, when she was ready.

We sold the ponies at auction, lot numbers on their rumps, led into horseboxes, mothers and their young, placid and unconcerned, noses in haynets. EL perched on the corral in a headscarf and breeches while the girls at the House of Laing packed pots into boxes of lemon and pink, their hair tied up. Although her stiff back was aching badly Marjorie drove her Land-Rover home, held the door-frame, eased herself out and gave me the keys.

They had calculated the depth precisely. Marjorie's coffin grated on the major's, the earth that would settle heaped over.

EL had bought an electric kettle so this time the teapots filled more swiftly. She threw the breadcrusts out for the birds and drank the last of the major's sherry from its dusty bottle, grimacing, as the guests came in, and wiping the crumbs from the surfaces. Someone had brought a cake. Townspeople forget about baking.

'I expect you'll be putting the place on the market, will you?'

'I expect so,' said EL.

'No,' I said. 'We're keeping it.'

We made my garden together, but alone, weekend work, buying books to teach us. You can fashion plant life, you can choose it, plan where to place it, imagine how it will grow, then control it so that it does. My knuckles bled when I rolled away the barbed-wire.

We set rhododendrons and azaleas in basins of peat and hammered in stakes to hold the poplar saplings against the wind. We worked until we were too tired to speak, weekend after weekend, driving home in silence to the markets and the tubes of cleansers and moisturisers. Douglas firs, quick-growing, shallow-rooted, marshalled the boundary; when they were grown the fallen needles carpeted the ground beneath. Had things been otherwise Joanna might have scooped them into roads and tunnels and fortress walls. Yellow cypresses meshed into a wall, and I planted a copse of prunus, bluebells at their feet. In winter the red-barked willows vied, orange, with the crimson dogwood. With the passing seasons the old horizon vanished.

'Come with me, let me show you.' But they were nervous, my parents, frail I thought, fearful of wild country. 'Just for the day, then.'

My mother's high heels sank in the soft grass and on my arm she sought refuge on the brick terrace I had made, carrying bricks with old expertise, laying them with new competence, finding new muscles, passing time. She sat on a wrought-iron garden seat massaging the ankles she had feared for and surveyed her son's inexplicable obsession. Her mouth worked as she hunted in vain for words of appreciation. 'So much work,' she said, stupid, stupefied.

Their tour of inspection complete, EL brought my father back, her arm in his as if he were the escort. 'A lot of good wood, you'll have.' He gave his approval, visualising pine tables and cabinets of walnut. 'Not in my lifetime, though. They're so small, your trees. Can't you make them grow faster?' Just for the day, for they missed the pavements and my mother conceded, distressed, that this was not a house you could clean.

I tried again.

Giusè came, bringing his family, and the garden filled with the children's running. 'Busman's holiday.' He cooked a cauldron of spaghetti and brought it out into the garden but, carrying our plates, we fled back to the house, pursued by wasps. 'Bloody damn things. No bloody good to anyone.' And he laid about him, afraid. 'Can't see the purpose of wasps. Don't make honey, don't do nothin' but get in your nosh and sting you.'

EL, warming to him, scoffed. 'Keep still. If you don't wave your arms about they'll leave you alone.'

'They won't leave my dinner alone. Now look.' Leonora held out a swollen hand, swallowing her sobs in front of her siblings.

'Oh, honey, come here.' Barbara folded her away.

'Try this.' EL unwrapped the mother's arms and pulled the child away. Leonora had heard about Uncle Leo's wife and stood to attention, her puffy hand unwilling but obedient on EL's knee. Soap was rubbed on the red spot, which subsided.

'Where the 'eck you learn that?'

'We always had wasps. Jam sandwiches and wasps, fizzy lemonade and wasps. Wasps with everything.'

'Bloody marvellous. Come on, chuck, come to yer dad. Give us a kiss.' But Leonora did not move. She stood between EL's knees gazing at the fine white face, the bent head with the hair swept up, EL examining her handiwork, until the heat of those brown eyes lifted EL's face and she took in the round cheeks and the tear-glued lashes.

'Go. Go on now to your father.' She swung Leonora round by the shoulders and with a shove which all but sent her sprawling propelled the girl into Giusè's waiting embrace. And was gone.

Barbara restrained me. 'Leave her be. Giusè, keep the kids.'

'Domenica, wash! Sandro, dry! The rest of you, shut up.'

I left them and climbed the stairs to our bedroom, the Laings' room, to spy on my wife, who walked among the nursery of trees, pointing with sweeps of her arm, her hands describing in angular motion for an invisible companion the shapes of sheds and stables. The trees melted into fencing posts and the flowering shrubs crunched hay. It was a mistake, I thought, keeping the place. But the mistake had been in the changing of it. I had dislodged EL's childhood to plant a new one for myself. But only the trees were rooted.

That night, all the young Tolinis in sleeping-bags on the old sitting-room floor, I lay wedged between them and said, surprising them, 'There was once a girl called Janie, who was like no other girl who ever was. For when other girls were playing waitresses, and doctors and nurses' – Domenica and Leonora giggled – 'Janie was away in the fields talking to horses – and the horses talked back.' The door to the kitchen was open. I could hear the movements of someone opening and closing cupboards, tidying, restoring chairs to the table. 'No one would have believed that Janie spoke horse-language, so she kept her secret to herself. One night, she was woken by a thunderstorm. The house shook and her room blazed white with every flash of lightning. Out in the field the horses ran together panicking, away from the tree that had sheltered them from the rain. Janie was warm in her bed' – the children drew their sleeping-bags up to their chins – 'but she knew she must go out and reassure her friends. So she pulled her dungarees on over her pyjamas, stepped into her wellingtons and went down the stairs. She took her father's big black torch and went out into the awful night. For a moment she thought she had lost the animals but then she saw them huddled together, unmoving and amazed. The field under her feet rumbled as if there was an earthquake. Coming across the field, as big as a house, was a gigantic black horse, galloping and galloping. For a moment she thought it would run her down but she stood her ground. Then all of a sudden she felt a great head bending to touch hers, she felt the hot breath. "Janie," said the horse, jet black in the torchlight, at least six foot to the shoulders.'

'Sixteen hands, and it's withers.' EL squatted in the threshold.

'Sixteen hands. Thank you. She reached up and grasped a handful of hair . . . mane, and tried to leap on to the horse's back, but he was too tall. "Allow me," said the horse, and knelt before her as if she was the queen. Janie scrambled up and the horse rose and rose until Janie thought she was about to fly. "Perhaps I should introduce myself. The name is King Kong." '

Away they went, Janie and her horse, in a partnership that was to last another five years. EL placed her feet uncertainly among the sleeping-bags, bending forward. I held out a hand, still talking. She took it and squirmed down on to the floor beside me, stretched herself full length. 'Do you do this often?' she whispered.

'Most nights. Ssh.' She lay in the crook of my arm, listening with the children. The story trickled from my mouth and EL's eyes were wide open as she stared at the ceiling, listening and wondering. '. . . at that moment the gate creaked. Janie saw the outline of a man with a gun creeping towards the house. If she had been at home she could have warned her parents. There was only one thing she could do. That's it, kids. More next time.'

'Uncle Leo!' Only a practised choir could produce such unison.

'At least it means you know there'll be a next time. I mean, I want to know what happens as much as you do.' I made to get up but EL pressed on my arm: stay, stay here.

Around us the children slept, one by one, their breathing lighter, their bodies heavier. The floor was hard and the space narrow. Like a bunk in a shed full of sleeping men, below me a man in silent agony, writhing from his own bones and listening to me muttering EL's name in my sleep. *You've got to sort her out*, gripping my arm as we walked to the gate, leaving the traces of pain in the sand, the grizzled cropped head turned to me, trusting me to pick the safest path. Meyer. Of all people to be without. EL, relaxed, slipped off my arm. Thinking she would roll on to a child I scooped her back, holding her weight, and eased her under me.

'What a waste,' she said, her cheeks sweet and salty as blood and syrup on her lips. I tried a hand between her legs and found her slippery wet, worked my fingers deep into the warm soft tunnel so that, pinioned, she lost her breath and drew me to her. With my elbows on the carpet and my hands under her head I made love with my wife in silence among the dreaming mounds of my friend's children.

Twenty-one

Tolini's opened up in Brighton and Manchester and tripled its clientele overnight. Giusè was nonplussed and put a hand in his trousers to scratch a lower region of his paunch. 'You was right, then' – having doubted my assurance – 'they're all over, too much money and not enough sense. Still, 's all right by me if they want to throw it away.' False modesty, Giusè. Quality costs, we have never pretended otherwise. And we worked for that quality, more hours, it seemed, than there were in a day. I did not regret them. What else should I have done with them?

Meanwhile, my trees grew, their branches overarched and weaving corridors as I directed; dark foliage glowered behind light as I had envisaged. The sap of all the seasons was in my control, for I shaped my small Eden with a pruning-knife.

I had not been back to St Matthew's, and I was growing older. Frail as paper my parents were fading in consort, a day nurse and a night nurse on my payroll, watchful but surplus. My mother tottered to my father's needs, and he helped her do it.

Andrea, at twenty-five, had long left school – successful, armed with a future, his teachers jubilant and proprietorial – but with pastry fingers which drove him. Tolini's pâtisseries became all his own. His brothers, growing their hair, were banned, undismayed, from the kitchens. Domenica's pony was put out to grass because she preferred to sit, still astride, on her mother's velveteen stool redesigning her face. Giusè thundered but was ignored, for had he not always shouted? Irritable with youth, Leonora had long since wrenched herself from his obsolescent embrace. She had been our last one left. Until.

He must have sat toying with the telephone, lines of distress crumpling his face, but resorted finally to his fountain pen, eschewing a waiting secretary. 'Dear Mr and Mrs Beck, I have difficulty in writing this to you . . .'

EL opened, read the letter, laid it on the table beside her coffee-cup gone cold so that I came upon her first, gripping the basin and retching over it. I thought she was ill and held her head, but the retching was dry and she shook me off, coughing. 'Go. Go and look.'

'. . . I cannot think how it can have happened and I blame myself. We have discovered that Joanna is pregnant. Naturally she doesn't realise, she doesn't understand. She is well, I would say robust, but somewhat overweight for lack of exercise as she has always been. I have to admit that my staff failed to recognise her condition partly for this reason and because her cycle has been irregular. We estimate that she might be in the fourth month of pregnancy. She could certainly carry the child to term, on the other hand I ask you to consider Joanna's interests. We have to consider what childbirth would entail for Joanna herself. Although the law does not favour it, I am convinced a case could be made for a termination should you feel this to be the most suitable course of action. I would ask you both to consider what you want done and then, perhaps, we could meet to discuss the case further. I can only apologise for what is undeniably negligence on the part of St Matthew's. You have both suffered so much distress already. Please accept my warmest good wishes and my condolence . . .'

Condolence. What a word to use, a word for the bereaved where he was talking about a child, a new child. Overhearing my thoughts I was revolted. A child got how? A child perpetrated on my child. Joanna asleep and the thing done before she could put up a shout – if she still had shouting in her – by someone stalking a prepared and helpless body, a womanly body, good enough for the purpose. Joanna had grown into a woman's body, perhaps surging with a woman's urges; perhaps it had welcomed. But it had not chosen. It could not choose, unaware of being unaware, no sense of the past, no notion of any future, contentment only in warmth and food, bodily sensations. Perhaps then it *had* welcomed. Impossible. There could be no welcome without agreement; the word implied as much. You were offered, you considered, you welcomed or rejected. This body could only have taken what was put into it,

286

struggled or not struggled. *Overweight*. Immobile, he meant, in her cart on wheels. Presumably a giant affair now. What did they do? Did they pull her by tractor, someone permanently rostered to tow Joanna, a fat almost-woman with a farting mouth and windmill arms, or did they keep her indoors, on a mat, in a bed with caged sides to prevent her toppling out and cracking that emptied head?

The Director had said there was nothing that you might call mind. 'You can't know.' 'I do know.' But he might have been wrong, and Joanna knew what it was she was growing inside her, how it got there, but could not let us know she knew. And we were supposed to decide for her, just as the prowler had decided for her. Where were they, where had they been, those devoted employees? Had it been one of them, or a gardener? A building contractor leaving his ladder under the window? *I ask you to think of Joanna's interests*. The interests of a creature less than chimpanzee over its potentially human child.

Stop this talk of 'less'. Neither is more nor less than the other, said Meyer impatiently. *Each one is suited to what it is, and where it is. That's why it's there and not somewhere else. That's why it's still there at all. The child is not the pinnacle of creation nor the aim of evolution.*

But, I said, don't you see? Don't you understand what's happened? She's less of a human being than she was supposed to be, because she hasn't the mind, and she's not as much as a chimpanzee either, because she hasn't its instincts. She's not suited to anything. So what is she? I know what she was, for those few moments – with her violet eyes. But what is she now? Tell me that, Meyer.

In his silence he only said, *That is for you to decide.*

'Bastard!' Giusè sweated in his tall white hat in the chrome kitchen of Tolini's, and his minions ran from pot to pot. ''E's got a bloody nerve. Course she's got to 'ave it. It's a kid, it's there, it's alive. You don't throw it away just like that. An' I tell you what. It's probably 'im what done it.'

'He wouldn't.'

'Why not? 'Cos 'e's the Director? Do what 'e likes, can't 'e, with them kids, and who's to stop 'im? People like that oughtn'ter be allowed. I'd 'ave 'im closed down. I'd tell the law.'

'That's not the point. What are we to do?'

'I already told yer. God never made men so as they could keep one or chuck one as they fancy. You got a kid there. A baby.'

'I had a baby once.'

'Yeah, mate. I know.' Giusè dipped his mouth over a spoon held out for his approval and lingered there. The baby I had had once had made his jaw drop and he didn't care for the memory. When Giusè re-emerged his features were in place again. 'Look. You gotta talk to your EL. It's none of my business. But if I was you I'd get down on my knees and pray.'

'There's no one I can pray to, you know that.'

'Then you'd better find someone and pretty damn quick.'

God never made man at all, I thought but did not say. Besides, what sort of God does one pray to who keeps and chucks as he fancies, denying the decision to the creatures they say he made in his image, pulling rank as proof of godhead, doling out humanity and instantly withdrawing it, leaving only the empty shell of image? How could my friend believe what he believed? Too easily, for his belief had never been challenged, tripping weekly with his flourishing family to his church with its candles and incense, giving thanks and washing his soul clean. Anger gushed up in me that he dared offer his unthinking advice, as insubstantial as the thin cinnamon biscuits Andrea fashioned to accompany the Tolini ice cream. Wafers. How simple to be Giusè. How enviably simple. Inwardly I spat. Outwardly too.

Giusè grabbed my lapels. 'Just in case you forgot. Just in case you forgot why we got together, you an' me, my dad was prayin' for me when 'e went under. 'E knew where 'e was goin' an' 'e knew where 'e come from. I know, an' I bring my kids up to know. If you don't know it's not my fault an' it's not my problem, but just because you got rid of your kid, don't get rid of hers as well . . . I'm sorry. I'm sorry. I didn't mean that. I gotta big mouth, Barbara always says. But you get up my nose, sometimes, Leo, you know that? Now do us a favour and get out before I land you one.'

I walked, heel toe, heel toe, away from Tolini's. Giusè had grown to look like his father, one might have thought deliberately, despite his greater height, his greater strength. Andrea, no doubt, would do the same. But not the others. Sandro and Paulo, brought up by their father as he had been brought up, had not been paying attention. Maybe it didn't matter. Maybe all you needed was one to be the standard-bearer of Bologna and the church, only one to light candles and pass on the story of Tolini's, the story of the soft-bellied man who had started up in London to better his family but finished as food for scavenger fish because London had taken fright. It wouldn't do. So long as Giusè wanted them all, Andrea's delicate mille-feuilles and walnut meringues could not compensate for Sandro's shoulder-length hair and Paulo's affected disaffection. Even his daughters – especially his daughters. One was not enough. Something was impelling Giusè to teach his children to live as his grandfather had lived but in another place. He had learned the lesson. Why wouldn't they?

I felt his hands on my lapels – he had almost frightened me – the heat of his breath in my face. Why did it matter so much? Why couldn't he accept that his grandchildren would most probably not speak Italian, they might no longer be Catholics, they might in the end consider themselves only children of London, meeting and fornicating and procreating with others like them, spreading the Tolini genes without the Tolini culture? Yet he presumed to instruct me, who had one daughter to whom nothing could be taught, reduced to a body involuntarily nourishing another, like a queen bee extruding eggs, unable to refuse, unaware that there was such a thing as refusal, the processes of that body trundling unstoppably through time until it was no longer viable. Giusè had advised what he had to advise, for his convictions would not allow him to do otherwise. But I had a choice.

'There are no choices,' my grandfather had shouted while I squatted in the corridor outside his room. 'Make no mistake, Benjamin, it was not God who chose the Jews but the Jews who chose God and all His difficult ways. No one else was prepared to accept the laws, to obey the commandments, but us. We undertook it knowing that it would be a struggle, and it remains one. But it defines us. If once we give up the struggle we cease to exist. And you are teaching the boy it doesn't really matter. Why don't you simply slit his throat? I'll get you a knife from the kitchen, and you can do it now, in front of me. Well, what do you say?' And my father had demurred, but to himself, in a low voice, angered, put out. 'Don't be so extreme, it's not the end of the world. You're not Abraham, you know.' So that my grandfather, his ears sharpened, pounced. 'Abraham. Precisely. And do you know what would have happened if the Lord had not prevented Abraham from sacrificing his only son? Do you know? There would have been no Jewish people, that's what. You would not be here. I would not be here. The boy would not be here. Nothing.'

But he was wrong. If Abraham had not stayed his hand, with or without God's help, there might have been no Jewish people but there would not have been nothing. If the commandments and the laws, great and small, had not been obeyed the Jews would have been indistinguishable from everyone else, simply people, one of the many tribes who swarmed over the pages of the Old Testament, and then disappeared. Only they had not disappeared. They had gone to great lengths to ensure that they did not disappear, so determinedly, so self-consciously, that their very success had spawned catastrophe. Why? Why struggle to become and remain a people unlike all others? Why wasn't it enough simply to be? *Well done*, whispered Meyer. *I'm proud of you.* But I found myself answering reproachfully, on my grandfather's behalf: That question is the privilege only of those who have never had to ask it.

Stop this, I thought. I have to decide about one particular life – no, two. What to do with my second chance, another child, but one whose birth might damage and terrify the first. 'I will teach it to ride,' EL had said. 'And I will teach "it" nothing at all, I will tell bedtime stories.' Had I not discovered that one can also tell stories to other people's children? I should not insist on my child's child, condemning its mother to pain and fear, and the child itself at best to the pleasant passing of time. Not for my sake. Nor in the name of anyone's unnecessary god.

EL was buttering scones. 'Hallo, there you are.' The bottom of her face was a sculpture of good humour. 'Are you hungry?'

'I've just been to see Giusè.'

'Then you can't be hungry. What a pity. I haven't made scones for such a long time.'

'I showed him the Director's letter.'

'Why?' EL crashed the butter dish on to the table. 'Why always Giusè this and Giusè that? What the hell has anything got to do with him? I don't want to know what he said. I can guess, but it's none of his damn business.'

'That's what he said.'

'Good. The first sensible thing I've heard in a long time.'

'But he made me think.'

'What about?'

'EL, please. The letter. We are being asked to decide.'

'You decide. Decide what you like.'

'I can't. I mustn't decide by myself. You're Joanna's mother.'

'I am not.'

'You are. Stop pretending, just for once. You were her mother and you are her mother. Joanna is in St Matthew's where she has been for sixteen years. She's likely to stay there for the rest of her life. She is pregnant and we have to decide whether or not she has this baby because, things being as they are, she cannot decide for herself.'

'Let them decide.'

'EL, don't be silly. You know perfectly well they —'

'Yes, I know, I know. Look, Leo. I don't want to decide. I don't want to have anything to do with it. I don't want to go there. I don't want to see this . . . the . . . Joanna. I don't want to and I'm not going to.'

I heard myself asking, completely failing to obstruct my voice, 'What if she had a baby? A perfect healthy baby? What would we do then?'

Still holding her knife, EL buttered on, scooping the excess gathered at the edges and wiping it on to the next scone as if butter were in short supply. She laid out her scones on a platter for the guests she had not invited, waited long enough for everyone to make a choice, then selected, with hovering fingers, from the centre and took a bite. The piece of pastry sat in her mouth. She held it there, ran and spat it out, threw the rest of the scone into the bin, swept the scones from the platter in after it.

I said as she wiped her mouth, 'I'm going down. Come with me.'

'No.'

'Come with me.'

'No.'

'Come with me. Just this once and never again. I can't manage without you and it's got to be done. We owe it to her. It's not her fault and it's not our fault but we owe her something now.' Which would be more powerful, guilt reawakened or the old enduring fear? I reached for the guilt. 'Remember your pregnancy' – she did not want to – 'all that clumsiness and the indigestion. And you were lucky, by all accounts . . . in the pregnancy. Joanna doesn't understand. She's a pregnant woman who doesn't understand. We've got to see how she looks, how she seems to be taking it.'

EL was smoothing papers, slitting the day's neglected post with a knife, perfect incisions, practised and brisk as no nonsense. She scanned her mail, piece by piece, and her rapid decisions took shape on the table, these to discard, these to reply to, these deserving a little unwilling time; when you read letters you bend your head. 'I wouldn't know how she's taking it. I have nothing to compare.'

'EL,' I said, 'neither have I.'

'You saw her. Day after day. You saw her, you were down there, you were never at home. You spent all your time there.' You were never here.

'But that was years ago. She was a child, and now she isn't. I have little more to go on than you have.' *She's got as far as she's going to get. Don't count on any improvement.* I had lied to my wife as, one way or another, one lies all the time. 'The Director will help us. If need be we can rely on him.'

'Why do you always have to rely on someone? Why can't you rely on yourself?' she said, on whom many relied at her behest. But her coat was over her arm, in readiness, for it was mid-January. A gesture was being made, for my sake. A gesture of support.

The woman who preceded me through our front door, opting for my car rather than her own, might shortly become a grand-mother for life, having been a mother for a few hours only. She was slender as a pencil but the hair twisted around a single silver pin on her neck had paled into the colour of cinnamon.

So we drove and mentioned the traffic and the wind scudding the trees; we noticed the change in the weather and I remarked upon the motorway which was sending us to our destination more rapidly than we had intended. We discussed the wisdom of pulling into a service station and topping up the tank to be sure of an uneventful return journey. We considered pausing for motorway coffee. In this way, alone together, we passed the time until we arrived.

The circumstances which brought Mr and Mrs Beck to St Matthew's to see the Director over the unfortunate business of their daughter, Joanna Beck, embarrassed the staff. They gave us a wide berth. We walked, chins high, along a corridor familiar to me, virgin land to EL though no observer could have told, to the Director's office, a courtesy, gaining time. But there sat the matron wearing an outsize watch which seemed to tell me how many years late I was for my appointment. Her face was as many years thinner, more grey.

On her feet, she circled the big desk and approached with her hand already extended. 'Mrs Beck, how do you do? Mr Beck, of course, I know. How are you, Mr Beck? You'll be wanting to see Joanna, I have no doubt, but if you wouldn't mind waiting . . . Won't you both sit down?' She motioned us to a settee for two, a new acquisition. Where had she been when she should have been at her post? Did she feel the question in my eyes, the same question in EL's? 'Some tea? It's nearly four, after all. How was your journey, by the way? That new motorway should have made some difference. I find it cuts a full half-hour off the time when I go up to town. It was the bottleneck at Egham that used to be so bad before. I'll get some tea and biscuits for us all. I like a biscuit with my tea, don't you?'

She hurried away and I crossed the room to find an ashtray, the better to see my wife's face on which I thought I detected relief. A cup of institutional tea and a digestive biscuit were her stay of execution.

'Ah, good afternoon to you both.' Bravely doing his duty, the Director welcomed Mrs Beck, and then Mr Beck, but guilt-ridden, unable to meet their eyes. 'Let's go directly and see Joanna. I'd like to be able to say she's been waiting but . . .'

'Shouldn't we talk first?'

'Mrs Beck, we will, we will talk but we'll be talking about someone. Someone you should see. Please. Only a brief visit, if that's what you want.' It was his business, his institution. The Director was in charge, and we found ourselves on our way, each with a hand under the elbow, propelling us without force, promising no escape.

Through the open doors of rooms to the left and right young men and women sat at low tables talking to discarded children, sat on the floor moving wheeled objects for their interest; the children sat. In other rooms they were no longer children. Joanna was no longer a child.

Manners or policy had caused the Director to nudge EL into the room ahead of us. She stopped dead in the doorway and I saw Joanna over her shoulder. She was draped in an armchair by the window so that she could look out, a loose green dress covering the ins and outs of her. About her head her hair was polished copper, piled away from her face in a soft cloud and clipped in place with a pink plastic pin shaped like a duck. A child's duck. An indignity, I thought, to hold the hair of a young woman with a child's duck, even if as a child she had not recognised its significance, even if she did not recognise it now. Then whose dignity was injured? The dignity of her potential, the Director would doubtless answer, but he was in control here, he must know which clips were placed in the hair of his charges. Yet under her dress Joanna was swelling. Her arms were round, her ankles puffy. There were creases in her neck. These, we were to believe, were normal.

His hands on her shoulders, the Director eased EL, blocking the entrance, further into the room so that she stood at her daughter's outstretched feet. He placed himself behind her lest she try to make a getaway.

'Hallo, Joanna. Is that right? What do I say?'

'It's fine. Say what you want.'

Joanna lifted an arm. Oswald's trunk, all that remained of him, dripped from her fingers like a mangled limb.

EL shuddered back into the Director's hands held at the ready for her upper arms. 'What's that?'

'It's Oswald,' I said.

'Who?'

Up came the other arm and slowly, restrained by weight and lassitude, Joanna see-sawed through the air, a wide beam bisecting her face from which gurgled a continuous raspberry.

'She's greeting you. It's her greeting.'

294

'Indiscriminately to everyone,' I added, realising the truth of that for the first time.

EL drew in a breath and stepped closer. She laid a finger on Joanna's cheek and the arms halted. 'Her skin's so soft.'

'She's a young girl.'

'And her hair.'

'Like yours.'

'Used to be.' EL looked out of the window at the scene Joanna could not turn away from, the cows in their field behind the wire, lying in the grass under the single oak. 'Doesn't she get bored?'

'Hardly. She always seems content.'

The old anguish rose in me. 'Stop talking across her!'

'Mr Beck, please, we've been through all this.'

'All the same.'

EL met my eye. We were her parents. We had once seen something flicker and vanish, but the Director had been entrusted only with the debris. Joanna's arms subsided on to her lap and the green fabric caught under the protruding mound which tugged at our attention.

EL leaned over our daughter. 'May I?' She cupped a palm over her incipient grandchild. Joanna's hands pounced like a pair of cats and EL yelped, shocked, not wounded, but trapped. 'It's moving,' she said. 'The baby's moving.' Outside, the clouds tore along the sky and the sunlight flickered off and on, reflecting in the eyes Joanna had turned on her mother, lending them momentarily a shade of the palest violet. EL extracted her hands. 'Who did this to her? Who's responsible?' The question she was bound to ask and only one of the questions the Director could not answer. He shook his head. 'It makes a difference to know, doesn't it, who that will be? Where it comes from?' She pointed to the mound shifting under Joanna's green covering. Joanna gazed at it too. 'I mean, Joanna's all right, in principle. When she was born she was all right. So on *her* side her baby ought . . .'

'You're asking if the father was another patient?'

'Well, yes.'

'Because you think there might be some genetic problem so that you'd have another Joanna. And if that were so you'd think differently about what to do.'

'You're not helping me,' said EL. (You're supposed to be helping me.)

'I'm trying to be sure you're saying what you want to say.' (I have to be brutal or we won't get anywhere.) 'Is that what you meant?'

'Well, yes.'

'I can't help you. I don't know who it was or how or why or when. What she's carrying is a life. That's all we know. That's all we will know until the time comes to find out.'

'Unless we stop it.' They were moving too quickly. I had to intervene. 'You said it might be traumatic. You said . . . you've always said . . . she's not suffering. It's the one thing she has the capacity to do – not to suffer – unless it's imposed on her.'

The Director shuffled. 'It's not so simple, of course. A termination isn't so simple.'

'But she wouldn't know what it was, would she? She wouldn't have any sense of loss?'

He shrugged – I can't say; I daren't know. 'The trouble is . . .'

'What is the trouble?'

'When I wrote to you I said, I think, we were guessing that she was in the fourth month. Well, we were wrong.'

'It's more, isn't it?' said EL. 'I could have told you that.'

The Director shuffled again and muttered to one side, 'Pregnancy isn't what we expect to deal with here. It isn't something I'm familiar with.'

But EL was taking no excuses. 'You're a qualified doctor, aren't you? You must have come across pregnancy when you trained.'

'I didn't specialise. It wasn't my area. It wasn't my interest. One forgets.'

'Oh, for Christ's sake!'

'EL, steady on. He's apologised. That's not the point any more.'

'It may not be the point but anyone can apologise. And what's the matter with you, Leo? People do the most appalling things but for you they always come up smelling of roses.' Major Laing lowered his gun and held out a sherry glass. 'You put Joanna in this man's care – okay, because I asked you to . . . to do something – and he has been monumentally negligent. There's Joanna we're asked to think about and there's the baby, whatever it's going to turn out to be, in a couple of months time, isn't that right?' She turned to the Director. 'That's how soon it's going to be, isn't it? So there's no question of terminations or whatever other word you wanted to fish out for it. She's going to have this baby, which may terrify her, and the baby may be another, you know . . . and you're saying, "Oh, leave him alone, he's apologised." He ought never to have been put in charge of a place like this. He ought to be dismissed. We ought to bring charges . . .'

In her chair Joanna began bouncing Oswald's trunk from her knee to the window-frame and back, farting through a beatific smile. The Director crossed over and stood behind her, stroking her hair, twirling a lock of it round and round his fingers. I thought, he's the one who really cares about her. 'All I can promise is that we'll try and see it goes as painlessly for her as possible. I'd rather not let them operate because she won't leave the stitches alone afterwards. I'm sorry. I don't think you understand how sorry.'

'I want to stay.' EL sounded suddenly deflated, tired.

'I beg your pardon?'

'I want to stay down here. Until she's had the baby.'

'But you don't have to. She doesn't know it's you, Mrs Beck, you do see that, don't you?'

'Yes, yes. I just want to be here, on hand. I don't want to look after her or anything. I don't think I could. I know it doesn't make any difference. I know it makes no sense.'

'It makes some. And you, Mr Beck? What about you?'

I had no desire to stay at all any more, listening to this man's professionally trained concern. 'If you think it makes sense.'

We left Joanna communing with herself as the door closed on her, insouciant of the future that approached and could not now be averted. So there was to be a baby. All the argument had been neither here nor there.

We took a room in the Horse and Hound, whose beams were genuinely old and whose soft furnishings, said EL, smelled of toast and tom cats. I lay on the spongy mattress of our bed with my arms behind my head and wondered how the nose distinguished such particular information. Toast and tom cats. What was it to recognise those aromas, to announce their provenance without giving the matter thought? EL liked toast. Tom cats less. Had she taught her nose to discriminate or were her judgements directed by her sense of smell, so that what she imagined was an opinion reasonably arrived at was no more than a reaction she could not control? She sold her scents and toilet waters to millions. Millions must share a nose. I had seen noses wrinkle even at the mention of an offensive smell with a unanimity the other senses never achieved. Or perhaps it only seemed so to someone in an odourless world. Yet people surely did not agree so easily on what they found beautiful or harmonious. Or delicious. But there again. Each of the senses, I thought, had its own prejudices. Together they orchestrate what we call taste; take away one of them and the incapacitated individual's assessments are flawed; he's aware that something is lacking, but he'll never even guess what difference the possession of the missing sense might have made. And yet my daughter, deprived of the conductor of her senses, couldn't ask herself these futile questions, for having no mind she did not know to regret it. Unaware of being unaware. And if her child should turn out the same, whose loss would that be? Not the child's. 'Joanna's always seemed quite content.' The discontented were her parents. Always 'seemed'. Seemed. It was that damned 'seemed' which would not go away.

At first EL went daily to St Matthew's and busied herself there in activities which she admitted profited no one and failed to muzzle her trepidation. So she took to walking the countryside for longer hours each day, enveloped in an oilskin against the sodden wind of the season and striding in the teeth of the wind to induce a fatigue designed to bring instant sleep. Her limbs protested and her mind, racked with apprehension, kicked the sleep away. But it need not turn out like that. We could not know. We could, perhaps, begin again.

Part IV

Twenty-two

Joe, I may have misbehaved, in which case I apologise. Honestly, I cannot remember. I know, though, that I was overcome by the conviction that my presence at your birth was essential to prevent another mishap. I think there may even have been a minor tussle outside the labour ward to which Joanna, elephantine and contorting, had been wheeled. I have asked my doctors, I have asked EL, but the manner in which they deflect my questioning leads me to assume my suspicions, based on the haziest of recollections, cannot be far from the truth. They are solicitous. They have to be. It is the prerogative of the seriously ill that those around him will be solicitous. It is also his misfortune that they will be nothing else. When people suspect the truth may kill you, you cannot tease from them so much as its silhouette.

We were made to wait in a neighbouring corridor, pacing up and down in opposite directions, both ignoring the hospital's request not to smoke. Double doors insulated us from sound. Outside it was almost Easter; chocolate eggs and bunnies were sweating in the shop windows as we drove past. Like rabbits, EL had said, whenever Barbara, shouting, splayed her wide thighs and pushed out her young, never in doubt. Eggs at Easter, symbolic of new lives; but what a kerfuffle for some of us to procure just one.

Half an hour, an hour, the corridor was still. Along its walls others sat, whispering. A door would open, releasing a nurse in blue and white checks – student's garb, as a matter of fact, I know them all – who passed us by at a brisk pace and disappeared. From another direction came a doctor, necklaced by his stethoscope, and went, keeping his secrets. Every movement that interrupted the susurrating silence seemed commotion, presaging someone's drama.

They pushed a tea trolley, two fat women, their ankles

overspilling their shoes. We bought tea, boiled water poured on to a brown dust in thin plastic cups, and Penguin biscuits which we unwrapped but hid, with the plastic cups, under distant chairs. A young man burst from a door, pulling coins from his pocket, running to the phone box. Mother first, then mother-in-law, mates at work, her sister. He garbled and gobbled his message which I strained to hear.

'Mrs Beck? Mr Beck?' A doctor and a sister together. So much news. 'Mr Beck? Mr Beck?'

But I was covered in ants, a termites' nest had split over me, or I was its hub the way they rushed, phalanxes of them up and down my skin, under my clothes, which I ripped at to claw the ants away. I was on the floor writhing to escape but the movement seemed to encourage them. Then they gathered as one and pressed with an incredible weight on my chest compressing the breath out of me.

'Mr Beck! Can you hear me, Mr Beck?'

'Leo?'

'Too many eggs. That's what's done it. All in all it's a wonder it hasn't happened before.' I was in bed because my feet were pushing up a grey cellulose blanket. Mr Benson dressed as a doctor stood beyond my feet talking to a clipboard in his hand. 'Extraordinary, the way some people choose to live – or die.'

'Symbol of life,' I said.

'Oh. You awake? What?'

'Symbol of life. Eggs. Symbol of life. Can't have too much life. Can't have too much symbols.' My tongue was too large for my mouth.

'What was that?' A voice behind my ear.

'Don't worry, sister. It's the morphine talking.' There was something in my nose, the back of my hand was sore. I moved to free my nose. 'Now keep still there or you'll have us all jumping again.' I took a deep breath to sneeze out the obstruction in my nose but could not – the breath cracked my ribcage apart. 'You're a bit bruised, I'm afraid, but that'll pass in a few days. We may have damaged a rib or two, but better that than curtains, wouldn't you say? Nearly was, too.'

'What?'

'Heart, my dear fellow. Yours is unhappy.'

'Always been unhappy, heart.'

'Yes, well, the way you've been treating it. Hunky-dory now, though. You're in good hands, isn't he, sister? I'll leave you in her care. Look in later.'

'Got a good price. Giusè tell you.'

'What did you say?'

'Had to do it. Thought you could throw us all out, throw us away.'

He melted away. The sister said, 'Now that's nice and steady. You're going to have to try and keep it that way. Do you hear? We don't want any nonsense.'

'What steady?'

'Look.' She held out an arm so that I had to twist my head to follow its direction. A small television screen fixed to the wall bleeped a white roofscape across a green ground.

'What that?'

'That's your heartbeat. It's as it should be – well, nearly, under the circumstances.'

'How it know?'

'You're wired up to it. Look.' She drew back the cellulose blanket. Pads were glued to my chest; wires stretched from the pads to the wall. She gave one of the wires a gentle tug.

'No! Careful. Help!' If she disconnected me from the machine on the wall, if she withdrew the pulsing white roofscape from my heart I would surely die.

'It's all right. All nice and firm, or the message wouldn't be getting through.' I knew that, still alive. 'I'll go and tell your wife she can come in and see you now.'

'Whole family. All together one place. Funny. All unner one roof.'

'Whatever you say.'

They were playing something, four men whose faces I should have recognised, on violins, beautifully, something I thought I knew but couldn't place. The desire to remember what the music was creased my mind and distorted the music, which made me angry because I had wanted to listen.

303

'He's very restless.'

'He never was a good sleeper. Kicks, you know.' Your grandmother's hand was laid on mine on top of the blanket, but it was immense, its fingers wide and cumbersome. They grew, then waned, until my hand encompassed hers as if she were a tiny plastic doll drawn dusty from a lucky dip.

'We expect him to stabilise.' Leonora had had stabilisers, Giusè running ahead of her, pulling her tiny plump-wheeled pink bicycle so quickly that her legs couldn't keep pace with the whirring pedals. She stuck her feet out to the sides, screaming while Giusè ran without looking, forgot the width of the outriders until one lodged in a ridge, toppling the bicycle forwards and propelled Leonora on to her nose. 'You some kinda maniac, Giusè, or what are you?' Barbara pulled a handkerchief from her bag, wiped the sore nose, licked the handkerchief, wiped again. Giusè, out of breath and appalled, tried to laugh it off. 'You okay, though, in't yer, eh, princess?' And Leonora, in her mother's lap, squeezed an extra tear from finished eyes, tasted another wail, but sat on Giusè's shoulders so that he had to clamp her ankles in one hand and pull the miscreant bicycle with the other. 'Sometimes you just don't think, you know that?' But Barbara's arm was on Giusè's waist.

'Come on, mate. You're not goin' ter stay in this place till fuckin' Christmas, are yer?'

'Giusè, hush up, honey, not so loud.'

'He can't bleedin' 'ear me, can 'e, if I don't turn it up a bit. Eggs. Would you believe it? 'Ow d'you ever get done in by an egg? I eat eggs. You eat eggs. Eat 'em all the time.'

'But you eat other things too, don't you?' EL so clipped, her hand growing again.

'Gotta feed people on what they like or they don't eat nothing at all.'

'Time to feed that kid of yours. Shall I go get him?'

'Thank you, Barbara, but I'll go.' The hand slipped away from mine just before it regained its full size.

'Look now, he's real cute, that one.' EL was suckling you, impossibly, I thought at first, she held you so close, but she bent to show me the bottle concealed between her fingers, under your wrappings. You were almost cross-eyed with concentration, drawing in the milk in huge draughts, staring up at your grandmother without blinking. I'd noticed all the small Tolinis gaze up with that uncanny purpose. Now our child was doing the same. Good thing it's a boy, I thought, got it right this time, boys are stronger. '*Rubbish*,' said Meyer. '*Don't confuse the muscle and the size of the male with the ability to withstand the pressures of nature. The females win every time.*' What about my daughter? '*Ja, sure. I was talking in averages, in generalities. Of course there are exceptions, and you were unfortunate. Particularly unfortunate. But it doesn't prove a thing. Anyway, she's strong as a horse.*' Strong as bad-tempered Mirabelle. I watched you, Joe, already with that black hair – I must remember to ask who on the premises had such raven hair . . . there he was, the negligent Director, so tentative, so hale, knowing no better, bringing grapes. 'There was a boy who worked with the gardener. He had black hair. Black eyes too. A kind boy. Used to pull Joanna out in the fine weather. Can't be sure he was there at the right time, though.' He must have been. What was his name? But the Director, shaking his head, wagging his head, left right, left right, on a hinge, 'Don't know. Don't think I ever knew. One doesn't have much to do with those sorts of people.' Have to give him a name, then, but can't think of one. Can't think of any names. The four men with their violins scraped away, less harmoniously, too shrilly, boring into my ears. Tell them to be quiet now, they'll wake Joe. Complaining for your sake. Nothing woke you.

An amazing year, that first one. Invalided out, away from the markets – 'those vegetable crates are too heavy for a man in your condition, a little light walking is what you need, but all in good time'; kept away from Tolini's – 'such a stressful business, catering, especially at your end of the market'; forced to remain at home where I most wanted to be.

Giusè brought a platter covered with a glass dome protecting our finest cheeses, but EL held up the flat of her hand and barred their entry.

'Vegetables,' she said.

'You'll be lucky.'

It was the year the House of Laing jettisoned the red and the yellow and opted instead for the colours of moorland and heath, wholesome honey and avocado and the crushed kernels of apricots from Syria. She opened a line for men. Man at Laing retailed in boxes of burgundy with gold lettering embossed London–Paris–New York. Out in the perfumeries and beauty shops EL's consumers pulled out their purses, again wondering how she had anticipated their unspoken desires so exactly. So she dusted her hands together. 'Well, that's that, then. The place can look after itself for a bit, I should think. Wouldn't you?' As I said, an amazing year.

She seemed to know, with uncanny certainty, what you wanted before you knew it yourself. You tested your repertoire of noises and she gave you food, she danced you on her knee, and held you up to see the leaves tacking in the breeze; she recognised, as I could not, when all you wanted was to sleep but in your excitement you had forgotten how. She talked to you in the voices of nonsense and you replied.

There was an impatience about you which would not be satisfied. We sat you on a blanket, folded on the floor, cushions tucked round to catch your toppling, all your toys, garish plastic things that could do no harm, within reach. But you whimpered for the objects across the room and when they were brought whimpered again, for it was not the objects you had wanted but the ability to collect them under your own steam. Then, overnight it seemed, you were on the move, comparing the world you saw with the reality of it in your mouth, hauling yourself to your fat feet, your legs bowed, impossibly soft.

You opened your mouth, sounds pressing to be released, closed it on them, opened and closed it and said, as one by one all the young Tolinis had said, 'mama', then 'baba'. Yes, yes, we shouted, echoing Giusè and Barbara and all people everywhere, but exchanged our doubts with our eyes, for it was not true. So we took you, just the once, to St Matthew's, knowing that you would no more understand than she would, but feeling conscience demand it. Even the matron clasped her hands to croon in disbelief with such penetrating falsetto that she brought the others running from their duties to marvel at the gleam in your eyes, at the intention in your movements. We showed you to Joanna, but at a distance, for Oswald's trunk hung ravaged from her rotating fingers. Taken by the windmilling limbs you lunged forward in my arms with a suddenness which caught her attention. The light lay on your hair, already a black mop, and she smiled to see it. Pursed her lips and farted through them for you. And you, fixing your eyes intently on her mouth, shaped your lips to match and breathed your first raspberry. So we stood there holding you while you set each other off, you and Joanna, higher and louder, united in your delight of that moment, oblivious of our silent shuddering, unaware that what was for you a new skill was your mother's only one.

The Director hovered behind us in the doorway, then borrowed you, unafraid but wary, set you on the floor, holding your hands above your head as you began the mechanical strutting that precedes walking. 'Unbelievable,' he said, a man relieved. 'I can't tell you.'

It was a year in which EL tossed salads and baked lean chickens, skimming away the skin. But Giusè was right. I swallowed enough only to stay alive, without relish, sustained instead by your growth. In the end you ate the chickens. It proved anyway to be too late. The eggs had done their malign work if I was to believe the accusations levelled against them. Shortly after your first birthday I found myself, with ribs bruised anew, veering in an ambulance through the wail-filled streets to the hospital bed where I still am.

They have not given me time. They are miserly with time. If I had not been paying more for this room than the services they offer deserve, I should have said they were anxious to have me out of here. Only this morning some cleric in black garb appeared at my door with the sister's hand behind his elbow. He did not seem to me yet to be rubbing his hands at the prospect of another soul to be gathered in, but he coincided with my parents, who have been wringing their hands, shrunken and transparent with the age that should have removed them first. At night I picture them lying on their backs, faces to the ceiling, concentrating on death, fulminating against an assault on their sense of chronology. We take all deaths ill, but those of our children come hardest. I could have told them that. The priest had happened by, perhaps at the sister's instigation. To my parents he was a black-hooded skeleton whetting his scythe, and my mother set up a thin wail of protest. Beyond my mother and father came Giusè, with Barbara, soberly dressed, just in case.

Giusè grasped the priest by the lapels of his dark jacket so that my sympathies went out to the mild-looking man who found himself suddenly in those big fists. I had once been there too. 'Out!' Giusè yelled, and Barbara's finger flew to her lips: this is a hospital, all these people are so sick, honey. 'Out! Vulture. Go on, go on. Get out an' don't come back.'

'I intended only to offer some comfort.'

'You're from the wrong bleedin' lot. Thought they'd've told yer. You can come an' see me any day, when my time comes. But not this one, gottit?'

I was a little regretful. I should have liked to hear what a new voice had to say about the passing of time to one with whom he could share no assumptions. But I had only the strength to raise one hand in a gesture no one could interpret.

'See?' Giusè whirled the priest round to face me. 'He's sendin' you out. Now clear off.'

'Gently, my son.' He had recognised one of his own. 'It hurts no one to think of redemption at this moment in their lives, and especially now. Remember the times.'

'What times?' My voice was something more than a whisper. It drew the priest to my bedside, sneaked from Giusè's faltering grip.

'The times? Now? Why, tomorrow is Good Friday. Easter is nearly upon us.' I had forgotten. I should have known that the season of eggs would lay me low a second time. 'It is the days when we –'

'No!' Giusè pulled his God's representative from my bedspread where he had begun to settle his buttocks. 'It's not right. You better leave 'im alone.'

They left me alone, all of them, eventually, for I drooped my eyelids, feigning an absent exhaustion. But my mind wandered back to the mild Father who had allowed Giusè to harry him away, unwillingly, for he was leaving a job barely begun. He knows more than I do, I thought, and waited to be afraid.

And then I saw my grandfather arched rigid on his bed, his beard on his chest, the tips of his fingers pressed on the covers, his angry but bewildered eyebrows. That had not been fear. He had not been afraid, not of death nor of anything to follow, if, indeed, he believed in any such thing. Now it seemed to me for the first time that his strange expression was entirely connected with this life on this earth. How unlike we were, he who had been so certain about that, knowing without question how it ought to be lived and why; I who was not convinced that there was any way of living superior to any other, or for that matter that life had to be lived at all. Some other notion had been worming its way about my grandfather's mind when death surprised him, caught him in the act of mulling over a displeasing thought, and preserved his displeasure in his twisted features like a figure trapped in volcanic flow.

He could not have been prescient. It would be too easy to suppose that he foresaw, but too late to warn anyone, what was going to happen to the Jews of Europe. No, my grandfather's imagination was troubled by something nearer, more domestic than that. I recalled his grimy entry into our apartment, provoking my mother's bourgeois distaste, quickly disguised by upbringing and her duty to the in-laws; how he ate by himself, how he glowered at me for daring to be born and deprive him of the wife he so needed to hate. Some might say that in its way your birth has hastened my death. If that's true I can't find it in me to reproach you. Who should be reproached for being born, least of all someone whose coming has been as unlikely as yours? Tomorrow being what it is, my grandfather, had he lived, would have been thinking about rinsing out his lettuce leaves in salt water, preparing to deliver himself of his narrative.

What was it he called me? Ill-mannered, stupid, indifferent, incapable of asking questions – the worst of them being indifference. He had told me the Passover story, as his law said he must, for that's what makes you a Jew – because your father, a Jew, told you the story, instructed by God to do so, and commanded you to pass it on. But even as he was telling it he knew it was too late. I was already terminally riddled with indifference. Perhaps that explained his grim deathbed expression: the last one of the family was lost and, one way or another, the failure was entirely his own. Because of him, my father had deserted his faith as well as the

309

battleground of his childhood only to bring up a son who would run out on his duty. 'I know where I come from, and I know where I'm going,' Giusè had said. 'And if you don't know, it's not my problem.' Well, I don't know. I don't know where I'm going. But why not placate the memory of the old man, who would, if he knew, add an epithet to the others? 'Hypocrite,' he'd snarl. 'Don't think it's so easy. This wasn't a story, it was the truth. Stories are a waste of time.'

But, tomorrow being what it is, let's pretend that you're old enough to pay attention, and to understand. Let me tell you the only story I can manage in the time we have left. Some people would say, my grandfather among them, that what I have to say was not intended for you, because I married out. You don't belong. Too bad. No one chooses my listeners but me. So come. Listen, and I will listen too. It won't be quite the one my grandfather told me, nor the one they sang in the desert for me but not for Meyer. It will be my rendering of our covenanted past, and if I tell it well enough I too may detect the echoes of connection. And then you will have to decide whether or not it is the truth, and what you want to do with it.